CHARMING
SMALL HOTEL
GUIDES

Britain

GW00720658

CHARMING
SMALL HOTEL
GUIDES

Britain

Series Editor
Andrew Duncan

★ EXCLUSIVE READER OFFER ★

Hotels marked with an asterisk ★ have exclusive
offers for *Charming Small Hotel Guide* readers.
These range from free drinks on arrival or at
meals to discounts at certain times of the year.
To find out more, contact the hotel in advance.
Be sure to take your copy of the guide with you.
Some proprietors may wish to endorse your copy
with an unobtrusive mark on the final page to
indicate that the offer has been redeemed.

DUNCAN PETERSEN

HUNTER
PUBLISHING

This new 1999 edition conceived, designed and produced by Duncan Petersen Publishing Ltd

Editor	Andrew Duncan
Revisions editor	Nicola Davies
Art director	Mel Petersen
Editorial director	Andrew Duncan
Maps	Christopher Foley

This edition published in the UK and Commonwealth 1999 by
Duncan Petersen Publishing Ltd,
31 Ceylon Road, London W14 OPY

Sales representation and distribution in the U.K. and Ireland by
Portfolio Books Limited
Unit 1C, West Ealing Business Centre
Alexandria Road
London W13 0NJ
Tel: 0181 579 7748

ISBN 1 872576 84 2

A CIP catalogue record for this book is available
from the British Library

AND

Published in the USA by
Hunter Publishing Inc.,
130 Campus Drive, Edison, N.J. 08818.
Tel (732) 225 1900 Fax (732) 417 0482
For details on hundreds of other travel guides and language
courses, visit Hunter's Web site at hunterpublishing.com

ISBN 1-55650-864-6

Typeset by Duncan Petersen Publishing Ltd
Printed by G. Canale & Co SpA, Turin

Contents

Introduction

This is the thirteenth consecutive edition of the *Charming Small Hotel Guide* to Britain, which along with *Charming Small Hotels France*, is the flagship of the *Charming Small Hotel Guides* series. This series now consists of 15 titles, including recent additions *Paris and the Ile de France*, *Venice and North-East Italy* and *Tuscany and Umbria*. For a full list, see page 240.

As usual, the guide has been updated for the new year, but only a few entries have had to be replaced because of declining standards, poor readers' reports or closure, although several hotels have undergone a change of owner. We are pleased to welcome to the guide an interesting range of new places, including two delightful hotels in Cornwall, a riverside hotel at Bucklers Hard, near Beaulieu, and a town house hotel in Edinburgh.

This remains the only independently inspected, UK-originated, selective colour accommodation guide to charming and interesting places to stay in Britain. No hotel pays for an entry. Beware of imitators who do not admit on the cover that they accept payments from hotels for inclusion, but only do so in small print on the inside pages. They say they are selective – but a quick comparison with this guide will prove that this is a hollow claim. And if money has changed hands, it is impossible to write the whole truth about a hotel.

Charming and small
There really are relatively few *genuine* charming small hotels. Unlike other guides, we are p
articularly fussy about size, rarely straying over 15 bedrooms. If a hotel has more than that, it needs to have the *feel* of a much smaller place to be in this guide.

We attach more importance to size than other guides because we think that unless a hotel is small, it cannot give a genuinely personal welcome, or make you feel like an individual, rather than just a guest. For what we mean by a personal welcome, see below.

Unlike other guides, we often rule out places that have great qualities, but are nonetheless no more nor less than – hotels. Our hotels are all special in some way.

We think that we have a much clearer idea than other guides of what is special and what is not; and we think we apply these criteria more consistently than other guides because we are a small and personally managed company rather than a bureaucracy. We have a small team of like-minded inspectors, chosen by the editor and thoroughly rehearsed in recognizing what we want. While we very much appreciate readers' reports – see page 11 – they are not our main source of information.

Last but by no means least, we're independent – there's no payment for inclusion.

Introduction

So what exactly do we look for?
- An attractive, preferably peaceful setting.
- A building that is either handsome or interesting or historic, or at least with a distinct character.
- Ideally, we look for adequate space, but on a human scale: we don't go for places that rely on grandeur, or that have pretensions that could intimidate.
- Decoration must be harmonious and in good taste, and the furnishings and facilities comfortable and well maintained. We like to see interesting antique furniture that is there because it can be used, not simply revered.
- The proprietors and staff need to be dedicated and thoughtful, offering a personal welcome, *without being intrusive*. The guest needs to feel like an individual.

Whole-page entries
We rarely see all of these qualities together in place; but our warmest recommendations – whole page, with photograph – usually lack only one or two of these qualities.

Half-page entries
Don't, however, ignore our half-page entries. They are very useful addresses: *all* are *genuine* charming small hotels, by no means just space-fillers. You can't have stars on every page.

Home from home
As might be expected, many of the full-page entries are given to those places that have the feel of a private house – a home from home – at the same time as being very professional operations. This is a difficult balancing act for the proprietors, but when it works well we think it makes for the most seductive form of accommodation. Those who've experienced it often turn their back on any other type of hotel, however luxurious or famous. Moreover, the 'CSH' experience need not be expensive: there are expensive places in this guide, but there are also very reasonable ones, that offer the same experience, but at different levels.

The hotel scene in Britain
When we started the *Charming Small Hotel Guides* the sort of place we like best was a relatively new phenomenon in Britian. Now it is well established, and the number of 'charming small hotels' has steadily increased. On the other hand, it hasn't increased dramatically. The real thing is still worth going out of your way for.

No fear or favour
Unlike many guides, there is no payment for inclusion. The selection is made *entirely* independently.

Introduction

Range of places included
Despite its title, this guide does not confine itself to places called hotels, or places that behave like hotels. On the contrary, we actively look for places that offer a home-from-home. We include pubs, guest-houses and bed-and-breakfast establishments; and we include quite a number of places that operate on 'house-party' lines, where you are introduced to other guests and take meals at a communal table. Many such places are part of a marketing group called Wolsey Lodges.

Caution: if you aren't gregarious, don't like making small talk to strangers or are part of a romantic twosome that wants to keep itself to itself, the 'houseparty' establishment may not be for you.

On the other hand, if you are interested in meeting people, and if, as a foreign visitor to the UK, you want to experience the locals at first hand, learning much about their country in the process, then you'll find it rewarding.

Check the price first
See page 10 for the system we adopt in giving prices; to avoid unpleasant surprises, always double check the price at time of booking. Sometimes they go up after we've gone to press, sometimes there is a seasonal or other variation from the printed version.

Our pet dislikes
Small hotels are not automatically wonderful hotels; and the very individuality of small, owner-run hotels makes them prone to peculiarities that the mass-produced hotel experience avoids. For the benefit of those who run the small hotels of Britain – and those contemplating the plunge – we repeat once more our list of pet hates.

The Hushed Dining-room This commonly results when an establishment falls between the two stools of a really small place, where the owner makes sure the ice is broken, and the not-so-small hotel, where there are enough people to create a bit of a hubbub.

The Ordinary Breakfast Even hotels that go to great lengths to prepare special dinners are capable of serving prefabricated orange juice and sliced bread at breakfast.

The Schoolteacher Mentality People tempted to set up small hotels should perhaps undergo psychometric testing to determine whether they are sufficiently flexible and accommodating to deal with the whims of travellers; some of them certainly are not.

The Excess of Informality At one not-cheap London address this year (one which did not find its way into the guide) we were shown around by a young man in jeans (which might be acceptable) and socks (which is not).

Introduction

The Inexperienced Waiter Or waitress. Running a small operation does not excuse the imposition on the paying public of completely untrained (and sometime ill-suited) staff who can spoil the most beautifully cooked meal.

The Imposing Name An unimportant one, this, but an irritant nonetheless. A charmingly cosy whitewashed cottage in the Lake District does not, in our view, constitute a 'country house hotel'.

The Lumpy Old Bed Surely, every hotel proprietor knows that they should occasionally sleep in each of the beds in each of their rooms? Otherwise, it's the easiest thing in the world to fail to spot the gradual decay of a mattress.

Readers' reports

To all the hundreds of readers who have written with comments on hotels, a sincere 'thank-you'. We attach great importance to your comments and absorb them into the text each year. Please keep writing: for further information, see page 11.

How to find an entry

In this guide, the entries are arranged in geographical groups. First, the whole of Britain and Ireland are divided into five major groups, starting with Southern England and working northwards to Scotland; Ireland comes last.

Within these major groups, the entries are grouped into smaller regional sub-sections such as the South-West, Wales, the Midlands and the Highlands and Islands – for a full list see page 5.

Within each regional sub-section, first come the full-page entries, arranged in alphabetical order by nearest town; if several occur near one town, they are arranged in alpha order by name of hotel.

These are followed by the half-page entries for that section, again organized alphabetically by nearest town.

To find a hotel in a particular area, use the maps following this introduction to locate the appropriate pages.

To locate a specific hotel, whose name you know, or a hotel in a place you know, use the indexes at the back, which list entries both by name and by nearest place name.

How to read an entry

At the top of each entry is a coloured bar highlighting the name of the town or village where the establishment is located, along with a categorization which gives some clue to its character. These categories are as, far as possible, self-explanatory. 'Country house hotel' needs, perhaps, some qualification: it is reserved for places whose style is appropriately gracious.

Fact boxes
The fact box given for each hotel follows a standard pattern which requires little explanation; but:

Under **Tel** we give the telephone number starting with the area code used within the United Kingdom; when dialling from another country, omit the initial zero. We also list **Fax** numbers, and **E-mail** and **Website** addresses where available.

Under **Location** we give information on the setting of the hotel and on its parking arrangements, as well as pointers to help you find it.

Under **Food & drink** we list the meals available. A 'full' breakfast is a traditional British hot meal of bacon, eggs and so on; such a breakfast may be available at extra cost, even in hotels where we have not mentioned it.
   We also say what licence the hotel possesses for the sale of alcoholic drinks. A restaurant licence permits the sale of drinks with meals, a residential licence permits the sale of drinks to those staying in the hotel, and a full licence permits the sale of drinks to anyone over the age of 18 during certain prescribed hours.

All the **Prices** in this volume – unlike those on France, Italy, Spain, Germany and Austria – are **per person**.
   Normally, a range of prices is given, representing the smallest and largest amounts you might pay in different circumstances – typically, the minimum is half the cost of the cheapest double room in low season, while the maximum is the cost of the dearest single in high season.
   We give prices for bed and breakfast unless dinner is inescapable. After the B&B price, we give either the price for dinner, bed and breakfast (DB&B), or for full board (FB – that is, all meals included) or, instead, an indication of the cost of individual meals. After all this basic information comes, where space allows, a summary of reductions available for long stays or for children.
   Rates include tax and service. Wherever possible we have given prices for 1999, but for many hotels these were not available; actual prices may therefore be higher than those quoted, simply because of inflation. But bear in mind also that the proprietors of hotels and guest-houses may change their prices from one year to another by much more than the rate of inflation. Always check when making a booking.

Our lists of facilities in **Rooms** cover only mechanical gadgets, and not ornaments such as flowers or consumables such as toiletries or free drinks.

Under **Facilities** we list public rooms and then outdoor and sporting facilities which are either part of the hotel or immediately on hand; facilities in the vicinity of the hotel, but not directly connected with it (for example, a nearby golf-course) are not listed, though they sometimes feature at the end of the main description in the **Nearby** section, which presents a selection of interesting things to see or do in the locality.

We use the following abbreviations for **Credit cards**:
AE   American Express
DC   Diners Club
MC   MasterCard (Access/Eurocard)
V   Visa (Barclaycard/Bank Americard/
          Carte Bleue etc)

The final entry in a fact box is normally the name of the **Proprietor(s)**; but where the hotel is run by a manager we give his or her name instead.

Unfamiliar terms
'Self-catering' means that cooking facilities such as a kitchenette or small kitchen are provided for making your own meals, as in a rental apartment. 'Bargain breaks' or 'breaks' of any kind mean off-season price reductions are available, usually for a stay of a specific or minimum period.

Reporting to the guides
Please write and tell us about your experiences of small hotels, guest-houses and inns, whether good or bad, whether listed in this edition or not. As well as hotels in Britain and Ireland, we are interested in hotels in France, Italy, Spain, Austria, Germany, Switzerland and the U.S.A. We assume that reporters have no objections to our publishing their views unpaid.

   Readers whose reports prove particularly helpful may be invited to join our Travellers' Panel. Members give us notice of their own travel plans; we suggest hotels that they might inspect, and help with the cost of accommodation.

   The address to write to is: Editor, *Charming Small Hotel Guides*, Duncan Petersen Publishing Limited, 31 Ceylon Road, London W14 0PY.

   In this edition we have marked with a star * those hotels that have special offers for our readers. Contact the hotel for details, or write to us at the address above for a full list.

11

Hotel locations

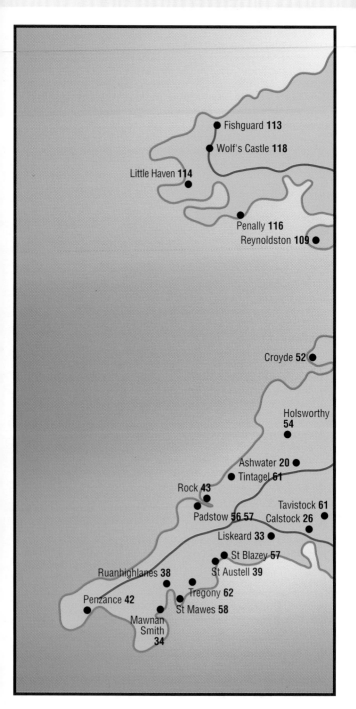

Fishguard **113**

Wolf's Castle **118**

Little Haven **114**

Penally **116**

Reynoldston **109**

Croyde **52**

Holsworthy **54**

Ashwater **20**

Tintagel **61**

Rock **43**

Tavistock **61**

Padstow **56 57**

Calstock **26**

Liskeard **33**

St Blazey **57**

Ruanhighlanes **38**

St Austell **39**

Penzance **42**

Tregony **62**

St Mawes **58**

Mawnan Smith **34**

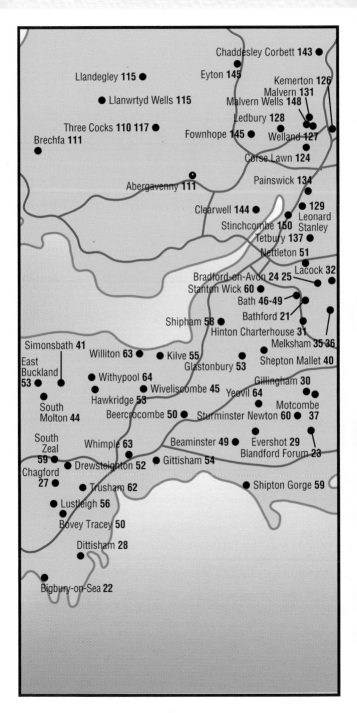

Chaddesley Corbett **143**
Llandegley **115**
Eyton **145**
Kemerton **126**
Malvern **131**
Malvern Wells **148**
Llanwrtyd Wells **115**
Ledbury **128**
Three Cocks **110 117**
Fownhope **145**
Welland **127**
Brechfa **111**
Corse Lawn **124**
Painswick **134**
Abergavenny **111**
Clearwell **144**
129
Leonard Stanley
Stinchcombe **150**
Tetbury **137**
Nettleton **51**
Lacock **32**
Bradford-on-Avon **24 25**
Stanton Wick **60**
Bath **46-49**
Bathford **21**
Shipham **58**
Hinton Charterhouse **31**
Melksham **35 36**
Simonsbath **41**
Williton **63**
Kilve **55**
Shepton Mallet **40**
East Buckland **53**
Glastonbury **53**
Withypool **64**
Gillingham **30**
Wiveliscombe **45**
Yeovil **64**
Motcombe
Hawkridge **53**
South Molton **44**
Beercrocombe **50**
Sturminster Newton **60**
37
South Zeal **59**
Whimple **63**
Beaminster **49**
Evershot **29**
Gittisham **54**
Blandford Forum **23**
Chagford **27**
Drewsteignton **52**
Trusham **62**
Shipton Gorge **59**
Lustleigh **56**
Bovey Tracey **50**
Dittisham **28**
Bigbury-on-Sea **22**

Hotel locations

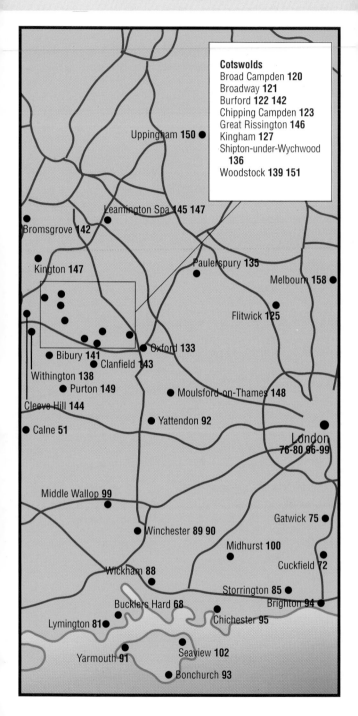

Cotswolds
Broad Campden **120**
Broadway **121**
Burford **122 142**
Chipping Campden **123**
Great Rissington **146**
Kingham **127**
Shipton-under-Wychwood
136
Woodstock **139 151**

Uppingham **150**

Leamington Spa **145 147**

Bromsgrove **142**

Kington **147**

Paulerspury **135**

Melbourn **158**

Flitwick **125**

Oxford **133**

Bibury **141**

Clanfield **143**

Withington **138**

Purton **149**

Moulsford-on-Thames **148**

Cleeve Hill **144**

Yattendon **92**

Calne **51**

London
76-80 96-99

Middle Wallop **99**

Gatwick **75**

Winchester **89 90**

Midhurst **100**

Cuckfield **72**

Wickham **88**

Storrington **85**

Bucklers Hard **68**

Brighton **94**

Lymington **81**

Chichester **95**

Yarmouth **91**

Seaview **102**

Bonchurch **93**

Hotel locations

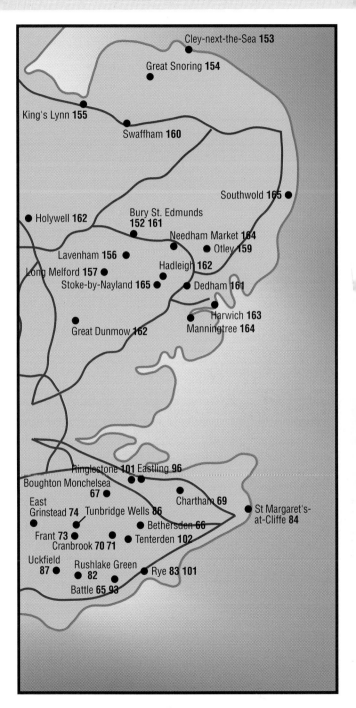

Cley-next-the-Sea **153**

Great Snoring **154**

King's Lynn **155**

Swaffham **160**

Southwold **165**

Holywell **162**

Bury St. Edmunds
152 161

Needham Market **164**

Otley **159**

Lavenham **156**

Hadleigh **162**

Long Melford **157**

Stoke-by-Nayland **165**

Dedham **161**

Harwich **163**

Great Dunmow **162**

Manningtree **164**

Ringlestone **101** Eastling **96**

Boughton Monchelsea
67

Chartham **69**

East
Grinstead **74** Tunbridge Wells **86**

St Margaret's-
at-Cliffe **84**

Bethersden **66**

Frant **73**

Cranbrook **70 71** Tenterden **102**

Uckfield
87

Rushlake Green
82

Rye **83 101**

Battle **65 93**

Hotel locations

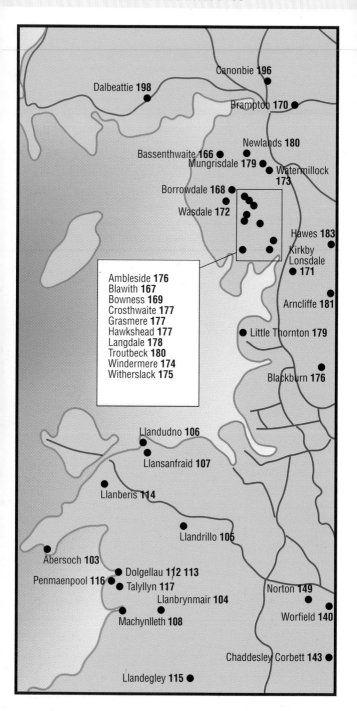

Canonbie **196**

Dalbeattie **198**

Brampton **170**

Newlands **180**

Bassenthwaite **166**

Mungrisdale **179**

Watermillock **173**

Borrowdale **168**

Wasdale **172**

Hawes **183**

Kirkby Lonsdale **171**

Arncliffe **181**

Little Thornton **179**

Ambleside **176**
Blawith **167**
Bowness **169**
Crosthwaite **177**
Grasmere **177**
Hawkshead **177**
Langdale **178**
Troutbeck **180**
Windermere **174**
Witherslack **175**

Blackburn **176**

Llandudno **106**

Llansanfraid **107**

Llanberis **114**

Llandrillo **105**

Abersoch **103**

Penmaenpool **116**

Dolgellau **112 113**

Talyllyn **117**

Llanbrynmair **104**

Norton **149**

Worfield **140**

Machynlleth **108**

Chaddesley Corbett **143**

Llandegley **115**

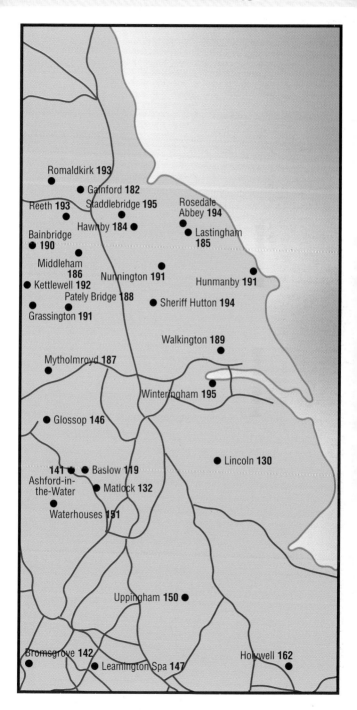

Romaldkirk **193**

Gainford **182**

Reeth **193** Staddlebridge **195**

Rosedale Abbey **194**

Hawnby **184**

Bainbridge **190**

Lastingham **185**

Middleham **186**

Nunnington **191**

Kettlewell **192**

Hunmanby **191**

Pately Bridge **188**

Sheriff Hutton **194**

Grassington **191**

Walkington **189**

Mytholmroyd **187**

Winteringham **195**

Glossop **146**

Lincoln **130**

141 Baslow **119**

Ashford-in-the-Water

Matlock **132**

Waterhouses **151**

Uppingham **150**

Bromsgrove **142**

Holywell **162**

Leamington Spa **147**

17

Hotel locations

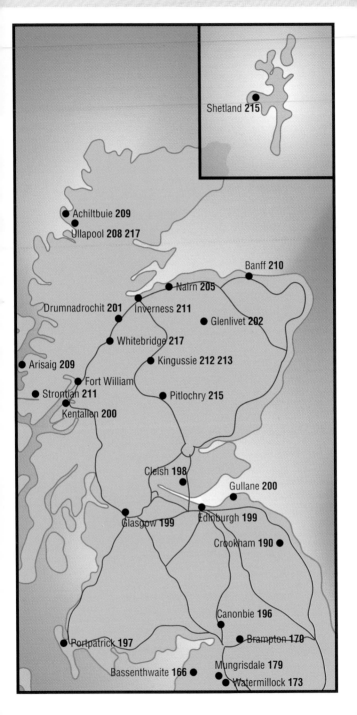

Shetland **215**

Achiltbuie **209**
Ullapool **208 217**

Banff **210**

Nairn **205**

Drumnadrochit **201**
Inverness **211**

Glenlivet **202**

Whitebridge **217**

Arisaig **209**

Kingussie **212 213**

Fort William
Strontian **211**

Pitlochry **215**

Kentallen **200**

Cleish **198**

Gullane **200**

Glasgow **199**
Edinburgh **199**

Crookham **190**

Canonbie **196**

Portpatrick **197**

Brampton **170**

Mungrisdale **179**
Bassenthwaite **166**
Watermillock **173**

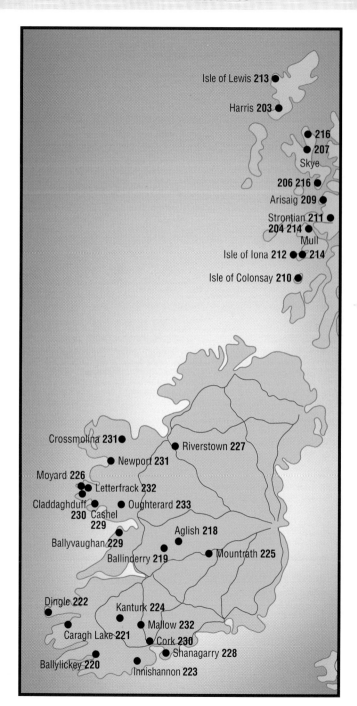

Isle of Lewis **213**

Harris **203**

216
207
Skye

206 216
Arisaig **209**
Strontian **211**
204 214
Mull
Isle of Iona **212** **214**

Isle of Colonsay **210**

Crossmolina **231**
Riverstown **227**
Newport **231**
Moyard **226**
Letterfrack **232**
Claddaghduff
230 Cashel
229
Oughterard **233**
Aglish **218**
Ballyvaughan **229**
Ballinderry **219**
Mountrath **225**

Dingle **222**
Kanturk **224**
Mallow **232**
Caragh Lake **221**
Cork **230**
Shanagarry **228**
Ballylickey **220**
Innishannon **223**

The South West

Blagdon Manor ★

Don't be put off by Blagdon Manor's isolated situation: it lies plum in the middle of the West Country, so no place of interest is very far away.

The Grade 11 listed former farmhouse, surrounded by rolling countryside, was derelict when Tim and Gill Casey discovered it on their return, in 1991, from Hong Kong, where they had spent many years. Having brought the building back to life, they opened it as a hotel in 1994. Their determination to succeed and attention to detail are evident everywhere, from the home-made jams and bowls of fresh fruit to the shortbread in the bedrooms and Belgian chocolates with the coffee.

Bedrooms are deliciously pretty and comfortable, with fluffy towels and crisp linen and plenty of thoughtful extras in the bathrooms. The dramatic dining-room dominated by a vast table and incredibly heavy matching chairs made specially in the Far East. The 'easy listening' music may not be to everyone's taste, but overall this is a relaxing, if expensive, small hotel, with near-faultless standards of service and delicious food: though entirely self-taught, Gill is a gifted cook of professional ability, and the food is beautifully presented. And some of her culinary products are available to take home as gifts.

Nearby National Trust Coast, 10 miles (16 km); golf courses.

Ashwater, Beaworthy, Devon EX21 5DF
Tel (01409) 211224
Fax (01409) 211634
Location just off A388 Launceston - Holsworthy road, 4 miles (6.5 km) S of Holsworthy, in 20 acres; ample parking and helicopter pad
Food & drink full breakfast, dinner; full licence **Prices** B&B £42.50-£70 (reduction for 5 nights or more May-Oct); dinner £19.50 **Rooms** 5 double, 2 twin, all with bath; all rooms have central heating, phone, TV, radio, tea/coffee kit, hairdrier **Facilities** sitting-room, library, dining-room, bar/snooker room, terrace, practice golf course, croquet **Credit cards** AE, MC, V **Children** welcome over 12 **Disabled** access difficult **Pets** not accepted **Closed** Christmas **Proprietors** Tim and Gill Casey

The South-West

Eagle House

No sign is displayed outside Eagle House, standing behind a stone wall and dignified wrought-iron gates, to suggest it is anything other than a fine, privately-owned, listed Georgian mansion. Inside, too, there is little to dispel that impression, particularly when sitting in the superb drawing-room which overlooks landscaped grounds and commands beautiful views across the Avon valley. John and Rosamund Napier are skilled hosts, combining professional service (John Napier trained at the Savoy and managed the Priory in Bath before moving here) with commendable informality – John firmly believes in trusting, not fussing over, his guests. The house is decorated without pomp – it is after all a guest-house rather than a full-blown hotel; the spacious bedrooms and adjoining bathrooms display simple wallpapers and an eclectic mix of furniture, ranging from the grand to the simple – some showing its age. Two additional bedrooms with a shared living-room and kitchen (for stays of 2 nights plus) have been created in a cottage in the old walled garden.
Nearby sights of Bath   abbey, Roman Baths; American Museum, 2.5 miles (4 km).

Church Street, Bathford, Bath BA1 7RS
Tel (01225) 859946
Fax (01225) 859430
E-mail Jonap@psionworld.net
Location 2.5 miles (4 km) E of Bath, off A363, in village; in 2-acre gardens, with ample car parking
Food & drink breakfast; residential licence
Prices B&B £24-£46; £2.80 extra for full breakfast; children sharing parents' room charged only for breakfast
Rooms 3 double with bath, 2 with shower; one single with shower; 2 family rooms with bath, one also with shower; all rooms have central heating, colour TV, phone, tea/coffee kit, hairdrier
Facilities sitting-room, dining-room; croquet, lawn tennis court
Credit cards MC, V
Children welcome; cots, baby-sitting available
Disabled access difficult
Pets dogs accepted
Closed 10 days over Christmas
Proprietors John and Rosamund Napier

The South-West

The Burgh Island Hotel

The solid white bulk of The Burgh Island Hotel hardly strikes one as charming and small, but we happily include it for the first time in this expanded edition of the guide for its novelty value and its unusual setting.

It occupies its own little island off a fairly unprepossessing part of the south Devon coast. It was built in 1929 in true Art Deco style, and its original Crittall iron windows are listed as an important feature of the building. The hotel became a fashionable hotspot for a whole string of glitzy pre-war names, and today, after extensive restoration by Tony and Beatrice Porter, it again exudes the style and atmosphere of that period.

Getting to the hotel is part of the experience: you are met at Bigbury-on-Sea by a sea tractor (or landrover at low tide) which wheezes its way across to the island. Once inside, the hotel feels a bit flimsy, rather like a film set, painted white, fabric rather skimpy, but there is a feast of Art Deco furniture and fittings in every room. We are advised by the owners that detailed restoration is continuing – feedback please.

The food has lately much improved, with the accent on presentation and quantity. Dining in the splendid Ballroom (live music on Saturday nights) is great fun.

Nearby Torquay, Buckfast Abbey, Polperro 30 miles (48 km).

Bigbury-on-Sea, Devon TQ7 4BG
Tel (01548) 810514
Fax (01548) 810243
Location on own 26 acre island off Bigbury-on-Sea, on B3392; parking in secure parking area; free transport by sea tractor or landrover to island
Food & drink breakfast, lunch, dinner; residential and restaurant licence
Prices DB&B £104-£129; special rates for extra nights
Rooms 14 suites, all with bath; all rooms have central heating, phone, TV, hairdrier, ironing board **Facilities** Palm Court, bar, sun lounge, 2 res-taurants
Credit cards AE, DC, MC, V
Children welcome; no children under 7 in Ballroom; special meals available **Disabled** access difficult **Pets** not accepted
Closed Jan, Feb **Proprietors** Tony and Beatrice Porter

The South-West

Country house hotel, Blandford Forum

Castleman Hotel and Restaurant

Chettle is one of those rare traditional estate villages that has hardly changed in the 150 years it has been in the benign ownership of one family – who live in the fine Queen Anne manor house, open to the public during summer months. Teddy Bourke, one of the family, took on the decrepid ex-dower house ("locals all thought it was haunted") in 1996, together with his partner, transforming it into a charmingly eccentric and very reasonably priced hotel and restaurant. Part of the building dates back 400 years, but it was much altered in Victorian times when it was tricked out with a galleried hall; a richly carved oak Jacobean fireplace was also installed in one of the reception rooms (the other is Regency style) with bookcases to match. Upstairs, the elegant proportions of the rooms have been left intact, and bedrooms are a model of the new style of hotel: comfortable and in good taste, but without unnecessary frills; several of the bathrooms have Victorian roll top baths. The 'large' rooms are enormous, one with a huge bay window overlooking the fields, whilst the smaller ones are still spacious.

The Castleman's restaurant – a long elegant room at the rear of the building – has a flourishing reputation. Barbara Garnsworthy cooks simple seasonal dishes with great panache – and the bill is not indigestible, either.

Nearby Kingston Lacy House; Cranbourne Chase; Salisbury.

Chettle, Blandford Forum, Dorset, DT11 8DB
Tel (01258) 830096
Fax (01258) 830051
Location in village, signposted of A354, 6 miles (9 km) north-east of Blandford; car park
Food & drink breakfast, Sunday lunch, dinner; residential and restaurant licence
Prices B&B £30-£40; dinner from £15.00
Rooms 8 double, all with bath; all rooms have central heating, phone, TV, hairdrier
Facilities dining room, 2 sitting-rooms, bar; garden
Credit cards MC, V
Children welcome
Disabled access difficult
Pets not accepted in house; 2 stables available for guests' own horses, and dogs
Closed February
Proprietors Edward Bourke and Barbara Garnsworthy

Converted windmill, Bradford-on-Avon

Bradford Old Windmill

'This is a very different kind of B&B,' says a reader who urged us to give it a full entry. Although it functioned as a windmill only briefly, the Roberts's extraordinary home was indeed built (in 1807) as one. It now appears something of a folly, with its four-storey Cotswold stone tower, conical tiled roof, pointed Gothic windows and restored sail gallery.

The sitting-room (cosy, round, with a log fire and books) and the principal bedroom each occupy a whole floor of the old tower. Bedrooms are romantic. A new suite with minstrel gallery has recently been created, with views across parkland to the White Horse at Westbury. One room has a round bed, another a waterbed. The Robertses travel far and wide, and the house is crammed with curiosities from around the globe.

There is a pretty terrace overlooking old Bradford, where breakfast and dinner are served, weather permitting.

Priscilla will cook dinner if given notice – you will encounter Mexican, Thai, Nepalese and other exotic influences. A soup tray is provided if dinner is unavailable.

Breakfast is taken at a communal table, but special provision is made for honeymoon couples who wish to eat late and alone. See also our other windmill B&B, page 153.

Nearby Bath, 8 miles (13 km); Kennet and Avon Canal.

4 Masons Lane, Bradford-on-Avon, Wiltshire BA15 1QN
Tel (01225) 866842
Fax (01225) 866648
Location just N of town centre; with cottage garden and parking for 3 cars
Food & drink full breakfast, dinner (Mon, Thur, Sat only)
Prices B&B £34.50–£49.50; dinner £20; reduction for children
Rooms 2 double, one with bath, one with shower; one suite; all rooms have central heating, colour TV, tea/coffee kit, alarm clock/radio
Facilities sitting-room, dining-room
Credit cards AE, DC, MC, V
Children welcome over 6 if well behaved **Disabled** access difficult **Pets** not accepted
Closed Jan, Feb, Christmas
Proprietors Peter and Priscilla Roberts

The South-West

Priory Steps

'This is a really lovely place,' writes a reporter – 'your current entry doesn't do it justice.' It is an amalgamation of a whole row of 17thC weavers' cottages, typical of Bradford, sympathetically decorated and furnished by Diana and Carey Chapman when they moved here from London in 1985.

Each of the bedrooms has a decorative theme. 'In spite of the cottage architecture, there is nothing cramped about the bedrooms – they are airy and light, with wonderful views.' They are beautifully decorated, too, each with its own character and furnished with antiques.

Diana Chapman is a keen cook – dinner is served either at a communal table in the elegant dining-room, or on fine days out on the terrace of a well-tended garden looking down over Bradford. Dinners are three-course, with no choice, but special requirements are happily met, given notice.

'Around the house you will find family photos, books, a comfortable sitting-room. The Chapmans are charming and relaxed. You feel like a house guest in a particularly well-run home. The atmosphere is pleasant and informal.'

The cottages stand high on a hill above Bradford, but are only three minutes' walk from the centre.

Nearby Barton Tithe Barn; Bath, 8 miles (13 km).

Newtown, Bradford-on- Avon, Wiltshire BA15 1NQ
Tel (01225) 862230
Fax (01225) 866248
Location close to middle of town, on N side; with car parking
Food & drink full breakfast, dinner; residential licence
Prices B&B £33-£53; dinner £19
Rooms 5 double, all with bath; all rooms have central heating, colour TV, tea/coffee kit
Facilities sitting-room, dining-room
Credit cards MC, V
Children accepted
Disabled access easy to one ground-floor bedroom; but dining-room on lower ground floor
Pets not encouraged
Closed never
Proprietors Carey and Diana Chapman

The South-West

Danescombe Valley Hotel

Danescombe has been a stalwart of this guide since our first edition, and the Smiths, resident since 1985, are maintaining standards here just as always. It is a colonial-style house, a hotel since 1860, once owned by the National Trust, whose Cotehele House is just 15 minutes' walk up through the woods. Every room in the hotel has a stunning view over a picturesque meander in the River Tamar, and the traditional slate floored bar leads directly on to the terrace. The antique furniture and traditional furnishings, the abundance of original paintings and natural light lend an airy and relaxed atmosphere.

Four-course dinners on Friday and Saturday nights feature salmon and local vegetables and cheeses, from chef Chris Dew.
Nearby Cotehele House; Morwelham Quay, 4 miles (6 km).

Lower Kelly, Calstock,
Cornwall PL18 9RY
Tel (01822) 832414
Fax (01822) 832446
E-mail Danescombe@aol.com
Website http://www.
inforamp.net/~lower/dvi/
Location 0.5 mile (0.8 km) W
of Calstock; private parking for
3 cars; further parking in lane
Food & drink breakfast, residential and restaurant licence
Prices B&B £50 (Sun to Thu);
DB&B £92.50 (Fri & Sat); dinner £30; discounts for 2 nights
or more **Rooms** 5 double
(single room by arrangement),
all with bath and shower; all
rooms have central heating
Facilities sitting-room, bar,
dining-room **Credit cards** DC,
MC, V **Children** welcome over
12 **Disabled** access difficult
Pets not accepted **Closed** Nov
to Feb **Proprietors** Martin and
Anna Smith

The South-West

Gidleigh Park

Duncan Petersen's art director, Mel Petersen, visited recently. His comments: 'Situated at the end of a long, narrow tree-lined lane which finally opens out to present an idyllic park setting. Behind the house are attractive terraced gardens, giving way to woods; in front, parkland and a rocky stream. This really is a spot to retreat to, and where you can indulge in understated luxury.'

'The oak-panelled sitting-room is large, with very comfortable furniture and stocked with interesting magazines, including *Private Eye*. Bedside books included volumes of Ted Hughes' poetry, a pleasant change from *Johanssen's Guide*, all indicating a style and a confidence rarely matched.' All the bedrooms give an immediate feeling of comfort and friendliness. Two especially attractive ones are next to the main building in a converted chapel.

The Hendersons, Americans with no previous hotel experience before taking on Gidleigh in 1977, aim to provide nothing but the best. Service is meant to be 'always friendly and enthusiastic, sometimes efficient', and it works. The eclectic food is wonderful – even the cheeses are remarkable – while wines run to 400 bins plus 250 bin-ends. Gidleigh continues to deserve its long entry in the guide.

Nearby Castle Drogo, 4 miles (6.5 km); Dartmoor.

Chagford, Devon TQ13 8HH
Tel (01647) 432367
Fax (01647) 432574
Location 2 miles (3 km) W of Chagford; in 40 acre grounds with ample car parking
Food & drink breakfast, lunch, dinner; restaurant and residential licence
Prices DB&B £175-£385
Rooms 14 double, all with bath and shower; one cottage in the grounds; all rooms have central heating, TV, radio, hairdrier
Facilities sitting-room, bar, loggia, 2 dining-rooms; croquet, fishing, tennis, bowls, putting
Credit cards DC, MC, V
Children welcome only if adult in behaviour
Disabled no special facilities
Pets welcome **Closed** never
Proprietors Paul and Kay Henderson

The South-West

Manor house hotel, Dittisham

Fingals

Fingals *is* different, and those who love it will *really* love it – which sums up why we remain enthusiastic about this manor farmhouse in a secluded valley, close to the River Dart. Owner Richard Johnston, calls it a 'hotel and restaurant', but in practice, Fingals comes much closer to the 'country house party' type of guest-house, where it is normal (though not obligatory) for guests to share a table in the wood-panelled dining-room at mealtimes.

The house – 17thC with Queen Anne front additions – has plenty of charm, with a stylish blend of new and old furniture, pine and oak. An adjacent self-catering barn is ideal for a family or for those wanting extra space and privacy.

It is an exceptionally relaxed place – you pour your own drinks, eat breakfast whenever you like – and those who insist on everything being just so are likely to be disappointed. The four-course dinners which are chosen from a short menu are modern in style, competent in execution, and ample in quantity.

Nearby Dartmouth Castle, 3 miles (5 km).

Old Coombe Manor Farm, Dittisham, near Dartmouth, Devon TQ6 OJA
Tel (01803) 722398
Fax (01803) 722401
E-mail richard@fingals.demon.co.uk
Website www.fingals.co.uk
Location 4 miles (6 km) N of Dartmouth, one mile (1.5 km) from village; with garden and ample car parking
Food & drink breakfast, snack lunch, dinner; residential and restaurant licence
Prices B&B £35-£80; dinner £27.50; reductions for 3 nights or more
Rooms 11 double, 10 with bath, one with shower; one family room, with bath; all rooms have central heating, phone, radio/alarm, tea/coffee kit; TV on request
Facilities dining-room, bar, library, TV room; swimming-pool, jacuzzi, sauna; snooker, croquet, tennis, table-tennis, wind-surfing, boating
Credit cards AE, MC, V
Children welcome if well behaved **Disabled** access difficult **Pets** accepted if well behaved, but not allowed in public rooms
Closed New Year to Easter
Proprietor Richard Johnston

The South-West

Summer Lodge

The Corbetts are the living evidence that not all 'professional' hoteliers are mediocre; we don't know what contribution they made to guests' happiness when they were at the Savoy, but the dedication they have applied to that cause since they escaped to Dorset is remarkable indeed. A recent inspection visit confirmed that their standards, and enthusiasm, remain unchanged.

For many visitors, Summer Lodge is all that a country house hotel should be. The Georgian/Victorian building is on just the right scale to give a sense of slight extravagance without being intimidating, and the Corbetts and their staff are masters at making guests feel at home in it. French windows lead from the public rooms (William Morris fabrics, open fires) to the beautiful flowery garden. Charming bedrooms range from the merely delightful to the quite grand. Bathrooms are spacious and have large white fluffy towels. The excellent cooking – 'not mean, but not heavy' – is offered as a monthly changing *carte* with daily specials.

Nearby Minterne Gardens, Maperton Gardens, Parnham House, 6 miles (10 km); Montacute House.

Summer Lane, Evershot, Dorset DT2 0JR
Tel (01935) 83424 **Fax** 83005
E-mail sumlodge@sumlodge.demon.co.uk
Website www.integra.fr/relaischateaux/summer
Location 15 miles (24 km) NW of Dorchester, off A37 on edge of village; ample parking
Food & drink full breakfast, lunch, dinner; residential and restaurant licence
Prices B&B £125-£235; DB&B £160-£305; reductions for children sharing; bargain breaks
Rooms 13 double, 3 single, 1 suite, all with bath; all rooms have central heating, phone, tea/coffee kit, hairdrier; TV, radio
Facilities dining-room, sitting-room, bar, reading-room; croquet, outdoor heated swimming-pool, tennis
Credit cards AE, DC, MC, V
Children welcome by arrangement **Disabled** access good to ground-floor bedrooms **Pets** By arrangement (£4 per night) **Closed** never
Proprietors Nigel and Margaret Corbett

The South-West

Country house hotel, Gillingham

Stock Hill House

This restored Victorian manor house, reached up a long drive through wooded grounds, has been beautifully furnished and decorated, with many of the Hausers' personal possessions in evidence. Sanderson and Baker designs abound, although each of the luxurious bedrooms is individual in style. The public rooms, too, are full of character and charm.

But your lasting memory of Stock Hill House is more likely to be of the Hausers' boundless enthusiasm and obvious delight in their work. Peter does all the cooking and produces superb results. His Austrian roots are reflected in the menu, which changes daily. Fruit and vegetables come from Peter's own immaculate walled kitchen garden. While he works away in the kitchen, guests pop in for a chat or to see what he is planning for dinner that evening. Before the evening meal, Chef Hauser draws his guests together before the grand fireplace in the entrance hall by playing his zither: thus begins an evening of good food and wine, hosted by a charming couple. Ties must be worn at dinner.

Nearby Shaftesbury, 5 miles (8 km); Stourhead House and Gardens, 6 miles (10 km); Salisbury and Longleat within reach.

Gillingham,
Dorset SP8 5NR
Tel (01747) 823626
Fax (01747) 825628
E-mail reception@stockhill.net
Website http://www.stockhill.net
Location 5 miles (8 km) NW of Shaftesbury on B3081; in 10-acre grounds with ample car parking
Food & drink breakfast, lunch, dinner; restaurant licence
Prices DB&B from £120-£140 per person (including morning tea and newspaper); reductions for 3 nights or more; winter breaks
Rooms 9 double, all with bath (1 with shower); 1 single, with bath; all rooms have central heating, radio, colour TV, phone, alarm clock, hairdrier, trouser-press
Facilities sitting-room, dining-room, breakfast room; tennis court, croquet (Easter to Oct), trout fishing, putting green **Credit cards** AE, DC, MC, V **Children** welcome over 7 if well behaved
Disabled access difficult, except to ground-floor suite
Pets not accepted
Closed never **Proprietors** Peter and Nita Hauser

The South-West

Country house hotel, Hinton Charterhouse

Homewood Park

Homewood Park, has been in these pages since 1988, and when it used to be in the hands of Stephen and Penny Ross (now at the Queensberry – see page 48) won high praise from every other notable guide. It therefore comes as no surprise to find that Sara and Frank Gueuning have stuck to the same successful formula of mixing the informal with the solicitous in supremely elegant surroundings. The Gueunings (he's Belgian) originally met at the hotel school in Lausanne and together successfully ran The Manor House in Moreton-in-Marsh for 10 years.

Bedrooms are individually decorated in country-house style – matching curtains, bedcovers and canopied bedheads in soft prints – while in the bathrooms Italian tiles and stencilling have been introduced to give a slightly exotic air. A heated outdoor swimming-pool has been added, and flowers from the large garden and the restored greenhouses are used to decorate the hotel. Although David Backhouse's bronzes still adorn the drawing-room, a much softer style of decoration has been introduced.

Chef, Andrew Hamer, formerly at The Manoir aux Quat' Saisons and Necker Island, has been maintaining high standards of cooking at Homewood Park for the past two years. And Sara's mother still produces the home-made jams, as well as the tantalizing bottled fruits in liqueur for winter months.

Nearby American Museum, 4 miles (6 km); Bath, 5 miles (8 km).

Hinton Charterhouse, Bath, Avon BA3 6BB
Tel (01225) 723731
Fax (01225) 723820
Location 5 miles (8 km) S of Bath, close to A36; in 10-acre grounds with ample car parking
Food & drink breakfast, lunch, dinner; restaurant licence
Prices B&B from £135; dinner £40-£55; bargain breaks
Rooms 17 double, 2 suites, all with bath and shower; all rooms have central heating, TV, phone, radio, hairdrier
Facilities sitting-room, bar, 3 dining-rooms; tennis, croquet; swimming-pool
Credit cards AE, DC, MC, V
Children by arrangement
Disabled access easy; 2 ground-floor bedrooms
Pets not accepted **Closed** never **Proprietors** Frank and Sara Gueuning

The South-West

Inn, Lacock

At the Sign of the Angel

Lacock and The Sign of the Angel go hand-in-hand: the 'perfect' English village (almost entirely in the preserving hands of the National Trust) and the epitome of the medieval English inn – half-timbered without, great log fires, oak panelling, beamed ceilings, splendid old beds and polished antique tables within.

There are many such inns sprinkled around middle England, but most are better enjoyed over a beer or two, or a meal, than overnight. Even here, the rooms vary in comfort and none could be called spacious. But they are all cosy and charming nonetheless, and full of character. The Angel is emphatically run as a small hotel rather than a pub – tellingly, there are no bars, and the residents' oak-panelled sitting-room on the first floor is quiet.

The Angel has belonged to the Levis family for over 40 years, and is now jointly run by daughter-in-law Lorna Levis and George Hardy with the help of village ladies. Lorna and George also share the cooking – traditional English food such as roasts, fish direct from Cornwall, and vegetarian options. Breakfast offers old-timers such as junket and prunes, as well as a huge cooked meal if you want it.

If the rooms in the inn itself are booked, don't turn down the cottage annexe, which is equally attractive and pleasantly secluded.

Nearby Lacock Abbey; Bowood House, 3 miles (5 km); Corsham Court, 3 miles (5 km); Sheldon Manor, 5 miles (8 km).

6 Church Street, Lacock, near Chippenham, Wiltshire SN15 2LA
Tel (01249) 730230
Fax (01249) 730527
Location 3 miles (5 km) S of Chippenham off A350, in middle of village; with gardens, and some car parking
Food & drink full breakfast, lunch, snacks, dinner Mon-Sun; full licence
Prices B&B £45-£52.50; dinner £10-£27.50; lunch from £5, Sun lunch £10-£20; bargain breaks
Rooms 10 double, all with bath; all have central heating, phone, tea/coffee kit
Facilities 3 dining-rooms, sitting-room
Credit cards AE, MC, V
Children welcome
Disabled wheelchair access
Pets dogs accepted, but not allowed in public rooms
Closed Christmas; Mon lunch
Proprietor George Hardy

The South-West

Country hotel, Liskeard

Well House

We've had consistently satisfied feedback on this hotel in recent years. Attention to detail is part of Nicholas Wainford's policy of providing a comfortable and restful background at this Victorian hill-top house with an outdoor heated swimming-pool. Everything here has been carefully chosen to create an atmosphere of calm and stylish luxury – up to country-house standard, but on a smaller scale (and at lower cost).

The house itself was built by a tea-planter in 1894, obviously with no expense spared. The beautifully tiled entrance hall, the staircase and all the woodwork are as new. The dining-room, the terrace and most of the richly decorated bedrooms look out over wooded grounds to the Looe valley.

The contemporary decoration and paintings on the walls are in no way at odds with the atmosphere of the old stone house. Nor is the modern style of the dishes on the daily changing menu. This is one of the best places to eat in Cornwall. It is also one of the most attractive too, with its soft yellow colour scheme. The wine list is extensive and largely French, with a heavy slant towards prestigious clarets. The lunch and dinner menus change daily.

Nearby Looe, Plymouth; Bodmin Moor.

St Keyne, Liskeard, Cornwall PL14 4RN
Tel (01579) 342001
Fax (01579) 343891
Location in countryside just outside village of St Keyne, 2 miles (3 km) S of Liskeard, off B3254; in 3.5-acre gardens with ample car parking
Food & drink breakfast, lunch, dinner; fully licenced
Prices B&B £42.50-£80; lunch, dinner from £21.95; 10% reduction for 4 nights or more
Rooms 8 double, one family room, all with bath; all have central heating, phone, radio, hairdrier, TV, trouser-press
Facilities dining-room, sitting-room, bar; tennis, heated swimming-pool, croquet
Credit cards AE, DC, MC, V
Children welcome; only over-8s in restaurant (high tea available for younger ones)
Disabled no special facilities
Pets by arrangement
Closed never
Proprietor Nicholas Wainford and Ione Nurdin

The South-West

Nansidwell

We had such a favourable unsolicited report on Nansidwell recently that we decided to give it a full page – a decision confirmed by an inspection visit in 1996.

It is a 1901 Arts and Crafts stone-mullioned house located in a superb spot close to the sea, with five acres of sub-tropical gardens – daffodils in January and banana trees bearing fruit as late as October. As you would expect, there are great sea views.

The reception area is large and welcoming; a wood fire burns year-round. The comfortable oak-floored sitting-room is full of paintings and photographs, magazines and books; there's a handsome antique desk, chintzy fabrics and fresh flowers. It could almost be the drawing-room of a private English country house; indeed the Robertsons (he an ex-London restaurateur and she an ex-banker) are determined to make you feel as if you are staying not in a hotel but in a well-run country house.

Our inspector found the bedrooms colourful, some quite small, but, most medium-sized. The food is ambitious and imaginative, and includes home-smoked salmon. Tea comes with home-made biscuits and is served in attractive china cups – 'very pleasant'. A quintessential charming small hotel in an ideal area for several days' break. The Cornwall Coast Path is a stroll away.

Nearby Glendurgan and Trebah gardens, both one mile (1.5 km).

Mawnan Smith, Falmouth, Cornwall TR11 5HU **Tel** (01326) 250340 **Fax** (01326) 250440 **Location** 0.5 mile (0.8 km) SW of village, SW of Falmouth; in gardens, with ample parking **Food & drink** breakfast, lunch, dinner, residential and restaurant licence **Prices** B&B from £102 (for 2 people); DB&B from £152 (for 2 people)	**Rooms** 12 double, all with bath; all rooms have central heating, colour TV, phone **Facilities** 2 sitting-rooms, dining-room; tennis **Credit cards** MC, V **Children** accepted **Disabled** access possible – 2 ground-floor bedrooms **Pets** accepted by arrangement **Closed** Jan **Proprietors** Jamie and Felicity Robertson

The South-West

Manor house, Melksham

Shurnhold House

Yet another grand old house rescued from decay in the late 1980s and put to new use – in this case, a bed-and-breakfast guest-house, in business since late 1988. The house is a beautifully proportioned stone-built Jacobean affair dating from 1640. It sits quite close to a busy main road on the outskirts of an unremarkable town, but is well shielded by trees (look for the signs, because you will not spot the house) and well placed for touring in several directions. A recent Swiss visitor gave it a rave report.

Inside, all is as you would wish. A flagstone floor in the bar/sitting-room, oak beams, log fires and pretty floral fabrics here and in the breakfast-room and sitting-room, which is full of books. Period furnishings are used wherever the opportunity arises and the budget allows. The beamed bedrooms are spacious, with restrained decoration – perhaps rich floral drapes against plain white walls – and several different styles of bed; several have fireplaces. Smoking is not allowed in the bedrooms.

Prices have been set at just the right level – higher than your typical B&B, but at half the rate of many 'country house hotels' occupying similarly splendid buildings. The licensed bar is an unusual feature for a B&B place.

Nearby Lacock, 2 miles (3.5 km); Bradford-on-Avon.

Shurnhold, Melksham, Wiltshire SN12 8DG
Tel (01225) 790555
Fax (01225) 793147
Location in countryside, one mile (1.5 km) NW of Melksham on A365 to Bath; in large garden with ample car parking
Food & drink breakfast; residential licence
Prices B&B £50-£88
Rooms 8 double, one family room, all with bath; all rooms have central heating, phone, TV, radio, hairdrier, tea/coffee kit
Facilities dining-room, sitting-room, bar/sitting-room
Credit cards AE, MC, V
Children welcome
Disabled no special facilities
Pets dogs accepted by prior arrangement
Closed never
Proprietor Sue Tanir

The South-West

Toxique

Our initial reporters were attracted to Toxique by a Michelin recommendation for its excellent stone farmhouse restaurant, but their curiosity was aroused by the pictures of its four bedrooms, and they decided to return for a night of decided luxury.

Melksham itself is not a pretty place, but the house is on the road towards the National Trust village of Lacock and stands in a stone-walled garden which is currently being upgraded from simple to 'show standard'. In the house itself, there are two dining-rooms, both candle-lit, one 'Mediterranean' with a pastoral mural across one wall, the other dark blue. They are separated by a cocoon-like sitting-room, its dark walls eccentrically studded with fir cones. Chairs are draped in deep purple and piled high with gold cushions which only adds to the general impression of a cosy and intimate cottage swept away by contemporary style. This finds its freest expression in the extremely comfortable bedrooms and *en suite* bathrooms, each one appropriately named: Desert, in summer lemon and blue, with sand around the bath; Oriental in black and white, with seagrass matting, low bed and spa bath with perfumed oils; Rococo with deep red walls, black velvet and gold brocade; and Colonial – basketwork furniture and mosquito netting.

Nearby Lacock, Bath, Bradford-on-Avon.

187 Woodrow Road, Melksham, Wilts SN12 7AY
Tel (01225) 702129
Fax (01225) 742773
Location turn left off Melksham High Street signposted Calne for 0.5 mile, then take left hand exit, Forest Road, for 1 mile; ample car parking
Food & drink breakfast, dinner
Prices DB&B £80-£95
Rooms 4 double with bath (one with jacuzzi); all rooms have central heating, one has colour TV
Facilities 2 dining-rooms, sitting-room, garden
Credit cards AE, MC, V
Children accepted
Disabled access difficult
Pets not accepted
Closed restaurant only, Sun to Wed
Manager Clare Ballinger

The South-West

Country Inn, Motcombe

Coppleridge Inn

An inviting 18thC farmhouse standing in an elevated position above the Blackmore Vale, and surrounded by its own meadows and woodland. Ranged around a large central courtyard are the former farm buildings, now converted into the hotel's ten spacious bedrooms. They are unpretentiously furnished with pine, bright fabrics and comfortable armchairs.

Guests wander across to the farmhouse for dinner where proprietor Chris Goodinge has created a homely atmosphere – flagstones, log fire, candlelight – and an eclectic menu. The bar is noted for its traditional beers and wines by the bottle or glass, and bistro-style meals can be taken here or in the charming dining-room where a more elaborate *à la carte* menu is also served. Children are well catered for and breakfasts are imaginative.

Those prone to exercise will do well here: apart from the tennis courts, cricket pitch and skittles available on site, an equestrian centre, leisure centre, clay pigeon shooting and trout fishing are all on hand in the village.

Nearby Shaftesbury, 2 miles (3 km); Stourhead House and Gardens, 6 miles (9 km); Salisbury and Longleat within reach.

Motcombe, Shaftesbury, Dorset SP7 9HW
Tel (01747) 851980
Fax (01747) 851858
Location 2 miles (3 km) NW of Shaftesbury at the N end of Motcombe on the minor road to Mere; 15-acre grounds with ample car parking
Foor & drink breakfast, lunch, dinner; licence
Prices B&B £37.50-£42.50; dinner £10-£20; reduction for 7 nights or more and special breaks

Rooms 10 double, all with bath; all rooms have central heating, TV, radio, phone, mini-bar
Facilities lounge, bar, garden room, dining-room, 2 tennis courts, cricket pitch, skittle alley (party bookings), children's play area
Credit cards AE, DC, MC, V
Children welcome
Disabled access easy
Pets welcome **Closed** never
Proprietor Christopher Goodinge

The South-West

Crugsillick Manor

Situated on the lovely Roseland Peninsula, with its many coves and harbours, Crugsillick is a beautiful listed Grade II* Queen Anne manor house. Lying in a sheltered hollow twenty minutes' walk from the Coastal Path and Pendower beach, it has a truly peaceful atmosphere, with views across the attractive gardens to a wooded valley beyond.

The antique-filled house is the home of the Barstow, who are superb hosts, treating their visitors as house guests whilst at the same time recognizing their desire for privacy. Their elegant drawing room, with its log fire and its highly unusual ceiling and scalloped friezes – reputedly moulded by French prisoners during the Napoleonic wars – is for the use of guests, and a four-course dinner is served by candlelight at a communal table in the 17thC dining-room, often using fruit and vegetables from the garden. Bedrooms are extremely comfortable, with cosy beds, prettily decorated and furnished with antiques. One satisfied reader writes of his enchantment with 'this wonderful old house', of the high standards and the warmth and hospitality of his hosts. In his view it was 'by far the most beautiful and pleasant place' he stayed in during a two week tour of the south-west. Guests are advised to arrive in the late afternoon. New to the guide last year; more reports please.
Nearby St Mawes, gardens of Heligan, Trelissick and Trewithin.

Ruanhighlanes, Truro,
Cornwall TR2 5LJ
Tel (01872) 501214
Fax (01872) 501214/501228
E-mail barstow crugsillick@csi.com
Location on road to Veryan off
A3078; in extensive garden
with ample car parking
Food & drink breakfast, picnic
lunch on request, dinner;
residential licence
Prices £35-£48; dinner £25
Rooms 3 double, 2 with bath,
one en-suite, one adjacent, one
with shower; all rooms have
central heating, tea/coffee kit,
hairdrier
Facilities drawing room,
dining-room, large hall
Credit cards MC, V
Children accepted over 12
Disabled access difficult
Pets accepted
Closed never
Proprietors Oliver and
Rosemary Barstow

The South-West

Boscundle Manor

A visit by one of our most experienced reporters confirms that Boscundle Manor continues to deserve its place in this guide. She was especially impressed by the attractive breakfast-room, the high standard of the bedrooms and the easygoing atmosphere, despite up-market trappings such as spa baths and a helicopter landing pad. The Flints continue to exude enthusiasm, still attend as carefully as ever to the needs of guests, and still find time to tend the large terraced garden themselves. Mary is the chef and her daily changing menu of simple but imaginative dishes is an important ingredient.

The delight of the place is its happy informality – the house is the Flints' home, with assorted furniture (some luxurious modern, some stripped pine, while some are elegant antiques). There are pictures, flowers, books and postcards everywhere. A snooker table, table tennis and darts are available in a beautifully converted barn.

Nearby Fowey, 5 miles (8 km); Restormel Castle, 6 miles (10km)

Tregrehan, St Austell, Cornwall PL25 3RL
Tel (01726) 813557
Fax (01726)814997
Location 2.5 miles (4 km) E of St Austell, close to A390; in 10- acre woodland gardens; ample car parking
Food & drink full breakfast, light lunches and snacks, dinner; residential licence
Prices B&B £55-£85; DB&B £75-£110; reductions for half-board (more than two nights)
Rooms 10 double, 8 with spa bath; 2 single, both with shower; all rooms have central heating, phone, colour TV with Teletext, radio/alarm, minibar, tea/coffee kit
Facilities 2 sitting-rooms, bar, 2 dining-rooms, conservatory/breakfast room; exercise room, heated indoor and outdoor pool, croquet, 2 practice golf holes, snooker, table tennis, darts **Credit cards** AE,MC, V **Children** welcome
Disabled access difficult to house; easy access to bungalow in grounds **Pets** accepted by arrangement but not allowed in public rooms
Closed Nov to Easter
Proprietors Andrew and Mary Flint

The South-West

Bowlish House

The formal appearance of this fine Palladian house seems to suggest that new arrivals should perhaps knock before barging in, but Bob and Linda Morley's regime behind the elegant façade is anything but pompous. These days, the public rooms of the house have rather less of the slightly battered air of an ageing dowager – there are new sofas in the sitting-room – but the atmosphere is still relaxed and home-like rather than august.

The restaurant and its food are the main focus of interest. You can sink into armchairs for pre-dinner drinks in the panelled bar, before moving into a pale yellow dining-room, hung with Italian architectural prints, to sample Linda Morley's polished culinary efforts and a fine wine list. A stylish conservatory extension offers a congenial space for coffee and liqueurs overlooking the well-kept gardens at the rear of the house, where there is seating for the summer months.

Up the fine wood-panelled staircase (an imported but appropriate feature), there are just three bedrooms – all comfortably furnished, with large *en suite* bathrooms and a formidable array of giveaways.

Nearby Wells, 4 miles (6 km) – cathedral, Bishop's palace; Glastonbury, 7 miles (11 km) – Tor, abbey; Mendip Hills – walking, caving; Bath within reach.

Wells Road, Shepton Mallet,
Somerset BA4 5JD
Tel (01749) 342022
Location just W of Shepton
Mallet on A371; with walled
garden and parking for 15 cars
Food & drink breakfast,
dinner; full licence
Prices B&B £29; dinner £22.50
Rooms 3 double, all with bath;
all rooms have central heating,
TV, radio/alarm, tea/
coffee kit

Facilities dining-room, bar,
sitting-room, conservatory
Credit cards MC, V
Children welcome
Disabled access difficult
Pets welcome in bedrooms
Closed 1 week in spring and
autumn
Proprietors Bob and Linda
Morley

The South-West

Simonsbath House

The first house on Exmoor when it was built in 1654, this long, low whitewashed stone building still presides over an isolated stretch of the moor, well placed for exploring (either by car or on foot) all the corners of the splendidly varied National Park. But the hotel itself is anything but desolate: Mike and Sue Burns, who arrived some years ago, inherited a tradition of providing unstinting comfort, generous and interesting food and a warm welcome in almost wickedly luxurious surroundings – and they carry on that tradition with vigour. Original features abound – wood panelling and large open fires in the sitting-room and bar/library, four-posters in some of the bedrooms – and great efforts have been made to keep the furnishings and decorations in harmony with the antiquity of the building. There is a modest but relaxing lawned garden, and beyond it the expanse of the moor.

The view of one of our most widely travelled reporters sums up Simonsbath: 'Very suave and comfortable; I'd love to go again, but it would have to be at someone else's expense.'

Nearby Lynton, 10 miles (16 km); Exmoor.

Simonsbath, Exmoor, Somerset TA24 7SH
Tel (01643) 831259
Fax (01643) 831557
Location 10 miles (16 km) S of Lynton, on B3223, in village; in one-acre grounds, ample car parking
Food & drink breakfast, lunch, dinner; residential and restaurant licence
Prices B&B £48-£66; DB&B £68-£86; reductions for 2 nights or more
Rooms 7 double, all with bath,

6 also with shower; all rooms have central heating, colour TV, phone, hairdrier
Facilities library with bar, sitting-room, dining-room
Credit cards AE, DC, MC, V
Children welcome over 10
Disabled access difficult – steps to entrance
Pets not allowed in house
Closed Dec to Jan
Proprietors Mike and Sue Burns

The South-West

The Abbey

When we last visited the Abbey, one of our over-riding impressions was of consistent good management. We don't often get reports about it, but this doesn't change our continuing belief that it is one of the most exceptional places to stay in the West Country. Jean and Michael Cox have taken a characterful house in the heart of old Penzance (it was built in the mid-17th century and given a Gothic façade in Regency times); they have decorated and furnished it with unstinting care, great flair and a considerable budget; and they have called it a hotel. But they run it much more as a private house, and visitors who expect to find hosts eager to satisfy their every whim are liable to be disappointed.

For its fans, the absence of hovering flunkies is of course a key part of the appeal of The Abbey. But there are other attractions – the confident and original decor, with abundant antiques and bric-a-brac, the spacious, individual bedrooms (one with an enormous pine-panelled bathroom); the welcoming, flowery drawing-room and elegant dining-room (both with log fires burning 'year-round'); the delightful walled garden behind the house; and not least, the satisfying dinners. Front rooms overlook the harbour and the dry dock.

Nearby Tregwainton Garden, 1.5 miles (2.5 km), St Michael's Mount, 3.5 miles (5.5 km); Land's End, 10 miles (16 km).

Abbey Street, Penzance,
Cornwall TR18 4AR
Tel (01736) 366906
Fax (01736) 351163
Location in middle of town, overlooking harbour; with private parking for 6 cars in courtyard
Food & drink breakfast, dinner; residential and restaurant licence
Prices B&B £50-£70; dinner £24.50

Rooms 6 double, 3 with bath, 3 with shower; one suite with bath; all rooms have central heating, tea/coffee kit, colour TV **Facilities** sitting-room, dining-room **Credit cards** AE, MC , V **Children** welcome if well behaved
Disabled access difficult
Pets dogs allowed in bedrooms **Closed** Christmas
Proprietors Jean and Michael Cox

The South West

Seaside hotel, Rock

St Enodoc

Well-heeled British families have flocked to Rock for their bucket-and-spade holidays for generations, but hotels which are both stylish and child-friendly have always been thin on the ground – until, that is, the 1998 emergence of the old-established St Enodoc Hotel from a change of ownership and total makeover.

The imposing building is typical of the area: no beauty, but solid and purposeful, with pebbledash walls and slate roof. Emily Todhunter's interior decoration suits its seaside location perfectly with its bright colours (paint, fabrics, painted furniture, modern art), clean lines, and easy-going comfort. The Californian-style Porthilly Bar and split-level Grill is popular with non-residents, although early reports indicate that the Pacific Rim food could improve. It has panoramic views, with a wide terrace for outdoor dining. Bedrooms feel like bedrooms rather than hotel rooms, with marvellous views across the Camel Estuary.

The hotel has a swimming-pool, a squash court, a sauna and a gym, and borders the two-course St Enodoc Golf Club, across which you will find the enchanting church of St Enodoc and the lovely gravestone of Sir John Betjeman.

Nearby Polzeath 2 miles (3 km); Padstow (by ferry).

Rock, Cornwall PL27 6LA
Tel (01208) 863394
Fax (01208) 863970
E-mail Enodoc@aol.com
Location overlooking the Camel Estuary, bordering St Enodoc golf course in Rock, 2 miles off B3314 from Wadebridge; car park (expensive)
Food & drink breakfast, lunch, dinner; full licence
Prices B&B £57.50-£100
Rooms 15 double, 3 suites, all with bath; all have individually controlled central heating, phone, TV, radio, hairdrier, fan **Facilities** sitting-room, library, dining-room, bar, billiard room; gym, sauna, squash court, swimming-pool
Credit Cards AE, DC, MC, V
Children welcome
Disabled ramp side entrance; adapted WC on ground floor
Pets not allowed **Closed** never
Proprietors Marler family

The South-West

Whitechapel Manor

Our most recent visitor to this Grade I Elizabethan manor house, comments on the 'excellent service and meals'; another, noted the 'admirable understatement' of the decoration in the public areas; the size and comfort of the bedrooms; the elegant bathrooms; the William and Mary plasterwork and Jacobean carved oak screen in the Grand Room which is used as a sitting-room.

A few years ago, Whitechapel Manor underwent a change of ownership, but we understand that the same high standards of hospitality set by former owners, the Shaplands, are continuing, with the emphasis on comfort, not on appearances and ceremony. This is not to say that the house lacks visual style – on the contrary, it is richly furnished with great taste (and at great expense).

Food is a highlight, with chef, Mathew Corner, still in charge of the cooking. Other features, small and large, noted by our inspector were breakfast cereal and fruit lavishly presented in unique pottery bowls; and the tranquil location, overlooking wooded farmland and low hills, in lawned terraced gardens, with flowering shrubs and old yew hedges.

Both external and internal renovation work is planned by the new owners, and we would welcome reports on any changes.
Nearby Exmoor.

South Molton, Devon
EX36 3EG
Tel (01769) 573377
Fax (01769) 573797
Location 3 miles (5 km) E of
South Molton, two miles from
A36l; with car parking
Food & drink full breakfast,
lunch, dinner; restaurant
licence
Prices B&B £55-£85; dinner
from £34; special breaks
Rooms 9 double, 2 single; all

with bath and shower; all
rooms have central heating,
colour TV, radio, hairdrier
Facilities 2 sitting-rooms, bar,
dining-room; croquet
Credit cards DC, MC, V
Children accepted
Disabled access difficult
Pets not accepted
Closed never
Proprietor Margaret Aris and
Charles Brown

The South-West

Langley House

This is the first hotel the Wilsons can call their own, but they are hardly beginners in the business: Peter, who cooks, came to it via the Lygon Arms at Broadway and then Ston Easton Park (both excellent hotels, in different ways, and excluded from this guide only because they fall outside our price and size limits); while Anne, who fronts, used to run the British Tourist Authority's Commendation Scheme – gamekeeper turned poacher, as it were. Between them, they ought to know what they are about.

The house is a modest building with a rambling garden in delectable, rolling Somerset countryside which is neglected by most visitors to the West Country. (Anne Wilson is happy to advise guests on where to go touring during the day and provides them with maps.) It is not ideally furnished – less elegance, more informality would be our prescription, both for the sitting-rooms and some of the bedrooms – but the Wilsons' warmth of welcome overcomes such reservations. Peter's four-course dinners help too. They are entirely fixed until the dessert, when there is an explosion of choice. His food is light and unconventional, lovingly presented, in the best modern British manner, and elicits plenty of praise from his guests – 'the Wilsons are exemplary in their care'.

Nearby Gaulden Manor, 2.5 miles (4 km); Exmoor; Quantock Hills; Taunton within reach.

Langley Marsh, Wiveliscombe, Somerset TA4 2UF
Tel (01984) 623318
Fax (01984) 624573
Location one mile (1.5 km) NW of Wiveliscombe, off B3227; in 4-acre gardens with ample car parking
Food & drink breakfast, dinner; residential and restaurant licence
Prices B&B £45-£75; dinner £25.50-£31; reductions for 2 nights or more
Rooms 7 double, 6 with bath, one with shower; 2 single, both with bath; one family room, with bath; all rooms have central heating, TV, phone, radio, hairdrier
Facilities bar, 2 sitting-rooms, restaurant; croquet
Credit cards AE, MC, V
Children welcome
Disabled access to ground floor easy but no lift to bedrooms
Pets accepted
Closed never
Proprietors Peter and Anne Wilson

The South-West

Fountain House

Fountain House offers an unusual formula in a provincial British city, but one which now seems to be gaining popularity: serviced apartments, combining the convenience of living and cooking space with the services of a bed-and-breakfast hotel. The building is a fine old Georgian townhouse. The suites vary widely in size, shape and style – some are essentially open-plan (one has the bed on a mezzanine), others divided into several separate rooms. Furnishings are smartly luxurious, in a variety of modern and reproduction styles. Fountain House is well placed for restaurants.
Nearby Assembly Rooms, Museum of Costume.

9-11 Fountain Buildings,
Lansdown Road, Bath, Avon
BA1 5DV
Tel (01225) 338622
Fax (01225) 445855
Location in middle of city,
close to main shopping area
Food & drink breakfast
Prices B&B from £125
Rooms 14 suites, sleeping 2 to
4 people, all with one or 2
baths; all suites have kitchen,
central heating, satellite TV,
phone, hairdrier, entry-phone

Facilities suites are serviced
daily as in a hotel
Credit cards AE, DC, MC, V
Children welcome
Disabled access possible;
lift/elevator
Pets accepted
Closed never
Proprietors Susan and Robin
Bryan

Haydon House ★

Complimentary sherry and home-made shortbread in the bedrooms add to the warm welcome at this elegantly furnished Edwardian house in a quiet residential street and yet just a ten-minute walk to the centre of Georgian Bath. The proprietors aim to provide a 'secluded retreat'. Bedrooms have pale decorative schemes, set off with delicately patterned floral fabrics, as does the spacious drawing-room overlooking the stylish garden, which has been landscaped into several courtyards. Porridge with a dash of whisky, and eggs Benedict are on the breakfast menu.
Nearby Bath city centre sights – abbey, Roman baths, museums.

9 Bloomfield Park, Bath
BA2 2BY
Tel (01225) 444919/427351
Fax (01225) 444919/427351
Location in a quiet residential
street with ample parking
Food & Drink full breakfast
Prices £35-£55
Rooms 3 double, 1 with shower
and bath, 2 with shower; one
twin, one family room with
shower and bath; all rooms
have central heating, TV,

phone, tea/coffee kit
Facilities sitting-room, garden
Credit cards AE, MC, V
Children by arrangement
Disabled limited access
Pets not accepted
Closed never
Proprietors Gordon and
Magdalene Ashman-Marr

The South-West

Holly Lodge

George Hall is well established on the Bath bed-and-breakfast scene, having run the highly regarded Haydon House (page 46) for several years. He opened up in this larger Victorian house in 1986 having rescued it from dereliction, and has again produced a base for tired sightseers which is pretty and restful as well as thoroughly comfortable. There are grand views of Bath from the garden, breakfast-room and some of the bedrooms, which are large and carefully furnished. The sitting-room too is spacious with comfy sofas, antiques and fresh flowers. Breakfast is impressive.
Nearby sights of central Bath.

8 Upper Oldfield Park, Bath, Avon BA2 3JZ
Tel (01225) 424042
Fax (01225) 481138
Location in residential area, half a mile (1 km) SW of city centre off A367; in garden, with car parking
Food & drink full breakfast
Prices B&B £37.50-£55
Rooms 5 double, all with bath and shower, one single with shower; all have central heating, satellite TV, phone, tea/ coffee kit; most have trouser-press, hairdrier
Facilities sitting-room
Credit cards AE, DC, MC, V
Children accepted by arrangement
Disabled access difficult
Pets not accepted
Closed never
Proprietor George Hall

Paradise House

David and Annie Lanz have taken over from the Cuttings who first rescued this 1720s house from decay over two decades ago and have now retired. The house, in a quiet cul-de-sac, is a steep walk or a winding drive up the wooded hill to the south of the city. This accounts for one of the guest-house's main attractions – the fine views shared by the secluded rear garden and several of the spacious, prettily decorated rooms. The Lanzes have plans to upgrade the bathrooms. Reports would be welcome.
Nearby Abbey, Roman Baths and Pump Room, Holburne Museum, Victoria Art Gallery (most within 10 min walk).

86-88 Holloway, Bath, Avon BA2 4PX
Tel (01225) 317723
Fax (01225) 482005
E-mail paradise@apsleyhouse.easynet.co.uk
Website www.s-h-systems.co.uk/hotels/paradise.html
Location on S side of city off A367; in 0.5-acre gardens; 3 garages; ample street parking
Food & drink full breakfast; residential licence
Prices B&B £32.50-£45 (1-night bookings for Fri or Sat not accepted); reduction for 4 nights or more **Rooms** 9 double, 5 with bath, 2 with shower; all rooms have central heating, TV, phone, tea/coffee kit
Facilities breakfast room, sitting-room **Credit cards** AE, MC, V **Children** not suitable
Disabled access fair **Pets** not accepted **Closed** over Christmas **Proprietors** David and Annie Lanz

SOUTHERN ENGLAND

The South-West

Town guest-house, Bath

Queensberry Hotel

This Bath hotel is slightly large for our purposes, but cannot be allowed to escape the net. Its owners, Stephen and Penny Ross, opened it in 1988 and transformed three Georgian terraced houses into one of the most relaxing, stylish and personal places to stay in the city.

The sitting-room is beautifully furnished in muted colours; bedrooms are smart and spacious and equipped with easy chairs and breakfast tables. Informal dining in the Olive Tree restaurant, and there is a sunny courtyard garden.

Nearby Assembly Rooms, Museum of Costume, The Circus; Avon

Russel Street, Bath, Avon BA1 2QF
Tel (01225) 447928
Fax (01225) 446065
Location in middle of city, close to main shopping area; paved gardens behind; daytime car parking restricted
Food & drink breakfast, dinner; restaurant and residential licence
Prices B&B £55-£100; winter break available Nov to Mar
Rooms 22 double, all with bath; all rooms have central heating, phone, colour TV
Facilities sitting-room, bar, restaurant
Credit cards DC, MC, V
Children welcome; cots available
Disabled access possible; lift/elevator
Pets not accepted
Closed one week Christmas/New Year
Proprietors Stephen and Penny Ross

Town guest-house, Bath

Somerset House

The Seymours took the name of their established guest-house with them when they moved further up Bathwick Hill in 1985, and with it the formula for which they had become known: caring, personal service (not for those who seek anonymity), with harmoniously furnished rooms and thoroughly good food – mainly traditional English in style, but with an occasional excursion into foreign territory – at impressively modest prices. The Georgian character of the building has been carefully preserved; it is a strictly no-smoking house.

Nearby Holburne Museum and Pulteney Bridge.

35 Bathwick Hill, Bath, Avon BA2 6LD
Tel (01225) 466451
Fax (01225) 317188
Location on SE side of city; private car parking
Food & drink breakfast, dinner, lunch on Sun only; restaurant licence
Prices B&B £23.50-£52; DB&B £44.50-£70; reduction for 3 nights plus and for children sharing parents' room; bargain breaks Oct-May
Rooms 4 double, 5 family rooms all with bath and shower; one single, with shower; all have central heating, phone, radio **Facilities** sitting-room (with bar), dining-room
Credit cards AE, DC, MC, V
Children welcome
Disabled not suitable for severe disabilities **Pets** small dogs only **Closed** never
Proprietors J and M Seymour

The South-West

Sydney Gardens

Off the main tourist track in a quiet residential area of Bath overlooking a small park, Sydney Gardens is nevertheless conveniently close to Bath's popular sights. When the Beavens, took over this large, Italianate Victorian house they completely refurbished it. Bedrooms are individually and freshly decorated in well co-ordinated colours, and even those right at the top of the house have enough space for easy chairs. The breakfast room and sitting-room are light and gracious, and the smoking ban (in the whole house) ensures that non-smokers will enjoy their breakfast.

Nearby Holburne Museum, canal towpath walk.

Sydney Road, Bath, Avon, BA2 6NT
Tel (01225) 464818
Fax (01225) 484347
Location close to middle of town; in small garden with some private car parking and more on street
Food & drink full breakfast; no licence
Prices B&B £45-£75
Rooms 6 double, all with bath and shower; all rooms have central heating, phone, colour TV, tea/coffee kit, hairdrier, radio alarm
Facilities sitting-room, breakfast room
Credit cards AE, MC, V
Children welcome over 4
Disabled access difficult
Pets dogs by arrangement
Closed Christmas and Jan
Proprietors Geraldine and Peter Beaven

Bridge House

Originally a 13thC clergy house, this stone building includes decently sized (some grand-sized) bedrooms by Peter Pinkster, who first converted a coach house and then built the conservatory overlooking a walled garden. Pale pink panelling gives the restaurant a Georgian atmosphere and the accolade-winning cooking features local produce. A recent visitor comments on its 'welcoming freshness'; a party of walkers appreciated the food, comfort and location. No smoking in the dining-room or conservatory.

Nearby Parnham House, Mapperton Gardens, 1.5 miles (2.5 km); Kingcombe Meadows, 3 miles (5 km).

Beaminster, Dorset DT8 3AY
Tel (01308) 862200
Fax (01308) 863700
Location on S edge of Beaminster just off A3066; ample car parking
Food & drink full breakfast, dinner; full licence
Prices B&B £44-£80; DB&B £64-£98; dinner from £21.50
Rooms 8 double, 4 twin, 1 family room, all with bath, some with power showers, 1 single with shower; all rooms have central heating, tea/coffee kit, TV, most with phone
Facilities sitting-room, bar, restaurant, conservatory, walled garden
Credit cards AE, DC, MC, V
Children welcome
Disabled 4 bedrooms with easy access **Pets** not in public rooms or unattended in bedrooms
Closed never
Proprietor Peter Pinkster

The South-West

Frog Street Farm

This flower-bedecked Somerset 'longhouse' is hidden deep in the countryside and approached by a narrow lane. According to our latest reporter it is 'an ideal place to escape to, and in which to be entertained by the friendly Veronica Cole,' a farmer's wife with a big interest in national hunt racehorses. The house has considerable character and warmth, with a handsome oak-beamed inglenook in one sitting-room and some very antique panelling.

There is a carefully prepared set meal of English food.

Nearby Barrington Court, 5 miles (8 km); Vale of Taunton.

Beercrocombe, Taunton, Somerset TA3 6AF
Tel & fax (01823) 480430
Location 6 miles (10 km) SE of Taunton, one mile (1.5 km) from A358; car parking
Food & drink full breakfast, dinner; no licence
Prices B&B £25-£27; dinner £16; reductions for 4 days or more
Rooms 3 double, 2 with bath, one with shower; all rooms have central heating, tea/
coffee kit
Facilities 2 sitting-rooms
Credit cards not accepted
Children welcome over 11
Disabled access difficult
Pets not accepted
Closed Nov to Mar
Proprietor Veronica Cole

Bel Alp House

Recent owners, Jack and Mary Twist, have been busy implementing the alterations promised in our last edition, and have concentrated on increasing overall comfort at Bel Alp House without diminishing its character. Rooms have been refurbished, and new bathrooms and a patio have been added.

Peacefully set in 8 lush acres, this is a fine Edwardian house high above Haytor, enjoying magnificent views. Our latest reporter observed that the place has the comfortable, relaxed atmosphere of a large family home. More comments on the changes welcome.

Nearby Haytor Rocks, Lustleigh, Dartmoor.

Haytor, nr Bovey Tracey, Devon, TQ13 9XX
Tel (01364) 661217
Fax (01364) 661292
Location in countryside, E of Haytor, 2.5 miles (4 km) W of Bovey Tracey off B3387; private car parking
Food & drink breakfast, lunch, dinner; restaurant licence
Prices B&B £60-£80; dinner £30
Rooms 8 double (4 twin), all
with bath or shower; all have central heating, phone, radio, hairdrier, TV, tea/coffee kit
Facilities 2 sitting-rooms, dining-room
Credit cards AE, DC, MC, V
Children very welcome; games room
Disabled not suitable
Pets welcome
Closed never
Proprietors Jack and Mary Twist

The South-West

Chilvester Hill House

'All that you promise,' write a New York couple of Chilvester Hill House. The Dilleys 'genuinely enjoy hosting their guests and run an excellent operation.' They started taking guests into their stone-built Victorian house in the early 1980s, and since then have gone from strength to strength. The house has large rooms with high ceilings, elegantly furnished; family photos, books and ornaments mingle with antiques, velvet sofas and old prints. The three bedrooms are spacious, and carefully decorated in different floral styles. Meals are eaten at the family table.

Nearby Bowood; Avebury and Lacock, both 7 miles (11 km).

Calne, Wiltshire SN11 0LP
Tel (01249) 813981
Fax (01249) 814217
Location in rural setting, 0.5 mile (1 km) W of Calne just off A4, signed to Bremhill; with gardens and car parking
Food & drink breakfast, dinner by arrangement; residential licence
Prices B&B £35-£55; reductions for longer stays and in low season; dinner £18-£25 (4 courses plus coffee)

Rooms 3 double, all with bath; all rooms have heating, TV, radio, tea/coffee kit
Facilities dining-room, 2 sitting-rooms
Credit cards AE, DC, MC, V
Children accepted over 12
Disabled no special facilities
Pets not accepted
Closed one week low season
Proprietors John and Gill Dilley

Fosse Farmhouse ★

We revisited recently to discover that Caron Cooper's B&B (which also serves dinner) has been taken up by the Japanese (including three members of the Imperial family): apparently they come here for lessons in preparing cream teas. Talented Caron's house is a delightful confection of antique furniture, stripped pine, ornaments and confidently chosen fabrics and colours. An accomplished cook (she presented a short series on country cooking on BBC TV in 1997), her dinners offer no choice of main course, but vegetarians can be catered for.

Nearby Castle Combe, 2 miles (3 km); Cotswolds.

Nettleton Shrub, Nettleton, nr Chippenham, Wiltshire
Tel (01249) 782286
Fax (01249) 783066
E-mail CaronCooper@Compuserve.com
Location in countryside off B4039, 6 miles (10 km) NW of Chippenham; with 1.5 acre grounds, private car parking
Food & drink full breakfast, lunch, dinner; full licence
Prices B&B £42.50-£67.50; lunch from £7.50, dinner £25

Rooms 4 double, one with bath, 3 with shower; one single with shower, one suite, one family room with bath; all rooms have central heating, TV, tea/coffee kit, hairdrier
Facilities dining-room, sitting-room, tea-room
Credit cards AE, MC, V
Children accepted **Disabled** access not easy **Pets** by arrangement **Closed** never
Proprietor Caron Cooper

The South-West

The Whiteleaf

The Rayners took over this pleasant 1930s guest-house in 1997. It may appear small and unremarkable, but what it lacks in visual appeal is more than balanced by the high standard of comfort and hospitality.

The garden is a peaceful retreat from the lively seaside village of Croyde, which has an excellent beach. What's more, David's cooking goes from strength to strength – English/Continental, some original dishes, regularly changing menus – 'superb' was one visitor's verdict.

Nearby Exmoor, Lundy Island, North Devon Coast Path.

Croyde, Nr Braunton, Devon EX33 1PN
Tel (01271) 890266
Location quarter of a mile (400m) SW of village, on B3231; with car parking
Food & drink breakfast, dinner; restaurant and residential licence
Prices B&B £27-£37; dinner £17.50
Rooms 3 double, 2 with bath and shower, 1 with shower; 1 twin with bath and shower; one family room (2 adults and up to 3 children); all rooms have central heating, TV, radio, alarm, hairdrier, tea/coffee kit, minibar
Facilities sitting-room, dining-room **Credit cards** AE, MC, V **Children** welcome; no special meals
Disabled not suitable
Pets welcome
Closed occasionally
Proprietors David and Sue Rayner

Hunts Tor

Hunts Tor is a compact 17thC house with Regency additions near an old pub off the square of a small and peaceful village. The Harrisons quit the rat race to set up here, opening their doors in 1985. We revisited in 1996 and noted again how well they had restored the house. It is furnished in a distinctive style, indulging the Harrisons' affection for art deco. Bedrooms are simple and neat – but, according to a recent visitor, 'could be more lively'. Two of the rooms have sitting-rooms and one a sitting area. A key attraction is Sue's food: 'beautifully cooked and presented.'

Nearby Castle Drogo; Dartmoor.

Drewsteignton, Devon EX6 6QW
Tel & fax (01647) 281228
Location on village square, 12 miles (19 km) W of Exeter; with private parking for 2 cars and parking on the square
Food & drink breakfast, dinner; restaurant licence
Prices B&B £30-£35; dinner £20-£23
Rooms 3 double (1 twin), all with bath; all rooms have central heating, hairdrier, TV, tea/coffee kit
Facilities 2 dining-rooms (one with bar), sitting-room
Credit cards not accepted
Children accepted over 10
Disabled access difficult
Pets well behaved dogs accepted in bedrooms
Closed Nov to Mar
Proprietors Sue and Chris Harrison

The South-West

Number 3

Both the main house of this listed Georgian building and the recently converted coach-house are richly decorated, with oil paintings in gilt frames, antiques and rich colours in the public areas, and carefully co-ordinated fabrics in the large and comfortable bedrooms.

A Swiss visitor and his wife found the location 'utterly charming'. We would welcome further reports. Although food is not served at Number 3, guests are given advice on recommended local restaurants.

Nearby Abbey, Tor; Wells Cathedral, 5 miles (8 km).

3 Magdalene Street,
Glastonbury, Somerset
BA6 9EW
Tel (01458) 832129
Fax (01458) 834227
Location in middle of town; with walled garden and secure parking for 8 cars
Food & drink breakfast
Prices B&B £35-£55
Rooms 4 double, all with bath; family room by arrangement; all rooms have phone, central heating, tea/coffee kit, TV

Facilities bar, sitting-room, walled garden
Credit cards AE, MC, V
Children welcome
Disabled access difficult – two steps to front entrance
Pets not accepted
Closed Dec and Jan
Proprietor Pat Redmond

Lower Pitt Restaurant

As the name suggests, the emphasis here is firmly on food. Word is spreading fast about the Lyons' small restaurant in this quiet Exmoor hamlet. The house is pretty : a long, low white cottage with plants clambering around the porch. The rear gardens also indicate green fingers – conifers almost have to be restrained from bursting in on the diners in the airy conservatory. Guests perch for drinks in the small bar or sitting-room before dinner. The three comfortable bedrooms are small and cottagey, tastefully decorated but not luxurious. A relaxed and informal atmosphere prevails.

Nearby Exmoor, coast – about 15 miles (24km).

East Buckland, Barnstaple,
North Devon EX32 0TD
Tel & Fax (01598) 760243
Location in village, 5 miles (8km) NW of South Molton; with garden and car parking
Food & drink breakfast, dinner; restaurant licence
Prices DB&B £60; reduction for 2 nights or more; dinner about £25
Rooms 3 double, one with bath, 2 with shower; all have

central heating, hairdrier
Facilities bar, sitting-room, 2 dining-rooms
Credit cards AE, MC, V
Children accepted over 10
Disabled access difficult
Pets not accepted
Closed Christmas; restaurant only, Sun and Mon in winter
Proprietors Jerome and Suzanne Lyons

The South-West

Combe House

This imposing Elizabethan manor lies hidden behind ancient beech-woods and within acres of private woodland, meadows and pasture. Despite the grandeur of the house, new owners Ken and Ruth Hunt, who have run similar hotels in England and Australia, aim for an informal atmosphere. There is a country house feel; warm-toned, oak-panelled rooms have comfortable seating, antique furniture and an abundance of fresh flowers. Bedrooms are spacious and elegant, many with views to the Blackmoor Hills. Weekly changing country menu, using local seasonal food, from head chef, Kyan Hooper.

Nearby Cadhay House, 4 miles (6 km); east Devon coast.

Gittisham, near Honiton, Devon EX14 0AD
Tel (01404) 540400
Fax (01404) 46004
E-mail stay@combe-house.co.uk
Website www.combe-house.co.uk
Location one mile (1.5 km) SW of Honiton off A30; ample car parking
Food & drink full breakfast, lunch, tea, dinner; restaurant & residential licence
Prices B&B from £49-£95; suite £120; lunch £15; dinner from £25; special breaks **Rooms** 14 double (1 with 4-poster beds), 2 suites, all with bath; all rooms have central heating, colour TV, phone, hairdrier **Facilities** bar, sitting-rooms, 2 dining-rooms; fishing, croquet **Credit cards** AE, DC, MC, V **Children** welcome **Disabled** access easy to ground floor only **Pets** dogs by arrangement (£5 per night); not in dining-room **Closed** never **Proprietors** Ken and Ruth Hunt

Tarr Steps Hotel

This long, low, cream coloured building, once a Georgian rectory, nestles serenely against wooded slopes on the upper reaches of the River Barle. It is set in 11 acres of grounds and gardens, with delectable views across the valley to the moorland and woods beyond. Inside, you will find antique furniture, an abundance of flowers, country-style bedrooms, and roaring fires on colder days.

Menus emphasize light English cooking, using local produce. Plenty of outdoor pursuits: clay pigeon and rough shooting, fishing and riding (guests are welcome to bring their own horses).

Nearby Tarr Steps bridge; Exmoor.

Hawkridge, near Dulverton, Somerset TA22 9PY
Tel (01643)851293
Fax (01643)851218
Location 7 miles (11 km) NW of Dulverton, W of B3223, in countryside; ample car parking
Food & drink full breakfast, lunch, tea, dinner; licenced
Prices DB&B (including afternoon tea) from £57; special offers available
Rooms 9 double with bath; 2 single; all rooms have central heating **Facilities** bar, sitting-room, 2 dining-rooms **Credit cards** MC, V **Children** welcome **Disabled** access good to all public rooms; one ground-floor bedroom **Pets** dogs accepted in bedrooms, but not in public rooms; kennels available **Closed** 10 days early Feb **Proprietors** Sue and Shaun Blackmore

The South-West

Court Barn

Its food and wine win national awards for Court Barn, a four-square Victorian house where antiques, souvenirs, books and games jostle with sometimes unusual furnishings in a carefree medley of patterns. The result is reassuring: this home-like environment spells comfort far beyond the meretricious harmony of hotels colour-matched by designers. Beautifully kept grounds surround the house; croquet hoops, putting holes and badminton and tennis nets suggest plenty to do outside. Teas are a speciality. Our latest reader's report is positive.

Nearby Bude, 7 miles (11 km); Dartmoor within reach.

Clawton, Holsworthy, Devon EX22 6PS
Tel (01409) 271219
Fax (01409) 271309
Location 3 miles (5 km) S of Holsworthy, near Clawton church off A388; car parking
Food & drink full breakfast, lunch, tea, dinner; residential and restaurant licence
Prices B&B £35-£50; dinner £15-£21; bargain breaks £50-£58 per person
Rooms 7 double (1 4-poster),

5 with bath and shower, 2 with shower; one single with shower; all rooms have central heating, TV, phone, radio, tea/coffee kit, hairdrier **Facilities** 2 sitting-rooms, bar, 2 dining-rooms, TV room
Credit cards AE, DC, MC, V
Children welcome **Disabled** no special facilities **Pets** accepted in some bedrooms
Closed 1 week Jan
Proprietors Susan and Robert Wood

Meadow House

This former Georgian rectory with 16thC origins is set in grounds of 8-acres and has a beautifully peaceful setting between the Quantocks and the sea. It is furnished with real taste, and immaculately cared for; the bedrooms (and bathrooms) are large, the public rooms warm and inviting (with hundreds of books for guests' use).

A recent visitor appreciated the relaxed family atmosphere, but felt that the food was average. Nearby Kilve beach is interesting, with fossil-rich rocks; and the coastline here is dramatic.

Nearby Dunster Castle, 10 miles (16km); Quantock Hills.

Sea Lane, Kilve, Somerset TA5 1EG
Tel (01278) 741546
Fax (01278) 741663
Location N of village of Kilve, on A39 5 miles (8 km) E of Williton; ample car parking
Food & drink full breakfast, dinner; retail, residential and restaurant licence
Prices B&B from £37.50-£60; 6-course dinner £25; reductions for 2 nights or more

Rooms 10 double, all with bath; cottage suites available; all rooms have TV, central heating, radio/alarm, tea/coffee kit, hairdrier, phone
Facilities dining-room, sitting-room, study, bar, conservatory; croquet **Credit cards** AE, DC, MC, V **Children** welcome
Disabled access difficult
Pets by arrangement **Closed** never **Proprietors** Howard and Judith Wyer-Roberts

SOUTHERN ENGLAND

The South-West

Woodley House

The proprietor's previous establishment, Willmead Farm, which appeared in this guide, was always rated enthusiastically, not least for Hilary's conviviality. Hilary left the oak beams of her old farmhouse for a handsome, modern house with large leaded windows in an idyllic setting with uninterrupted views of hills and woodland.

Uniquely for this guide, there is only one bedroom, arranged as a sitting-room. Another room (no wardrobe or drawers) is sometimes available for a larger group. Hilary serves a hearty breakfast accompanied by freshly baked granary bread. No smoking.

Nearby Newton Abbot, 5 miles (8 km); Dartmoor.

Caseley, Lustleigh, nr Newton Abbot, Devon TQ13 9TN
Tel (01647) 277214
Location in a secluded hamlet 2 miles (3 km NW of Bovey Tracey, off A382
Food & Drink full breakfast
Prices B&B £24
Rooms 1 twin, with bath and shower, TV, tea/coffee kit, hairdrier, central heating
Facilities breakfast room, sitting-room; garden patio
Credit cards not accepted

Children over 10
Disabled not suitable
Pets by arrangement
Closed never
Proprietor Mrs Hilary Roberts

St Petroc's House

If you would prefer to stay somewhere a little removed from the bustle of Rick Stein's famous Seafood Restaurant (see page 57), you could try his establishment just up the hill. This is an attractive white-painted building, with views across the older parts of town as well as of the estuary. Rooms here are less expensive than at the Seafood Restaurant, but still comfortable and furnished with impeccable taste. Some are on the small side. The place exudes a friendly atmosphere, not least in the Bistro. A short, reasonably priced menu features meat and vegetable dishes as well as seafood.

Nearby surfing beaches; Trevose Head.

4 New Street, Padstow, Cornwall PL28 8EA
Tel (01841) 532700
Fax (01841) 532942
Location just off the main square; private garage parking
Food & drink breakfast, lunch, dinner (except Mon); residential and restaurant licence
Prices £35-£60; dinner £19.95
Rooms 12 double, 1 single, 9 with bath, 4 with shower; all rooms have central heating,
phone, TV, tea/coffee kit, hairdrier
Facilities sitting room, dining-room, garden
Credit cards MC, V
Children welcome
Disabled not suitable
Pets accepted
Closed Christmas and New Year
Proprietors Rick and Jill Stein

The South-West

Seafood Restaurant

A first-rate restaurant with attractive, spacious and more than adequately comfortable rooms above – some with wonderful estuary views. The real reason to stay here, though, is the superb seafood – straight from the fishing boats and served by friendly staff in a lively dining-room. What the place lacks in public rooms and grounds, it makes up for in laid-back atmosphere and its prime position on the quay.

One of our most seasoned inspectors found everything, not least the food, up to expectations. See also St. Petroc's (page 56).

Nearby Surfing beaches, Trevose Head.

Riverside, Padstow, Cornwall PL28 8BY
Tel (01841) 532485
Fax (01841) 533574
Location on quay in village, 4 miles (6 km) NW off A39 between Wadebridge and St Columb; car park opposite
Food & drink full breakfast, lunch, dinner; restaurant and residential licence
Prices B&B £45-£105; lunch £28, dinner £34; reductions for 2 nights out of season, and for children
Rooms 3 double, all with bath; all rooms have central heating, phone, TV, minibar, radio, tea/coffee kit
Facilities conservatory **Credit cards** MC, V **Children** welcome **Disabled** access difficult **Pets** dogs accepted **Closed** Christmas and New Year
Proprietors Rick and Jill Stein

Nanscawen House

'No problems about this entry,' writes an astute visitor: 'It really is an excellent bed-and-breakfast guest-house.' Another describes it as a relaxing retreat, and is impressed by 'first-class' breakfasts. The carefully extended old house is in beautiful mature gardens with a 'wonderfully located' outdoor heated pool. There are only three rooms, all comfortable with good bathrooms. Some may find the decoration a touch feminine, but this didn't detract overall. There is a welcoming drawing-room: you normally eat in the cane-furnished conservatory. No smoking.

Nearby beaches, coast path; Lanhydrock House, 6 miles (10 km)

Prideaux Road, St Blazey, nr Par, Cornwall PL24 2SR
Tel and **Fax** (01726) 814488
Location in countryside, 0.5 mile (1 km) off A390, NW of St Blazey, 3 miles (5 km) NE of St Austell; in 5-acre grounds, with car parking
Food & drink breakfast, residential licence
Prices B&B £34-£39
Rooms 3 double (one twin), all with spa bath; all have TV, phone, central heating, radio, hairdrier; video on request
Facilities drawing-room, conservatory dining-room; heated outdoor swimming-pool
Credit cards MC, V
Children not accepted under 12 **Disabled** access difficult **Pets** not accepted
Closed Christmas, 2 days
Proprietors Fiona and Keith Martin

The South-West

Town hotel, St Mawes

Tresanton

Opened in summer 1998 by Olga Polizzi, daughter of Lord Forte. This is very much her creation, one in which city sophistication fit for the pages of glossy magazines (with prices to match) is married to Cornish character, in this case a cluster of cottages on different levels. In the '40s they were a yachtsmen's club, before becoming a well-known hotel whose heyday was in the '60s. Early reports from the reborn Tresanton speak of hiccups with food and service, but no doubt these are teething troubles and hopefully the hotel has by now slipped into gear. More reports please.

Nearby Glendurgan and Trebah gardens.

St Mawes, Cornwall TR2 5DR
Tel (01326) 270055
Fax (01326) 270053
Location in town, just below castle, 14 miles (22 km) S of Truro; parking
Food & drink breakfast, lunch, dinner; full licence
Prices B&B £150-£250; dinner £25
Rooms 25 double, 2 family; all rooms have central heating, phone, TV, video, hairdrier
Facilities sitting-room, dining-room, bar, terrace, private beach, yacht for charter, water-sports
Credit cards AE, DC, MC, V
Children welcome
Disabled 3 rooms on ground floor
Pets not accepted
Closed Jan
Proprietor Olga Polizzi

Country hotel, Shipham

Daneswood House

The exterior of this tall Edwardian house does not immediately inspire confidence, with its pebble-dashing and fake beams. Don't be put off: inside is a welcoming, personal atmosphere and richly decorated bedrooms with traditional furniture. Less atmospheric, but perhaps more comfortable, are those rooms in a recently built wing, with spa baths.

Food and wine are taken seriously. But the winding drive hints at the key attraction: a high setting affording splendid views over the Mendips.

Nearby Cheddar Gorge and caves, 2 miles (3 km).

Cuck Hill, Shipham, nr Winscombe, Somerset BS25 1RD
Tel (01934) 843145
Fax (01934) 843824
Location 1.5 miles (2 km) off A38, 13 (21 km) miles S of Bristol; with 4-acre grounds and ample car parking
Food & drink breakfast, dinner; residential and restaurant licence
Prices B&B £65-£75; dinner £29.95
Rooms 12 double (4 twin), 10 with bath, 2 with shower; all rooms have central heating, TV, radio, tea/coffee kit
Facilities dining-room, sitting-room, bar **Credit cards** AE, DC, MC, V **Children** accepted **Disabled** no special facilities **Pets** tolerated if small **Closed** Christmas to New Year **Proprietor** David and Elise Hodges

The South-West

Innsacre

Log fires and beams add to the cosy air of Innsacre, a converted 17thC farmhouse and barns, set in 10 acres of orchards and hillsides. Inside are four comfortable bedrooms with carved dark-wood French or cottage-style beds, a large sitting-room with inglenook fireplace, and a secluded south-facing terrace. An imaginative 3-course set dinner is served at 8 p.m., and vegetarians are catered for. A hot tray supper is provided for guests arriving late.

The location is truly peaceful and remote. We had positive comments in a recent reader's letter.

Nearby coast, 3 miles (5 km); Abbotsbury, 7 miles (12.5 km).

Shipton Gorge, Bridport, Dorset DT6 4LJ
Tel & Fax (01308) 456137
Location in quiet countryside, 2 miles E of Bridport, S of A35; with ample car parking
Food & drink breakfast, dinner; residential licence
Prices B&B £29-£45 (50% reduction for children sharing); dinner £14.50; 'hot tray supper' £10.50 (except Saturdays, Easter to Oct)
Rooms 4 double (1 twin), all with bath; all have TV, radio
Facilities bar, sitting-room
Credit cards MC, V
Children over 9
Disabled no special facilities
Pets welcome
Closed Christmas
Proprietor Sydney and Jayne Davies

Oxenham Arms

Our latest reporter was struck with the character of this building, thought to be the only dwelling constructed around a standing stone. The creeper-covered granite inn has been serving the needs of the visitor since at least the 15th century. Plumbing and wiring apart, the building has changed little since Tudor times, with its wealth of mullions, flagstones, dark panelling and oak beams. It is more of a hotel than a pub – the bar is small (though cosy), and there is a pleasant sitting-room. Bedrooms are appropriately simple. Food is plain, too, but good value.

Nearby Okehampton Castle, Castle Drogo; Dartmoor.

South Zeal, near Okehampton, Devon EX20 2JT
Tel (01837) 840244
Fax (01837) 840791
Location 4 miles (6 km) E of Okehampton, just off A30, in middle of village; with garden at rear, and adequate car parking in forecourt
Food & drink breakfast, lunch, tea, dinner; full licence
Prices B&B £25-£45; dinner from £15.50
Rooms 8 double with bath, 4 also with shower; all rooms have colour TV, telephone, tea/coffee kit
Facilities bar with family room, dining-room, sitting-room
Credit cards AE, DC, MC, V
Children welcome
Disabled access difficult
Pets welcome **Closed** never
Proprietors Mr and Mrs James H Henry

The South-West

Carpenters Arms

The English country inn at its best. The flower-bedecked Carpenters Arms was formed many years ago in a row of 17thC miners' cottages, and has all the essential pub features. In other ways it is a world away from the norm. To find 12 spacious, prettily decorated rooms with *en suite* bathrooms above a pub is one distinction. Another is the food, for which the Arms is locally renowned. In the cosy restaurant the food is adventurous; in the informal Coopers Parlour the emphasis is on simplicity and value. 'Everything the guide promises,' says a recent reader's letter.
Nearby Bristol; Bath 10 miles (16 km).

Stanton Wick, Pensford, Avon BS18 4BX
Tel (01761) 490202
Fax (01761) 490763
Location in rural setting, 7 miles (11 km) S of Bristol, just off A37 (follow signs from A368 which crosses A37 at Chelwood); with ample car parking
Food & drink full breakfast, lunch, dinner; full licence
Prices B&B £34.75-£52.50; dinner about £12-£20

Rooms 12 double, all with bath; all rooms have central heating, phone, TV, radio, tea/coffee kit , trouser-press
Facilities 2 restaurant,1 bar
Creditcards AE, DC, MC, V
Children not suitable
Disabled access difficult
Pets not accepted in bedrooms
Closed Christmas Day; restaurant only, Sun evening and Mon
Proprietor Nigel Pushman

Plumber Manor

This is a handsome Jacobean manor house, 'modernized' earlier this century, that has been in the Prideaux-Brune family for well over 300 years. Since 1973 they have been running it as an elegant but relaxed restaurant with comfortable bedrooms. Richard Prideaux-Brune, described by a recent satisfied reporter as 'charismatic', is much in evidence. He and his brother Brian, who produces the highly-regarded food, draw in restaurant customers from far and wide – expect plenty of bustle on Friday and Saturday evenings, and non-residents in the dining-room.
Nearby Purse Caundle Manor, 6 miles (10 km).

Hazelbury Bryan Road, Sturminster Newton, Dorset DT10 2AF
Tel (01258) 472507
Fax (01258) 473370
Location 2 miles (3 km) SW of Sturminster Newton; private car parking
Food & drink full breakfast, dinner; full licence
Prices B&B £47.50-£75; dinner £17.50-£27; special breaks
Rooms 14 double, all with bath and shower; 2 small doubles, with bath and shower; all rooms have central heating, TV, phone, tea/coffee kit
Facilities dining-room, sitting-room, bar; croquet, tennis **Credit cards** AE, DC, MC, V **Children** welcome
Disabled easy access to stable-block bedrooms and dining-room **Pets** by arrangement
Closed Feb **Proprietor** Richard Prideaux-Brune

The South-West

The Horn of Plenty

Since they arrived here in 1990, Ian and Elaine Gatehouse have enhanced the already high reputation of the place by their natural talent for hospitality and sheer hard work. The secluded, creeper-covered 1830s house has a splendid location overlooking the Tamar Valley, a view shared by all seven of the bedooms in the converted coach-house, fifty yards from the main house. Dinner is the main event, skilfully prepared by chef Peter Gorton, and served in front of picture windows in the two-part dining-room. A recent reporter was impressed with Elaine's friendly, outgoing style.

Nearby Cotehele House, 3 miles (5 km); Dartmoor.

Gulworthy, Tavistock, Devon PL19 8JD
Tel (01822) 832528
Location 3 miles (5 km) W of Tavistock on A390; with ample car parking
Food & drink breakfast, lunch, dinner; residential licence
Prices B&B £47.50-£85; special 2-night breaks; meals £10.50-£32.50, (£21 special menu on Mon eves)
Rooms 7 double, 5 with bath, 2 with shower; all have central heating, phone, hairdrier, TV, minibar, radio
Facilities 2 dining-rooms, sitting-room
Children not accepted under 13 years
Disabled two suitable bedroom
Pets accepted in bedrooms
Closed Christmas; restaurant only, Mon lunch
Proprietors Ian and Elaine Gatehouse

Old Millfloor

A steep shady path is the only access to Old Millfloor, situated by a fast-flowing stream amid gardens. 'Leave the holiday traffic,' says our latest reporter, 'and enter the enchantingly detached world of Janice Waddon-Martyn's converted mill.' Janice runs the house with the help of her daughter, and succeeds admirably in giving her guests a relaxing 'away from it all' stay. She adores cooking, and likes nothing better than to be told of her guests' preferences so that she can be sure her creations will be enjoyed. Bedrooms are neat and pretty. Families are welcome, but not smokers.

Nearby Tintagel Castle, 2 miles (3 km); Bodmin Moor.

Trebarwith Strand, Tintagel, Cornwall PL34 0HA
Tel (01840) 770234
Location 2 miles (3 km) S of Tintagel on B3263; in 10-acre grounds with ample car parking
Food & drink full breakfast, tea, dinner; no licence (guests may supply their own wine)
Prices B&B £18.50; dinner £12; reductions for 2 or more days and for children
Rooms 3 double; all rooms have TV, hairdrier
Facilities sitting-room, dining-room
Credit cards not accepted
Children welcome
Disabled access difficult
Pets not accepted
Closed Dec to Feb
Proprietor Janice Waddon-Martyn

The South-West

Tregony House

We have always received a steady trickle of favourable reports from visitors to this guest-house which fronts on to the main street of Tregony, as it has since the seventeenth century – when this was an important river port. Andy and Cathy Webb took over Tregony House about three years ago, eager to maintain the standards set by the previous owners. Cathy's meals are based on local produce, including herbs from the flowery walled garden (where guests can relax and take tea). The rooms are comfortably and individually furnished. More reports welcome.

Nearby Trelissick Garden, 6 miles (10 km); Heligan gardens.

Tregony, Truro, Cornwall TR2 5RN
Tel (01872) 530671
Location 7 miles (11 km) E of Truro on A3078; with gardens and private parking for 5 cars
Food & drink breakfast, dinner; residential and restaurant licence
Prices B&B £19-£23; DB&B £30.50-£34.50; reductions for 7 nights or more
Rooms 4 double (2 twin), 3 with bath or shower; one single; tea/coffee kit
Facilities dining-room, sitting-room, bar
Credit cards MC, V
Children welcome over 7
Disabled access difficult
Pets guide-dogs only
Closed Nov to Feb
Proprietors Cathy and Andy Webb

Cridford Inn

The oldest house in Devon has become one of its newest inns, lovingly restored and refurbished over the past year or two by its enthusiastic and friendly owners. Unlike many inns, it has a pleasant sitting area, ideal for morning newspapers or afternoon tea, complete with ticking grandfather clock and other period pieces. Ye olde oak dining-room has an impressive fireplace plus a floor 'window' revealing a unique Saxon mosaic (circa 800). The cosy bar has suitably antique wooden seats, a stone floor and stained glass.

Nearby Bradley Manor, Stover Park, Bovey Tracey, Dartmoor.

Trusham, Newton Abbot, Devon TQ13 0NR
Tel (01626) 853694
Location 3 miles (5 km) off A38, along B3193, 3 miles (5 km) NE of Bovey Tracey
Food & drink full breakfast, lunch, dinner; full licence
Prices B&B £32.50-£45; dinner à la carte
Rooms 4 double (2 twin), 2 with bath, 2 with shower; all have central heating, TV, tea/coffee kit
Facilities dining room with sitting-room attached, bar
Credit cards MC, V
Children not suitable
Disabled not suitable
Pets by arrangement (£2.50 per day)
Closed Christmas Day
Proprietors David and Sally Hesmondhalgh

The South-West

Woodhayes

Antiques, watercolours, prints and fabrics of high quality characterize the public rooms of this gracious Georgian house, while the bedrooms (some exceptionally large) are individually and harmoniously decorated. Katherine's meals follow a satisfying dinner-party style but offer some choice, and are properly served at well-spaced tables in the elegant dining-room. All the public rooms have open fires in winter. 'The relaxed comfort is very much to do with the pleasant personalities of Katherine and Frank Rendle,' says our latest report.

Nearby Cadhay House, 3 miles (5 km); Exe valley.

Whimple, near Exeter, Devon EX5 2TD
Tel & Fax (01404) 822237
Location 9 miles (14.5km) E of Exeter, close to A30; in 3-acre grounds with parking for 12 cars
Food & drink full breakfast, dinner; lunch by arrangement; residential and restaurant licence
Prices DB&B £70-£90 (including afternoon tea); (no single rate); lunch £15,

dinner £25
Rooms 6 double, all with bath; all rooms have central heating, TV, phone, radio
Facilities 2 sitting-rooms, dining-room, bar; croquet, tennis court
Credit cards AE, DC, MC, V
Children welcome over 12 years **Disabled** access difficult
Pets not accepted
Closed never
Proprietors Katherine, Frank and Michael Rendle

White House ★

When we revisited White House we were again struck with Dick and Kay Smith's affability. They have been here for more than 25 years. The mostly Georgian house has a pleasant sitting-room and pretty co-ordinated fabrics in the comfortable bedrooms. Four are in the pleasant courtyard annexe.

The Smiths have a passionate interest in food and wine, which has resulted in several accolades and awards for the appetizing dishes on the daily changing menus and for their excellent wine cellar. Home-baked rolls for breakfast.

Nearby Cleeve Abbey, 1.5 miles (2.5 km); Quantock Hills.

11 Long Street, Williton, Somerset TA4 4QW
Tel (01984) 632306
Location 9 miles (14.5 km) SE of Minehead, in middle of village; ample car parking
Food & drink full breakfast, dinner; fully licenced
Prices B&B £37-£58; DB&B £68-£89; dinner £31; reductions for 2 nights or more
Rooms 10 double, all with bath, 4 also with shower; 1 fam-

ily rooms; all rooms have phone, radio, TV; 6 have central heating, hairdrier, tea/coffee kit **Facilities** sitting-room, bar, dining-room **Credit cards** not accepted **Children** welcome if well behaved; cots, high-chairs available **Disabled** ground-floor bedrooms **Pets** not in dining-room **Closed** Nov to mid-May
Proprietors Dick and Kay Smith

SOUTHERN ENGLAND

The South-West

Village inn, Withypool

Royal Oak

This popular Exmoor inn has much to recommend it besides its
Lorna Doone associations (Blackmore stayed here while writing
the novel in 1866). The two bars are kitted out with a variety of
antlers, fox's masks and hunting scenes – even the candlesticks are
fashioned from staghorn. Bar menus offer an assortment of home-
made food with interesting dishes such as venison sausages or local
trout. More formal dining takes place in the strikingly colour-
schemed restaurant. The quaint bedrooms vary in size, but are well
coordinated in cottagey prints. Recent owner, so reports please.
Nearby Exmoor; walking, riding, fishing, shooting.

Withypool, Somerset
TA24 7QP
Tel (01643) 831506
Fax (01643) 831659
Location in middle of village,
just off B3223, 15 miles SW of
Minehead; with ample parking
Food & drink breakfast, lunch,
dinner; full licence
Prices B&B £19.50-£33; bar
snacks; dinner from £18.50
Rooms 8 double, 7 ensuite, 1
with bath; 2 bedroomed cot-
tage for weekly rental; all
rooms have central heating,
phone, hairdrier, TV, radio
Facilities dining-room,
sitting-room, 2 bars
Credit cards AE, DC, MC, V
Children welcome over 10
years
Disabled access difficult
Pets welcome in bedrooms
Closed never
Proprietor Richard Howard

Restaurant with rooms, Yeovil

Little Barwick House

'The big plus of Little Barwick is the food,' writes a recent visitor.
But we continue to rate this listed white-painted Georgian dower
house for its friendly informality – it is first and foremost the family
home of the Colleys, with no sign of hotel rules or regulations. The
bedrooms are comfortable, but simply furnished – don't expect
four-star luxury – the public rooms are lived-in, not smart.
Veronica is the chef and Christopher looks after the restaurant,
ground floor sitting-room and bar. He has put together an interesting selection of realistically priced wines.
Nearby Brympton d'Evercy, 2.5 miles (4 km); Montacute House.

Barwick, near Yeovil, Somerset
BA22 9TD
Tel (01935) 423902
Fax (01935) 420908
Location 2 miles (3 km) S of
Yeovil off A37; car parking
Food & drink breakfast,
dinner; residential and
restaurant licence
Prices B&B £42.75-£57.50;
DB&B £60.75-£77.50; bargain
breaks
Rooms 6 double, 4 with bath,
2 with shower; all have TV,
central heating, tea/coffee kit
Facilities sitting-room, bar,
dining-room
Credit cards AE, MC, V
Children welcome if well
behaved
Disabled access difficult
Pets dogs welcome
Closed Christmas and New
Year
Proprietors Christopher and
Veronica Colley

The South-East

Little Hemingfold Farmhouse ★

Praise floods in for this 'truly rural haven hidden away from the tourist town of Battle'. 'A perfect getaway'. 'The epitome of a charming little country hotel.' Don't be misled by the word 'farmhouse': apart from the setting there is not much that is agricultural about this substantial, rambling building, part 17thC, part early Victorian. The house has a peaceful setting in 40 acres of farm and woodland; it is surrounded by gardens, and overlooks a pretty 2-acre trout lake (the Slaters are happy to lend fishing rods). Inside, intriguing nooks and crannies give the house a special charm. The two sitting-rooms and the cosy dining-room all have log fires. So do 4 of the 9 bedrooms, all individually furnished, and accommodated in the converted coach house and stables, grouped around a flowery courtyard. Allison and Paul emphasize fresh ingredients in their traditional cooking. Another happy customer calls them 'hard-working, friendly, and inconspicuous unless called upon'.

Nearby Bodiam Castle, 6 miles (10 km); Great Dixter, 6 miles (10 km); Rye, Sissinghurst.

Battle, East Sussex, TN33 0TT
Tel (01424) 774338
Fax (01424) 775351
Location 1.5 miles (3 km) SE of Battle, off A2100; in 40-acre garden, with trout lake, fields and woods; ample car parking
Food & drink breakfast, light lunch, dinner; restaurant licence
Prices B&B £38-£45; DB&B £60; 2 day breaks; Christmas and New Year breaks
Rooms 13 double, one family room; 10 with bath; all rooms have central heating, colour TV, phone, tea/coffee kit, radio clocks, electric blankets; 4 rooms have log-burning stoves
Facilities 2 sitting-rooms, dining-room, bar; boating, trout-fishing, tennis, croquet
Credit cards AE, DC, MC, V
Children welcome
Disabled access very difficult
Pets dogs accepted if well behaved
Closed 6 Jan to 12 Feb
Proprietors Paul and Allison Slater

The South-East

Country guest-house, Bethersden

Little Hodgeham ★

Most small hotels reflect the personality of their owner but some are virtually extensions of that personality; Little Hodgeham falls squarely into the latter category. Erica Wallace dominates this picture-postcard Tudor house, and although evidence of her care, attention and hard work abounds, it is the vitality of her character that makes a lasting impression on guests. (Ms Wallace is not past putting a greetings card on the bed of a couple arriving for a wedding anniversary celebration, and preparing heart-shaped mousses for that evening's first course.)

The lovingly restored house has just three bedrooms, all beautifully and carefully co-ordinated, right down to the choice of flowers. The split-level four-poster room is particularly striking. The sitting-room has a massive open fireplace, exposed beams and furnishings in complementary colours. The dining-room is small and intimate. Erica cooks whenever possible and displays an untutored 'natural feel for food' – check on booking whether dinner is available.

Nearby Sissinghurst Castle gardens, 8 miles (13 km); many other interesting houses and gardens within reach.

Smarden Road Bethersden, Kent TN26 3HE
Tel (01233) 850323
Location 2 miles (3 km) NW of Bethersden, 8 miles (13 km) W of Ashford by A28; in garden, with car parking
Food & drink full breakfast, dinner; residential licence
Prices B&B £36.50-£45.50; dinner £15.50; reduction for 4 nights or more, and for children sharing parents' room
Rooms 3 double, 2 with bath and shower, one with shower; all rooms have central heating, tea/coffee kit, hairdrier, radio
Facilities sitting-room, dining-room, TV room; carp fishing, small outdoor swimming-pool
Credit cards not accepted
Children accepted; usually fed earlier than adults
Disabled not suitable **Pets** by arrangement
Closed Sept to mid Mar
Proprietor Erica Wallace

The South-East

Tanyard

'Exactly the sort of place you are looking for – a most interesting building in a beautiful setting, not far from a busy town, run by a committed and sensitive proprietor and with top-class food.'

This report from a regular visitor pays proper tribute to Tanyard's setting and the contribution Jan Davies makes to the well-being of her guests, but underplays the attractions of the house itself. It is a dream of a building – timber-framed, built around 1350 and entirely without symmetry; red tiles and muted yellow paint outside, sparkling white between the mellow exposed beams within – set in a lovely country garden with glorious views. Another recent and satisfied reporter describes Tanyard as 'uniquely different'.

It is furnished with a cheerful mix of modern and antique pieces – all very natural and home-like – and both the sitting-room and bar area have large inglenook fireplaces. All the bedrooms are spacious, and there is one large open-plan suite.

The restaurant is in the oldest part of the building, serving a four-course menu which features local produce cooked in a modern but unpretentious style.

Nearby Sissinghurst, 7 miles; Leeds Castle, 4 miles.

Wierton Hill, Boughton Monchelsea, near Maidstone, Kent ME17 4JT
Tel (01622) 744705
Fax (01622) 741998
Location 4.5 miles (7 km) S of Maidstone, just off B2163; in 10-acre grounds with ample car parking
Food & drink full breakfast, dinner; restaurant licence
Prices B&B £52.50-£85; dinner £29

Rooms 4 double, 3 with bath, one with shower; one single; one suite with spa bath; all rooms have central heating, TV, phone, tea/coffee kit, radio, hairdrier
Facilities restaurant, sitting-room, bar **Credit cards** MC, V
Children welcome over 6
Disabled not suitable **Pets** not accepted **Closed** Christmas; Jan
Proprietor Jan Davies

The South East

Master Builder's House

A new entry to the guide, the superbly sited Master Builder's Hotel has long been ripe for a carefully judged overhaul, and when its lease from Lord Montagu of Beaulieu came up for renewal, Jeremy Willcock and John Illsley, proprietors of the George in Yarmouth, Isle of Wight (see page 91) were just the right pair to step in. Lord Montagu's daughter, interior designer Mary Montagu, undertook the redecoration, creating a straightforward traditional style with a maritime theme (plenty of old prints on the walls) in keeping with the spirit of Bucklers Hard, where some of Nelson's ships were built in the 18thC. Today it is a picturesque and popular marina, with a street of shipwrights' dwellings, including the Master Builder's, a popular bar for visiting yachtsmen, and a maritime museum.

The 18thC building has until now been lumbered by a modern annexe, the Henry Adams wing. Even Mary Montagu's best efforts cannot give the bedrooms here the character they lack, although they are now comfortable and attractive. Given their size, we feel they are somewhat ambitiously priced, too. Bedrooms in the main building have much more character. The sophisticated new entrance and reception is a vast improvement on the old, and in the smart dining-room, with absorbing views down to the river, delicious 'modern classical' dishes are served. Reports please.

Nearby New Forest; Beaulieu 2 miles (3 km).

Bucklers Hard, Beaulieu, Hants SO42 7XB
Tel (01590) 616253
Fax (01590) 616297
Location overlooking Beaulieu river at Bucklers Hard, 2 miles (3 km) SE of Beaulieu, 9 miles (14 km) SE of Lyndhurst; ample car parking.
Food & drink Breakfast, lunch, dinner, full licence
Prices B&B £65-£95; dinner about £25

Rooms 25 double, all with bath and shower; all rooms have phone, TV, radio, hair-drier; 2 self-catering cottages
Facilities sitting-room, dining-room, Yachtsman's bar, terrace, garden, private pontoon
Credit cards AE, MC, V
Children welcome
Disabled not suitable **Pets** not accepted **Closed** never
Proprietors Jeremy Willcock and John Illsley

The South-East

Converted oast house, Chartham

Thruxted Oast

There is nothing more Kentish than a red-brick oast-house; here you can actually stay in one, last used for hop-drying over 20 years ago and rescued from decay in 1986 by the Derouets. It is effectively a terrace of five oasts, and each of the three bedrooms occupies one; these rooms are spacious and welcoming, with patchwork quilts and stripped pine furniture. Each room has a shower but no bath.

The drawing-room is similarly appealing, with an open fire. Authentic Kentish artefacts are all around, picked up by the Derouets from all kinds of places. They make for eclectic and sometimes surprising *décor*: there is a hop press in the gallery that houses the Derouet's picture-framing business; doors, clay jars, even lavatories and baths redolent of old Kent, are all pressed into service. You are welcomed as part of the family here, taking breakfast in the kitchen. Smoking is not allowed in the bedrooms.

Our inspector was highly impressed with the originality of the place, feeling he was 'a guest in a living museum'.

No dinner is available at Thruxted Oast, but there are pubs and restaurants in the vicinity. Other reports welcome.

Nearby Canterbury; Chilham castle and gardens, 4 miles (6 km).

Mystole, Chartham,
Canterbury CT4 7BX
Tel (01227) 730080
Location in peaceful valley, 4
miles (6.5 km) SW of
Canterbury just off A28; with
garden and parking for 6 cars
Food & drink full breakfast
Prices B&B £39-£68 (no single
rate); reductions for 7-night
stay
Rooms 3 twin, all with shower;
all rooms have central heating,
phone, TV, radio, hairdrier
Facilities sitting-room; croquet
Credit cards AE, DC, MC, V
Children accepted over 8 years
by arrangement
Disabled access difficult
Pets not accepted
Closed Christmas
Proprietors Tim and Hilary
Derouet

The South-East

Manor house, Cranbrook

Kennel Holt

Having been dropped from our guide some years back after a crop of complaints, we now frequently hear excellent things from readers about the new regime at this Elizabethan manor of soft red brick and white wooden boards, set in 5 acres of secluded and flowery gardens, notable for its impressive yew hedging. Certainly no one complained about the building – which has Edwardian additions – or its setting; indeed you would be hard pressed to find a better-placed base for an exploration of south-east England than Cranbrook, and you certainly will not find a hotel which feels more at one with its Kentish surroundings.

It is a homely manor rather than a grand one, with capacious sofas before the open fires of its beamed sitting-rooms, and honest antiques dotted about. The Chalmers took over in 1992, and, judging from a recent reader's letter, have considerably improved both the food and the ambience, 'achieving what so many aspire to achieve, but never do. Leaving was a wrench'.

Neil Chalmers taught himself to cook when he took over, and now serves accomplished set menus of seasonal food, each course with six or seven choices, to both residents and locals. More reports please.

Nearby Sissinghurst Castle Gardens, 3 miles (5 km), Hole Park, 5 miles (8 km); Weald of Kent; Rye within easy reach.

Goudhurst Road, Cranbrook, Kent TN17 2PT
Tel (01580) 712032
Fax (01580) 715495
Location 1.5 miles (2.5 km) NW of Cranbrook, close to A262; in gardens, with ample car parking
Food & drink breakfast, lunch by prior booking, dinner; residential and restaurant licence
Prices B&B £62.50-£90; dinner £27.50-£32.50

Rooms 8 double, 2 single, 7 with bath, 3 with shower; all rooms have central heating, phone, TV, hairdrier **Facilities** 2 sitting-rooms, dining-room, gardens, croquet and putting lawns **Credit cards** AE, MC, V **Children** welcome, but those under 6 at proprietors' discretion **Disabled** access difficult **Pets** not accepted **Closed** 2 weeks in Jan **Proprietors** Neil and Sally Chalmers

The South-East

Manor house, Cranbrook

The Old Cloth Hall

Mrs Morgan's warmth of welcome has made her many friends among the guests who have made their way up the sweeping gravelled drive to this splendid 15thC half-timbered manor, which can count Queen Elizabeth I as one of its visitors.

Diamond-paned windows look out on to 13 acres of glorious Kentish gardens – magnificent rhododendrons and azaleas, a sunken rose garden, swimming-pool, tennis court, and a superb croquet lawn to complete the picture.

The interior, as you would expect, is also rather special. There are log fires in the inglenooks; the oak floors and panelling gleam; and the antiques, fine chintz fabrics, porcelain and flower arrangements are all evidence of Mrs Morgan's appreciation of how to make her home look its best. She is also a cook – house specialities include chicken with orange, mustard and tarragon and stuffed leg of lamb. The bedrooms, furnished with antiques, are exceptionally pretty, and offer a very high standard of comfort.

A couple who spent their autumnal wedding night at the Old Cloth Hall report in glowing terms on everything from the tranquil setting to the fruit fresh from the garden; and a recent inspection confirms that it thoroughly deserves its place in this guide.

Nearby Sissinghurst gardens 2 miles (3 km); Scotney Castle gardens 7 miles (11 km).

Cranbrook, Kent TN17 3NR
Tel and fax (01580) 712220
Location in countryside one mile (1.5 km) E of Cranbrook on road to Tenterden, before cemetery; in grounds of 13 acres with ample car parking
Food & drink full breakfast, dinner; lunch by arrangement; no licence
Prices B&B £42.50-£55; dinner £20
Rooms 3 double, one with bath, 2 with bath and shower; all rooms have central heating, hairdrier, TV
Facilities sitting-room, dining-room; swimming-pool, tennis-court, croquet
Credit cards not accepted
Children by arrangement
Pets not accepted
Disabled not suitable
Closed Christmas
Proprietor Mrs Katherine Morgan

The South-East

Ockenden Manor

A telling comment from the inspector we sent recently: 'Anne Goodman oversees the decoration herself, so gives it the personal touch, rather than simply splashing out on the finest.' She has made many changes for the better here since taking over this attractive 16th/17thC manor house.

Bedrooms are spacious and individual (and crammed with giveaways); a superb master suite with sombre panelling relies on reds and greens to give a feeling of brightness. Several of the bathrooms are notably spacious. The main sitting-room, though lavishly furnished, has a personal feel. Staff are friendly and obliging. (A notice in the hotel states that whatever a hotel's character and charm, it is only as good as its staff.)

Dinner, which is served in the oak-panelled restaurant with painted ceiling and stained glass windows, is another highlight. Food is based on local produce, with vegetables and herbs from the garden.

In Ockenden Manor we stray somewhat outside our usual size limit, but this is a human, comfortable hotel. It is also convenient for Gatwick and Brighton, and ideally placed for visiting the gardens at Wakehurst Place, Leonardslee, Sheffield Park, Sissinghurst and Nyman's.

Nearby Nyman's Garden, 3 miles (5 km).

Ockenden Lane, Cuckfield, West Sussex RH17 5LD
Tel (01444) 416111
Fax (01444) 415549
Location 2 miles (3 km) W of Hayward's Heath close to middle of village, off A272; in 9-acre grounds, with ample car parking
Food & drink breakfast, lunch, tea, dinner; residential licence
Prices B&B £125-£260; dinner from £32.50; half-price meals for children under 10
Rooms 21 double, 1 single, all with bath; all have central heating, TV, phone, radio, trouser-press, hairdrier
Facilities sitting-room, bar, dining-room, function room
Credit cards AE, DC, MC, V
Children welcome **Disabled** access easy to restaurant **Pets** not accepted **Closed** never
Proprietor Mrs Anne Goodman

The South-East

Country guest-house, Frant

The Old Parsonage

At the heart of the charming village of Frant, The Old Parsonage is set in three acres of gardens. This is a fine Georgian country house beautifully renovated by Tony and Mary Dakin. The tall and spacious reception rooms are filled with plants and decorated with lithographs and watercolours as well as Mary's unusual tapestries and Tony's photos of village scenes.

The centrepiece is the exceptionally large and airy atrium, which floods light onto the main staircase, landing and hall, and shows off the black and white photographic portraits in the picture gallery to advantage. The drawing-room is delightful, too, gracious in style, with Persian rugs, crystal chandeliers and antiques – impressive without being overpowering. The freshly decorated bedrooms (two with four-posters) have large bathrooms (one, with sunken bath, is almost a sitting-room). Their decoration and furnishing are constantly under review.

The Dakins are evidently enthusiastic and dedicated: 'This is our home, so we want it to look its best,' says Mary. Tony is responsible for breakfast, and for the pleasant garden. (Free sherry on the terrace.) An excellent base for visiting the several famous National Trust properties in the area – see below.

Nearby Bodiam, Leeds, Hever and Scotney Castles; Sissinghurst and Sheffield Park Gardens; Bateman's, Penshurst Place, Knole.

Frant, Tunbridge Wells, TN3 9DX
Tel and Fax (01892) 750773
Location near church in village 2 miles (3 km) S of Tunbridge Wells, in large gardens with ample car parking
Food & drink full breakfast
Prices B&B from £30
Rooms 3 double (one twin), all with bath and shower; all rooms have central heating, TV, tea/coffee kit, radio, hairdrier
Facilities sitting-room, breakfast room, conservatory
Credit cards MC, V
Children welcome
Disabled not suitable
Pets accepted in bedrooms
Closed never
Proprietors Tony and Mary Dakin

The South East

Gravetye Manor

The country house hotel, now so much a part of the tourist scene in Britain, scarcely existed when Peter Herbert opened the doors of this serene Elizabethan house over 40 years ago. It is scarcely surprising that in that time he and his team have got their act thoroughly polished; but it is remarkable that Gravetye is not in the least eclipsed by younger competitors. Standards in every department are unflaggingly high. Service consistently achieves the elusive aim of attentiveness without intrusion, while the ambitious food is about the best in the county. A recent visitor, who has known the hotel for 30 years, remained as impressed as ever: 'A sleek operation that doesn't compromise.'

The pioneering gardener William Robinson lived in the house for half a century until his death in 1935. Great care is taken to maintain the various gardens he created; Robinson was also responsible for many features of the house as it is seen today – the mellow oak panelling and grand fireplaces in the calm sitting-rooms, for example. Bedrooms – all immaculate – vary in size from the adequate to the enormous, and prices range accordingly.

Nearby Wakehurst, 3 miles (5 km); Nyman's Gardens, 6 miles (10 km).

Vowels Lane, near East Grinstead, West Sussex RH19 4LJ
Tel (01342) 810567
Fax (10342) 810080
Location 4.5 miles (7 km) SW of East Grinstead by B2110 at Gravetye; in 30 acre grounds with ample car parking
Food & drink breakfast, lunch, dinner; restaurant and residential licence
Prices B&B £93-£139; dinner £31-£60
Rooms 16 double, 2 single, all with bath; all rooms have central heating, TV, phone, radio, hairdrier
Facilities 2 sitting rooms, bar, dining-room; croquet, trout fishing
Credit cards MC, V
Children welcome over 7, and babes in arms
Disabled access difficult
Pets not accepted
Closed never
Proprietors Herbert family

The South-East

Manor house hotel, Gatwick

Langshott Manor

Coming upon this exquisite brick-and-timber Grade II Elizabethan manor house, in its own grounds amid the suburban sprawl of Horley, is akin to discovering a rare orchid in a swamp. Once inside, surrounded by oak panelling, the only sound is of a clock ticking.

Each of the rooms has a distinct character, but they are all luxuriously furnished and well equipped. Eight of the bedrooms are in a converted Victorian stable block across the award-winning garden, where you will find grass sofas, millstone benches, a Victorian rose garden and medieval moat. Dinner – traditional British, with modern overtones – offers at least five choices for each course. You can eat on the terrace, or in the dining-room, which our reporter found intimate – 'and I don't simply mean small'.

Everything at Langshott Manor seems to have been thought of, even down to the courtesy car to take you to the airport if necessary. It is not cheap. But you get what you pay for. The Hinchcliffes took over a few years ago and seem to be maintaining standards well. We look forward to receiving more reports.

Nearby Gatwick airport; Ashdown Forest; Hever castle, Chartwell.

Nr Gatwick, Surrey RH6 9LN
Tel (01293) 786680
Fax (01293) 783905
E-mail admin@langshottmanor.com
Location 0.75 miles (one km) E of A23, 2.5 miles (4 km) N of Gatwick Airport; in 3-acre gardens with ample car parking
Food & drink breakfast, lunch, dinner; residential and restaurant licence
Prices B&B £77.50-£220 (including newspaper, 7 days airport parking, and transfer to the airport); dinner £35
Rooms 15 double (7 in house, 8 in annexe in grounds (3 with own gardens); all with bath and shower; all rooms have central heating, TV, radio, minibar, safe, trouser-press
Facilities dining-room, sitting-room; croquet
Credit cards AE, DC, MC, V
Children accepted; but ponds dangerous for toddlers
Disabled ground floor rooms available
Pets dogs accommodated in kennels in the grounds
Closed Christmas
Proprietors Peter and Deborah Hinchcliffe

The South-East

Dorset Square

This striking hotel stands on the south side of the fine Regency garden square which was the original site of Lord's cricket ground. Outside is a discreet brass plaque bearing the hotel's name; inside, a delightful evocation of a traditional English country house – the work of co-owner Kit Kemp. The sensation that absolutely nothing has been left to chance may be slightly unnerving – but there is no denying that the whole effect is captivating. Colefax chintzes, striped wallpapers and clever paint effects are mixed with flair in the small public rooms, along with an abundance of flowers and pictures. Bedrooms – whose solid marble bathrooms include de luxe American showers that practically knock you over – are all fresh and supremely elegant, with not a jarring note to be found.

The Potting Shed restaurant, situated in the basement, is beautifully decorated with murals of cricketing and ballooning scenes, and serves modern English dishes.

Don't expect a sleepy, easy-going country-house atmosphere to go with the surroundings at Dorset Square. This is a slick city hotel with a carefully contrived image and a dynamic young management team.

Nearby Regent's Park; Madame Tussaud's; Oxford Street.

39 Dorset Square, London NW1 6QN
Tel (0171) 723 7874
Fax (0171) 724 3328
Location close to Marylebone and Baker Street station, in square with access to 2-acre private gardens, garaged parking close by
Food & drink breakfast, lunch, dinner, full room service; full licence
Prices £98-£195 (breakfast not included); dinner from £12

Rooms 31 double, 7 single; all with bath and/or shower; all rooms have central heating, satellite TV, clock/radio, mini-bar, phone; most rooms have air-conditioning
Facilities sitting-room, dining-room, bar **Credit cards** AE, MC, V **Children** welcome
Disabled access easy to ground-floor bedrooms
Pets not accepted
Closed never
Manager James Thomas

The South-East

Town guest-house, London

L'Hotel

A revisit in 1998 confirmed L'Hotel as a delightfully tranquil haven in busy Knightsbridge, especially considering that its chic little Metro restaurant in the basement has long made this a popular address with local residents and shoppers. The entrance is pleasantly understated which gives it the look of a private house. Inside, hand-stencilled motifs embellish the striped colour-washed walls and wooden floor. The small but well-equipped bedrooms, designed by Margaret Levin, have padded fabrics on the walls, in soft creams and beiges, wooden shutters and antique pine furniture, as well as double glazing and cooling fans. Some rooms can be interconnected to form a suite, which is popular with families.

The restaurant has a bright, continental brasserie look and it is also where the hotel guests have breakfast. Plain walls set off black-and-white photographs; the seating combines banquettes, mint green and chrome chairs at wooden-topped tables, and bar stools at the black marble bar. The food is 'modern British' which can include grilled tuna steak on a beetroot salad with capers, or magret of duck on shredded red cabbage braised with braeburn apples. The menus are devised by Phillip Britten, the head chef, who also presides at L'Hotel's sister establishment and neighbour, the Capital Hotel, where there is a smart, formal dining-room.

Nearby Knightsbridge; Hyde Park; Buckingham Palace.

28 Basil Street, London
SW3 1AS
Tel (0171) 589 6286
Fax (0171) 823 7826
Location between Sloane Street and Harrods; paying car park opposite
Food & drink breakfast; snacks, lunch, dinner available in restaurant/bar
Prices B&B £82.25-£188
Rooms 12 double, one suite; all with bath and shower; all rooms have central heating, radio, satellite TV, phone, minibar, tea/coffee kit, safe
Facilities wine bar
Credit cards AE, DC, MC, V
Children welcome
Disabled not suitable
Pets accepted by arrangement
Closed restaurant only, Sun lunch and dinner
Proprietor David Levin

The South-East

Number Sixteen

Number Sixteen is one of London's most characterful luxury bed-and-breakfast establishments. The original building has spread along its early Victorian South Kensington terrace, to encompass four adjoining houses – all extensively refurbished in the last few years.

Public rooms and bedrooms alike are brimful of pictures, including a huge eye-catching abstract in the reception room. Downstairs there are always big bowls of fresh flowers – sweet peas or roses perhaps – and the large rear patio garden is well kept and full of colour. Inside, the decoration is richly traditional and harmonious. A series of small sitting-rooms with Victorian moulded ceilings, polished antiques and luxurious drapes, lead to an award-winning conservatory, from where, on summer days, you can sit and admire the profusion of flowers outside.

Bedrooms are generously proportioned, comfortable and stylish, largely furnished with period pieces or reproductions; some have French windows opening on to the garden. Bathrooms are tiled and functional. Breakfast is served in your room. The hotel has no dining-room but there are plenty of restaurants on the Old Brompton Road nearby.

Nearby South Kensington museums; Knightsbridge; Sloane Square; Kensington Gardens.

16 Sumner Place, London
SW7 3EG
Tel (0171) 589 5232
Fax (0171) 584 8615
(US toll free: 1800 592 5387)
E-mail reservations@numbersixteenhotel.co.UK
Location off Old Brompton
Road; small garden, no private
car parking; nearest tube
South Kensington
Food & drink breakfast;
residential licence
Prices B&B £80-£125

Rooms 27 double, 23 with
bath and shower, 4 with
shower; 9 single with shower;
all rooms have central heating,
minibar, hairdrier, phone, TV,
radio, safe
Facilities sitting-room, bar,
conservatory **Credit cards** AE,
DC, MC, V **Children** accepted
over 12 **Disabled** not suitable
Pets not accepted
Closed never
Manager Jean Branham

The South-East

Sydney House Hotel

The hotel spreads across a terrace of mid-19thC townhouses in busy Sydney Street. Owned by a Swiss company, it was restored, designed and is managed by Swiss designer and hotelier Jean-Luc Aeby, who has created a comfortable, welcoming and very individual residence. A maze of stairways and dark but intimate passages lead to much lighter, fair-sized bedrooms, each of which has its own delightful character, enhanced by rich fabrics, artefacts, prints and paintings from around the world. The penthouse has a terrace overlooking Chelsea's rooftops, another room opens on to a sunny balcony, another has a gilded four-poster tented in silk and brocade, another leopard print fabrics and a Chinese theme. All have crisp white sheets and thick towels in the pristine bathrooms.

Public rooms are richly decorated and filled with interesting mirrors, carpets, marbles and furniture. Staff are unobtrusive, but efficient and friendly, as they should be at this price. Breakfast is excellent, the fruit plate a work of art.

Our one criticism is reserved for the somewhat uninspired room service menu. Take-outs, however, can be ordered from two good local restaurants with which the hotel has an arrangement, and if you ask nicely, the staff will serve them in your room.

Nearby King's Road, Michelin Building, museums.

9-11 Sydney Street, London SW3 6PU
Tel (0171) 376 7711
Fax (0171) 376 4233
Location in a street running between the Kings and Fulham Roads, near the Fulham Road end
Food & drink breakfast, light meals; 24-hour room service; full licence
Prices rooms £90-£150 + VAT; breakfast £8-£15

Rooms 14 double, 7 single; all with bath and shower, all rooms have central heating, satellite TV, minibar, phone, modem plug, hairdrier
Facilities sitting-room, breakfast room, restaurant/bar; business services
Credit cards AE, DC, MC, V
Children welcome
Disabled access difficult
Pets not accepted **Closed** never **Manager** Jean-Luc Aeby

The South-East

The Gore

We make no apology for including a hotel as big as this when it is run by the team who opened Hazlitt's (page 97). In 1990 they bought this Victorian town house (long established as a hotel) set in a wide tree-lined street near Kensington Gardens, and since then have given it the Hazlitt treatment: the bedrooms are furnished with period antiques, the walls are covered with old prints and oils, and they have recruited a young and friendly staff, trained to give efficient but informal service.

Our latest reporter gave it a rave review: 'Character by the bucketload; walls whose every square inch is covered with prints and oil paintings; bedrooms furnished with antiques, each with its own style – a gallery in one room, Judy Garland's bed in another.' She was also impressed by the dossier in each room describing what to do locally – 'put together with verve and a feel for what the guest might really want'. Her only criticism was the 'less than charming service' in the very busy ground-floor Bistrot 190 – some excuse for this at dinner, but not at breakfast, when it was almost empty.

Restaurant 190, which is in the same ownership as The Gore, is stylish with rosewood panels and deep red velvet chairs. Reports welcome.

Nearby Kensington Gardens, Hyde Park; Albert Hall; Harrods.

189 Queen's Gate, London
SW7 5EX
Tel (0171) 584 6601
Fax (0171) 589 8127
Location just S of Kensington Gardens; metered parking and public car park nearby
Food & drink breakfast, lunch, dinner; full licence
Prices £64-£287 (breakfast not included)
Rooms 31 double, 23 single (32 baths and 22 showers); all

rooms have central heating, phone, satellite TV, minibar, radio, hairdrier, safe
Facilities sitting-room, bar, restaurant, bistro
Credit cards AE, DC, MC, V
Children welcome; babysitting
Disabled lift/elevator; steps to front entrance
Pets by arrangement
Closed Christmas
Proprietor Peter McKay

The South-East

Stanwell House Hotel

Until its recent reincarnation, Stanwell House Hotel was a fading Georgian landmark in the prettiest part of Lymington's attractive High Street. When Jane McIntyre took over in 1995 the place was transformed: an Italianate stone-flagged courtyard now stretches the length of the building, affording inviting views from the street of a glass-roofed sitting-room strewn with velvet cushions; on one side of the entrance is a country clothing shop, Stanwells, on the other a bar and a cosy bistro in simple 17thC style – dark walls, oak settles, pewter plates and a *trompe l'oeil* fireplace complete with shaggy dog. Our meal here was delicious and inexpensive.

In contrast to the bistro, the candle-lit restaurant – steel chairs upholstered in purple, cerise, pink and deep red velvet, swathes of silk curtains – and the bedrooms, are theatrical, not to say over the top. The latter share a predilection for dramatic walls, rich hangings in silk, velvet and brocade, delicate bedspreads ("I'm learning my lesson as a hotelier, they'll have to go, the guests are spoiling them"), piles of white cushions and baths, some of them roll top, swathed in yet more fabric. The bedrooms in the extension have been more simply treated: ("for my corporate clients"). Quite a shake up; we had mixed feelings – what do you think?

Nearby New Forest; Beaulieu; Isle of Wight.

High Street, Lymington, Hampshire, SO41 9AA
Tel (01590) 677123
Fax (01590) 677756
Location on High Street, close to the quay and marina; public car parks nearby
Food & drink breakfast, lunch, tea, dinner; full licence
Prices B&B £47.50-£75; suite £110-£140; cottage £150; set dinner and à la carte
Rooms 31; 26 double, 3 luxury suites; 2-bedroomed cottage; all with bath, 1 with shower; all rooms have central heating , phone, TV, minibar, tea/coffee kit, trouser press, hairdrier
Facilities conservatory, bar, restaurant, bistro, conference room; garden; 50 ft yacht for charter **Credit cards** AE, DC, MC, V **Children** welcome
Disabled access difficult
Pets accepted **Closed** never
Proprietor Jane MacIntyre

The South-East

Coutry house hotel, Rushlake Green

Stone House

Our latest reporter enthusiastically agrees with everything we have said about Stone House in the past. It is Peter and Jane Dunn's ancestral family home, a glorious 16thC manor house, to which they moved after running another successful hotel on their estate, damaged by the 1987 hurricane. Their current enterprise is on a smaller scale and means that Jane now has time to do what she enjoys most – cooking, and looking after her guests individually. Her relaxed and friendly demeanour belies a very sure touch, and Stone House is run with great competence – which means it is much in demand for house parties, Glyndebourne visitors (luxury wicker picnic hampers can be prepared), shooting weekends and even small executive conferences. They have recently created a Victorian walled vegetable garden and an 18thC-style rose garden.

Bedrooms are beautifully decorated; two have fine antique four-posters and are particularly spacious (the bathrooms can double as sitting-rooms). Televisions are hidden so as not to spoil the period charm. An excellent place in which to sample authentic English country living at its most gracious – log fires and billiards, woodland walks and croquet – together with the atmosphere of a home. **Nearby** Battle; Glyndebourne 15 miles (24 km).

Rushlake Green, Heathfield, East Sussex TN21 9QJ
Tel (01435) 830553
Fax (01435) 830726
Location just off village green 8 miles (13 km) NW of Battle, in large grounds with ample car parking
Food & drink full breakfast, afternoon tea, dinner; residential licence
Prices B&B £49.75-£79 (reductions in winter); dinner £24.95
Rooms 6 double (2 four-posters, 3 twin); one single, all with bath; all rooms have central heating, telephone, radio, TV **Facilities** sitting-room, library, dining-room; billiards/snooker; croquet, fishing, shooting
Credit cards not accepted
Children welcome over 9
Disabled not suitable
Pets welcome, in bedrooms only
Closed Christmas to 2nd Jan
Proprietors Peter and Jane Dunn

The South-East

Town house hotel, Rye

Jeake's House

This splendid 17thC house has been lovingly restored to make a delightful small hotel – a verdict confirmed by several readers. The beamed bedrooms overlook either the old roof-tops of Rye or Romney Marsh. Bedsteads are either brass or mahogany, bedspreads lace, furniture antique. Downstairs, a galleried ex-chapel makes the grandest of breakfast rooms. A roaring fire greets guests on cold mornings, and Jenny Hadfield serves either a traditional breakfast or a vegetarian alternative. There are a comfortable sitting-room and a bar, with books and pictures lining the walls. 'Situated on *the* street in Rye (Mermaid Street) within walking distance of all the sights,' says our inspector.

Nearby Great Dixter, 6 miles (10 km); Ellen Terry Museum.

Mermaid Street, Rye, East Sussex TN31 7ET
Tel (01797) 222828
Fax (01797) 222623
Website http://www.s-h-systems.co.uk/hotels/jeakes.html
Location in middle of Rye; private car parking nearby
Food & drink full breakfast; residential licence
Prices B&B £25.50-£59; reductions for 4 nights plus, and for children sharing

Rooms 8 double, 7 with bath; one single; 2 family rooms with bath; one suite with bath; all rooms have central heating, phone, TV, radio
Facilities dining-room, 2 sitting-rooms, bar
Credit cards MC, V
Children not accepted
Disabled not suitable
Pets dogs, by arrangement
Closed never **Proprietors** Francis and Jenny Hadfield

The South East

Wallett's Court

'Amply plugs a gap in an area where there is a dearth of decent hotels, other than the standard and predictable ones that serve the Dover ferry traffic,' says a recent inspector, who adds that 'it feels like Kent ' – he should know, since he was raised in the county. It is located away from the main Dover-London route, off the road to Deal.

The Oakleys started doing bed and breakfast in their handsome old manor house in 1979, rescuing it from a poor state of repair. They developed in steps into a hotel with a restaurant that now has a reputation locally as well as with guests. The number of compact pine-furnished rooms in a converted barn, each with their own individual character and 'a delightfully rustic feel', has increased to eight now; there are three grander ones in the main house, with abundant beams and brickwork in the best Kent tradition, and robust antique furniture. The public areas include a panelled sitting-room with period furniture and a grandfather clock ticking calmly away. The breakfast room is pleasantly in keeping and there is an impressive old staircase.

Children enjoy seeking out the tree house in the orchard; there is also an indoor swimming-pool, steam room and hydro-spa.
Nearby Walmer Castle, 3 miles (5 km); ferries and Eurotunnel.

West Cliffe, St Margaret's-at-Cliffe, Dover, Kent CT15 6EW
Tel (01304) 852424
Fax (01304) 853430
E-mail Wallettscourt@compuserve
Location 3 miles (5 km) NE of Dover on B2058, off A258; garden and ample car parking
Food & drink breakfast, dinner; full licence
Prices B&B £37.50-£60.50; dinner £25-£35 **Rooms** 12 double, 1 family room, all with bath and shower; all rooms have central heating, tea/coffee kit, TV, phone **Facilities** sitting-room, 2 dining-rooms, children's playground, table-tennis; tennis **Credit cards** AE, DC, MC, V **Children** welcome **Disabled** access difficult to dining-room; 1 annexe bedroom **Pets** only in 1 bedroom, not public rooms
Closed never **Proprietors** Chris and Lea Oakley

The South-East

Country house hotel, Storrington

Little Thakeham

Little Thakeham takes us outside our normal price limits, but here is a house of irresistible character – an Edwin Lutyens Tudor-style manor built in 1902-3 and considered one of his finest. The Ractliffs have been running it since 1980 as a refined and luxurious hotel of rare quality. The centrepiece is a double-height sitting-room with a vast fireplace and minstrel's gallery, and the furnishings – some by Lutyens himself – are of a high standard throughout. The Ratcliffs collect antiques, and these are in evidence all about. The bedrooms, as you would expect, are in keeping with the rest; a master suite is virtually a small guest house with two bathrooms.

The part-paved, part-grassy gardens – 'beautifully laid out and kept up', says a satisfied visitor – are lined with walnut trees and were created in the style of Gertrude Jekyll, the much-respected 19thC landscape designer. Our latest reporter noted the serene setting – the human scale of the building: 'Big without being overpowering. It is both a country house and a hotel.' The atmosphere is genuinely relaxed.

The restaurant manages to be imposing as well as having some intimacy. Food is traditional French and English, making sensible use of local produce. The menu varies daily.

Nearby Parham House; Arundel Castle; Petworth; Goodwood; Sussex Downs.

Merrywood Lane, Storrington, West Sussex RH20 3HE
Tel (01903) 744416
Fax (01903) 745022
Location 1.5 miles (2.5km) N of Storrington, close to B2139; in garden with ample car parking
Food & drink full breakfast; lunch and dinner by arrangement; full licence
Prices B&B £85-£110; dinner £35.25

Rooms 9 double, all with bath; all rooms have central heating, Teletext TV, phone
Facilities sitting-room, bar, restaurant; tennis, helipad
Credit cards AE, DC, MC, V
Children welcome
Disabled access fair
Pets not accepted
Closed Christmas, New Year
Proprietors Tim and Pauline Ractliff

The South East

Hotel du Vin

The much praised Hotel du Vin & Bistro in Winchester has now replicated itself in Tunbridge Wells, and with the owners' plans for further expansion, the operation looks like becoming a chain. We have never included identical twins before in a Charming Small Hotel Guide – still less a chain hotel – but such is the panache with which Robin Hutson and Petter Chittick have carried out their vision of a mid-price town hotel that we have no hesitation in including the Tunbridge Wells version this year.

There are differences. Although once again the owners have alighted on a faded hotel, ripe for conversion, here there is an abundance of space and many more period features such as the billiard room (its walls charmingly decorated with hand-painted cigar designs), the staircase, the delightful terrace overlooking Calverley Park, and indeed the elevated position. Bedrooms are stylishly restrained, extremely comfortable, with huge bathrooms and deliciously deep tubs and spacious showers. The bistro is a faithful copy, right down to the garland of hops and the world-class sommelier. This one – Henri Chapon – has come from Manoir aux Quat' Saisons. We asked him why. 'At the Manoir, it was a case of keeping everything the same; here, with a new venture, we can move forward.' The food has a sunny Mediterranean bias.

Nearby Sissinghurst Castle Gardens, 14 miles (22 km); Rye.

Crescent Road, Tunbridge Wells, Kent TN1 2LY
Tel (01892) 526455
Fax (01892) 512044
E-mail reception@tunbridgewells.hotelduvin.co.uk
Location in centre of town, private parking
Food & drink breakfast, lunch, dinner; full licence
Prices B&B £37.50-£109; breakfast £6-50-£9.50; dinner from £30

Rooms 32 double, all with bath and shower; all rooms have central heating, TV, radio, CD, minibar, tea/coffee kit, hairdrier **Facilities** sitting-room, billiard room, bar, bistro **Credit cards** AE, DC, MC, V **Children** welcome **Disabled** access to ground floor; lift to 1st and 2nd floors **Pets** not accepted **Closed** never **Proprietors** Alternative Hotel Company

The South-East

Hooke Hall

We inspected recently and Hooke Hall came out as well as ever. The owners Alister and Juliet Percy, have turned their elegant Queen Anne town-house (built in the early 18thC) into a stylish yet informal hotel. It is situated in the centre of Uckfield. Mrs Percy runs her own interior design business and knows all about good taste in the traditional manner: designer fabrics, family portraits, panelled rooms, log fires, gentle lighting and lots of flowers all contribute to the effect. The combination of home and hotel is cleverly achieved; there is a domesticated air about the place despite the presence of such chain hotel standbys as minibars and trouser-presses in the rooms, and of an upmarket restaurant, open to non-residents, on the premises. The rooms vary in size, some sumptuous with four-poster beds, others with sloping ceilings. The restaurant, La Scaletta, is the domain of two Italian chefs from Liguria and Veneto and they produce interesting regional dishes at reasonable prices.

The hotel also accommodates private parties and small business conferences, for which Juliet Percy, herself a Cordon Bleu chef, does much of the cooking.

Nearby Sheffield Park, 3 miles (5 km); Brighton, 17 miles (27 km); Glyndebourne, 9 miles (14 km.

High Street, Uckfield, East Sussex TN22 1EN
Tel (01825) 761578
Fax (01825) 768025
Location on the A22, 10 miles SW of Tunbridge Wells; in the centre of town; ample private car parking
Food & drink full breakfast, lunch, dinner; restaurant licence
Prices B&B £40-£80; dinner from £18
Rooms 9, all double or twin, 7 with bath, 2 with shower; all rooms have central heating, TV, alarm, mini-bar, hairdrier, trouser-press
Facilities sitting-room, air-conditioned restaurant; garden
Credit cards AE, MC, V
Children welcome over 12
Disabled access difficult
Pets not accepted
Closed Christmas
Proprietors Alister and Juliet Percy

The South-East

Old House

The Old House has much that we look for in this guide: a lovely setting – at a corner of the main square of one of the finest villages in Hampshire; a superb building – Grade II listed early Georgian; a delightful secluded garden; an immaculately kept and interesting interior, with antiques and 'objets' arranged to the best possible effect; and a fine restaurant, created from the original timber-framed outhouse and stables, serving far-above-average food – French regional in style, and making excellent use of fresh ingredients.

Nothing is over-stated – except perhaps the generous arrangements of fresh flowers which adorn all the public rooms. Bedrooms vary considerably – some palatial, others with magnificent beams, one or two rather cramped – but again a mood of civilized comfort prevails. Our reporter remarked on the imposing carved bar and the attractive beamed dining-room. The Skipwiths, who had been here for nearly 30 years, have just sold the Old House and 'declared their innings closed'. The new owners intend to continue the style and tradition; we welcome further reports.

Nearby Portsmouth, (ferries), 9 miles (14.5 km); South Downs; Winchester, Chichester, New Forest within reach.

The Square, Wickham, Hampshire PO17 5JG
Tel (01329) 833049
Fax (01329) 833672
Location 2.5 miles (4 km) N of Fareham, on square in middle of village; car parking
Food & drink full breakfast, lunch, dinner; residential and restaurant licence
Prices B&B £50-£85; dinner from £22
Rooms 9 double, 3 single, one family room, all with bath; all rooms have central heating, TV, phone, trouser-press, hairdrier, radio
Facilities 2 sitting-rooms, dining-room, bar
Credit cards AE, DC, MC, V
Children very welcome; special meals provided **Disabled** access easy to dining-room
Pets not accepted **Closed** 1 week at Easter; 2 weeks in Aug; 10 days over Christmas; restaurant only, Sun **Proprietors** Mr and Mrs N. Ruthven-Stuart

The South-East

Town house hotel, Winchester

Hotel du Vin

Citizens of Winchester and critics alike have responded with enormous enthusiasm to the opening in early 1994 of this stylish hotel and restaurant, formerly the faded Southgate Hotel. Anyone who knew it can only gasp at the transformation that owners Gerard Basset and Robin Hutson have wrought inside its fine Georgian shell. We continue to receive highly favourable reports on both hotel and 'cheerful and relaxed' restaurant, which can be booked solid at peak times – so reserve well ahead.

In the sitting-room, a false ceiling was removed, reinstating the room's original lofty proportions. Walls are decorated in the form of *trompe l'oeil* Georgian panelling in delicious shades of caramel cream and pale green. The decoration sets the tone for the friendly, informal atmosphere, much aided by the charming young staff. The Bistro, praised for its inventive, modern English menu and superb wine list (including plenty of inexpensive choices) gives the place its buzz. Gerard Basset was the renowned head *sommelier* at Chewton Glen (and Robin Hutson its Managing Director). Bedrooms are stylish, with 'extras' such as TV and mini-bar cleverly disguised; there is no room service, keeping prices to a remarkably reasonable level. Another Hotel du Vin has recently opened in Royal Tunbridge Wells (page 86).

Nearby Cathedral, Venta Roman Museum, Winchester College.

14 Southgate Street, Winchester, Hampshire SO23 9EF
Tel (01962) 841414
Fax (01962) 842458
E-mail admin@winchester.hotelduvin.co.uk
Location in the centre, a minute's walk from the cathedral; own car park
Food & drink breakfast, lunch, dinner; residential and restaurant licence
Prices B&B £49-£92; dinner £25
Rooms 23 double, 22 with bath and shower, 1 with shower; all rooms have central heating, TV, radio, CD, mini-bar, tea/coffee kit, hairdrier
Facilities sitting-room, dining-room/breakfast-room, bar, wine-tasting cellar; garden; boules **Credit cards** AE, DC, MC, V **Children** welcome
Disabled access easy to ground floor bedrooms; one specially adapted **Pets** accepted by arrangement **Closed** never
Proprietors Robin Hutson and Gerard Basset

The South-East

Inn, Winchester

Wykeham Arms

'Enormously charming; tons of personality,' says our latest reporter. Tucked away in the quietest, oldest part of the city, with Winchester College only yards away and the Cathedral also close by, it is a natural port of call for senior members of the choir. This is primarily a well-frequented local pub, and a first-rate one: 250 years old with four cosy bars furnished with old school desks, one engraved with the Winchester motto *Manners Makyth Man*. Interesting objects – old squash rackets, peculiar walking sticks – line the warm brick-red walls. This quirky character runs to the bedrooms, which are small in proportion and low-ceilinged, but each furnished in its own style with a personal feel, and adapted to accommodate all the usual facilities.

Breakfast is served upstairs, over the pub, in a pleasant straightforward English country breakfast room with Windsor chairs and a fine collection of silver tankards. Hearty pub food at lunch time and in the evenings; real ales and an impressive list of 40 wines, changed regularly, 22 served by the glass. Outside is a cobbled courtyard. Over the road is the 'Saint George' annexe with five bedrooms, a suite with 'folly' bedroom in the old College Bakehouse, and the post office and general store, also owned by the Jamesons. **Nearby** Cathedral, Venta Roman Museum, Winchester College.

75 Kingsgate Street,
Winchester, Hampshire
SO23 9PE
Tel (01962) 853834
Fax (01962) 854411
Location in middle of city, between College and cathedral, on corner of Canon Street; small courtyard garden with some car parking
Food & drink breakfast, lunch not Sun), dinner; full licence
Prices B&B £40-£99;

dinner about £15
Rooms 11 double, 1 single, all with bath; 1 cottage suite; all rooms have central heating, phone, TV, tea/coffee kit, radio/ alarm **Facilities** sitting-room, 3 bars, sauna; patio
Credit cards AE, DC, MC, V
Children welcome over 14
Disabled access difficult **Pets** welcome **Closed** Christmas day
Proprietors Graeme and Anne Jameson, and Nigel Atkinson

The South East

The George Hotel

In many ways the George is a perfect hotel: an atmospheric building in the centre of a breezy and historic harbour town, with welcoming rooms, a buzzing brasserie with tables spilling across the waterfront garden, and a quieter, more formal restaurant where good, inventive food is served. When they took over the peeling and faded17thC former govenor's residence, owners John Illsley (bass guitarist of Dire Straits) and Jeremy and Amy Willcock took great care to restore and renovate with sympathy. A panelled and elegantly proportioned hall sets the scene, leading to a cosy wood-panelled sitting-room with thick velvet drapes at the windows, an amusing mid-Victorian evocation of the George above the fireplace and a roaring log fire in winter. Across the hall is the dark red dining room, and beyond the central stairs, the brasserie and garden.

Upstairs, the bedrooms are all inviting and all different: one has a four poster draped in tartan; another is a light and pretty corner room; two have wonderful teak-decked balconies with views across the Solent. (The hotel has its own motor yacht for outings.)

The George is a new entry to this guide; we have been taken to task for its omission by several readers. 'It is a sheer pleasure,' writes one, 'to hop on the ferry at Lymington, alight at Yarmouth, and settle in to the George for two or three days.'

Nearby Yarmouth Castle (adjacent); Newport 12 miles (19 km).

Yarmouth, Isle of Wight,
PO41 OPE
Tel (01983) 760331
Fax (01983) 760425
Location in town, close to the ferry port and overlooking the Solent; no car park
Food & drink breakfast, lunch, dinner, full licence
Prices B&B £65-£85; dinner £22 (brasserie), £35 (restaurant)
Rooms 13 double, 2 suites, 1 single, all with bath and shower; all have central heating, TV, phone, radio, hairdrier
Facilities sitting-room, dining-room, brasserie, garden, private beach, 36 ft motor yacht available for charter
Credit cards AE, MC, V
Children welcome over 8
Disabled not suitable **Pets** by arrangement **Closed** never
Proprietors Jeremy and Amy Willcock and John Illsley

The South-East

Royal Oak

This inn has had a new lease of life in the past few years – attractive refurbishment of rooms and now a new chef, Robin Zavou, who trained with Raymond Blanc at Le Manoir aux Quat' Saisons. It's not difficult to believe that the food is more stylish than when Oliver Cromwell dined there, as the hotel claims he did.

Lest you mistake it for a mere pub, the sign on the front of this cottagey, mellow red-brick inn announces 'Hotel and restaurant'. Certainly, the Royal Oak is no longer a common-or-garden local. Its two restaurants have a style and elegance not usually associated with ale and darts. But the Oak still has a small bar where residents and non-residents alike can enjoy a choice of real ales without having a meal.

Next to the bar dining area is the light, relaxed and comfortable sitting-room (with newspapers and books within easy reach of its sofas) and beyond that the dining-room, with its elegant reproduction furniture. Bedrooms are prettily decorated and equipped with every conceivable extra. Another attraction is the walled garden, full of colour and a delight during the summer months.

Nearby Basildon Park, 3 miles (5 km); Donnington Castle, 6 miles (10 km); Snelsmore Common, 6 miles (10 km).

The Square, Yattendon, near Newbury, Berkshire RG18 0UG
Tel (01635) 201325
Fax (01635) 201926
Location 7 miles (11 km) NE of Newbury, in middle of village; walled garden; parking for 30 cars
Food & drink full breakfast, lunch, dinner; full licence
Prices £90-£110; suite £120; breakfast £6.50 (continental) £9.50 (full English); dinner £20 (bar), £25-£29.50 (restaurant – must be booked in advance); weekend breaks
Rooms 4 double, 1 suite, all with bath; all rooms have satellite TV, tea/coffee kit, radio, phone, hairdrier
Facilities restaurant, sitting-room, dining-room, bar
Credit cards AE, DC, MC, V
Children welcome
Disabled access easy to restaurant and bar but otherwise difficult
Pets accepted by prior arrangement
Closed Christmas night
Manager Corinne Macrae

The South-East

Powder Mills

The extensive grounds are only one attraction of this elegant Georgian house. The Cowplands were big in the antiques trade, and have assembled an interesting variety of period pieces – without spoiling the comfort of the sitting-rooms. Some bedrooms have antiques, too, while others are more modern. Guests dine in the Orangery (also open to non-residents). 'Though family run, with helpful staff, this is for those who like a dash of luxury with their country living,' comments our latest reporter. Prices, however, are not unfair.

Nearby Bodiam, 6 miles (10 km); Bateman's, 8 miles (13 km).

Powdermill Lane, Battle, East Sussex TN33 0SP
Tel (01424) 775511
Fax (01424) 774540
Location on S side of town; in 150-acre grounds with ample car parking
Food & drink full breakfast, lunch, tea, dinner; full licence
Prices B&B £42.50-£75; dinner £25; low-season reductions; bargain breaks
Rooms 35; 6 suites; all with bath and shower; all rooms have central heating
Facilities sitting-rooms, library, separate restaurant, function room; outdoor swimming-pool, fishing; riding and golf nearby
Credit cards AE, MC, V
Children welcome if well behaved
Disabled access easy
Pets dogs welcome if well behaved **Closed** never
Proprietors Douglas and Julie Cowpland

Winterbourne

This spacious house is of 18thC origin, and much is made of the time Charles Dickens spent here writing; but 'Dickensian' is the last adjective that springs to mind. Elegant, polished and formal are among the first, along with peaceful: the house and immaculate grounds (with streams and pools) are deliciously secluded. Many of the rooms are in a separate coach-house, giving sea views. The set four-course meals are not notably ambitious, but freshly prepared with local ingredients, and include a thoughtful vegetarian option.

Nearby beach; Botanic Gardens, Ventnor, one mile (2 km).

Bonchurch, Isle of Wight
Tel (01983) 852535
Fax (01983) 853056
Location in Bonchurch, 0.5 miles (one km) off A3055; with 4-acre grounds and ample car parking
Food & drink breakfast, dinner, lunch by request
Prices DB&B £49.77 reductions for children sharing
Rooms 14 double (5 twin), 3 single, 2 family room, all with bath or shower; all have phone, TV, radio; most have central heating, hairdrier
Facilities sitting-room, dining-room, bar **Credit cards** AE, MC, V **Children** welcome; babysitting by arrangement; no under 5s in dining-room
Disabled not suitable
Pets dogs accepted on leads (small charge) **Closed** Nov to Mar **Proprietors** TA and PM O'Connor

The South-East

The Twenty One

This tall Victorian town house in quiet Kemptown proves that a small hotel can be beautifully furnished and caringly run without charging guests the earth. Bedrooms are light and harmonious, well supplied with special comforts – some with hand-made beds. One has Victorian furnishings and a balcony; another, its own ivy-clad courtyard. Public rooms are done out in a rich, modern style, and the dining-room is particularly prettily decorated. Breakfast ranges from the heathily organic to traditional English. Dinner – ordered 24 hours in advance – is a set meal with an Indian flavour.
Nearby Royal Pavilion; Sea World.

21 Charlotte Street, Brighton, East Sussex BN2 1AG
Tel (01273) 686450/681617
Fax (01273) 695560
E-mail rooms@the21.co.uk
Website www.s-h-systems.co.uk/hotels/21
Location just off seafront road in Brighton; with free on-street parking
Food & drink breakfast, dinner
Prices B&B £27-£65; suite £90; dinner from £18; special breaks

Rooms 6 double (2 twin with single four-posters), all en suite; all rooms have central heating, TV, phone, tea/coffee kit, radio, hairdrier; some have trouser-press, minibar
Facilities sitting-room, dining-room **Credit cards** AE, DC, MC, V **Cbildren** welcome over 12 **Disabled** not suitable **Pets** not accepted
Closed restaurant only, Sun and Mon
Proprietor Tariq Jung

Topps

'Courteous efficiency and a fierce desire to be the best,' is our latest reader's comment. The hotel consists of two terraced Regency houses. The reception area (neat and light, with prints and comfortable chairs) is the only public room. The emphasis is on the bedrooms, furnished with some charming antiques which make you feel immediately at home. 'You could arrive without a suitcase and find everything you need.' An exceptionally comfortable and stylish hotel, even for elegant Brighton. No restaurant, but plenty to choose from in the town. Recent owners; reports please.
Nearby Royal Pavilion; seafront.

17 Regency Square, Brighton, East Sussex BN1 2FG
Tel (01273) 729334
Fax (01273) 203679
Location in heart of town opposite West Pier; large public car park opposite
Food & drink full breakfast; fully licenced
Prices B&B £22-£49
Rooms 13 double, 2 single; all with bath; all rooms have central heating, colour TV,

phone, tea/coffee kit, minibar, trouser-press, hairdrier
Facilities sitting-room, dining-room
Credit cards AE, DC, MC, V
Children welcome
Disabled access difficult
Pets not accepted
Closed never
Proprietors Bernard Houssin and Sabina Davis

The South-East

Crouchers Bottom

Readers continue to send us warm reports on Crouchers Bottom. The Wilsons (joined now by son-in-law, Lloyd) have created a relaxed, welcoming atmosphere, and it seems that the place fulfills a need for family-style accommodation in the Chichester area. There are now seventeen bedrooms (no smoking), in a converted coach house, all prettily decorated, with thoughtful use of space. The sitting-room in the the main house provides room for a 'garden restaurant'. A goose and some ducks give a lively cabaret outside. The name derives from the Croucher family's 'lower property'.
Nearby Fishbourne Palace, Chichester, 2 miles (3km).

Birdham Road Apuldram, Chichester, West Sussex PO20 7EH
Tel (01243) 784995
Fax (01243) 539797
Location in countryside 2 miles (3km) S of Chichester on the A286
Food & drink breakfast, dinner, snack lunches by arrangement; residential and restaurant licence
Prices B&B £49-£95; dinner £19.50; reductions for 3 nights or more
Rooms 17 double, all with bath and shower; all rooms have TV, tea/coffee kit, radio alarm, hairdrier, phone
Facilities sitting-room, dining-room **Credit cards** AE, MC, V
Children accepted **Disabled** access easy – 7 ground-floor bedrooms, 2 with wheelchair access **Pets** by arrangement
Closed never
Proprietors Drew and Lesley Wilson, and Lloyd van Rooyen

Suffolk House Hotel

This Georgian-style town house, once owned by the Dukes of Richmond (Grade II listed), is a welcoming and comfortable haven in a quiet part of the old city. At a recent inspection we noticed the pleasant family ambience and the excellent housekeeping. Bedrooms and bathrooms are airy and comfortable; there is an inviting sitting-room, which is non-smoking, like the adjoining dining-room where traditional English and French dishes are served. Guests can relax in the cosy bar or outside in the neat walled garden.
Nearby Cathedral, festival theatre.

3 East Row, Chichester, West Sussex PO19 1PD
Tel (01243) 778899
Fax (01243) 787282
Location off East Street, in middle of city, with garden; parking in front of the hotel
Food & drink breakfast, lunch, dinner; full licence
Prices B&B £44-£82; lunch from £7.50; dinner from £15.75; reductions for children
Rooms 6 double, 3 single, 2 family rooms, all with bath and shower; all rooms have central heating, phone, TV, radio, hairdrier
Facilities sitting-room, dining-room, bar **Credit cards** AE, DC, MC, V **Children** very welcome **Disabled** 4 ground-floor rooms **Pets** not in dining-room **Closed** never
Proprietors Michael and Rosemary Page

The South-East

Frith Farm House

Frith is an extremely civilized late-Georgian building reached by a sweeping gravel drive amidst carefully tended lawns and gardens. The Chesterfields have furnished and decorated their home with flair: elegantly draped fabrics in bold, deep colours complement the antiques and the fine collections of china, and the sitting-room (with log fire) and dining-room are subtly lit and atmospheric. The bedrooms are also handsome (one has a four-poster). Susan Chesterfield cares genuinely for her guests (who are requested not to smoke). We visited recently and were duly impressed.

Nearby Canterbury, 15 miles (24 km); Chilham, 9 miles (14 km).

Otterden, Eastling, nr Faversham, Kent ME13 0DD
Tel (01795) 890701
Fax (01795) 890009
E-mail markham@frith.force9.co.uk
Location 2 miles SW of village, 6 miles SW of Faversham; in six acres of grounds, with ample car parking
Food & drink full breakfast, packed lunch, dinner; no licence **Prices** B&B £26-£29; dinner from £21; reductions for 2 nights or more

Rooms 3 double, all with shower; all have central heating, radio, TV, tea/coffee kit, hairdrier **Facilities** sitting-room, dining-room; riding by arrangement **Credit cards** MC, V (+ 3%) **Children** welcome over 12 **Disabled** not suitable **Pets** not accepted **Closed** rarely **Proprietors** Susan and Markham Chesterfield

Five Sumner Place

This townhouse is prettily decorated and modestly priced for central London. It has no pretensions to hotel status – there are no signs outside, and you get a key to the permanently locked front door – and the rooms are not as individual as some. Breakfast (a buffet) is in a pleasant conservatory, and there is a small patio.

We continue to feature Five Sumner Place because it seems to offer value for money – not least because of the pleasant and convenient location. We would appreciate more readers' reports.

Nearby South Kensington museums; Knightsbridge; Albert Hall.

5 Sumner Place, London SW7 3EE
Tel (0171) 584 7586
Fax (0171) 823 9962
Location in residential street off Old Brompton Road; with small rear garden, public car park nearby; nearest tube South Kensington
Food & drink buffet breakfast; room service
Prices B&B £69-£150
Rooms 10 double (5 twin),

3 single, all with bath or shower; all rooms have phone, TV, radio, minibar, hairdrier
Facilities conservatory breakfast room
Credit cards AE, MC, V
Children welcome
Disabled no special facilities
Pets not accepted
Closed never
Proprietor John Palgan

The South-East

Hazlitt's

There is no quarter of central London with more character than Soho, now lively and fashionable; and there are few places to stay with more character than Hazlitt's, formed from three 18thC terraced houses off Soho Square. Character is the name of the game here. Old prints line the walls; Victorian taps grace the bathrooms; furniture is chosen more for its antiquity and decorative value than its function. Continental breakfast is served in the rooms. Nothing stuffy about the atmosphere, and no shortage of good restaurants nearby: it is located in the heart of Soho.

Nearby Oxford Street; Royal Opera House, theatres, cinemas.

6 Frith Street, Soho Square, London W1V 5TZ
Tel (0171) 434 1771
Location between Oxford Street and Shaftesbury Avenue; 2 public car parks within 2 minutes' walk
Food & drink breakfast
Prices B&B £101.50-£146; suite £276; continental breakfast £7.25
Rooms 17 double (1 twin), all with bath; 5 single, 4 with bath, one with shower; one suite with bath; all rooms have central heating, phone, TV, hairdrier
Facilities sitting-room
Credit cards AE, DC, MC, V
Children welcome; cots and baby-sitting available
Disabled access difficult
Pets dogs accepted by prior arrangement
Closed Christmas
Manager Lisa Wood

Pembridge Court

On a recent visit we found Spencer and Churchill, the ginger cats, sitting at the front desk with general manager Valerie Gilliat. The atmosphere of this Victorian house is nothing if not friendly and informal. The sitting-room is prettily furnished and features a large collection of framed Victorian fans, which also adorn the walls of the tastefully decorated bedrooms. The lovingly restored building is very cosy. Guests can eat in Caps, the hotel restaurant, or select from a fine room service menu.

Nearby Kensington Gardens; Kensington High Street and its shops; Portobello Road.

34 Pembridge Gardens, London W2 4DX
Tel (0171) 229 9977
Fax (0171) 727 4982
E-mail RESERVATIONS@PEMCT.CO.UK
Location a short walk N of Notting Hill Gate, in residential street; garage for 2 cars; nearest tube Notting Hill Gate
Food & drink breakfast; residential licence
Prices B&B £72.50-£115; dinner from £18
Rooms 17 double (14 with extra sofa bed; 3 twin); all with bath; 3 single with bath and shower; all rooms have central heating, satellite TV, radio, phone, hairdrier; some have air-conditioning
Facilities bar, sitting-room
Credit cards AE, DC, MC, V
Children very welcome
Disabled access difficult
Pets accepted if well behaved
Closed never
Manager Valerie Gilliat

The South-East

Portobello Hotel

An established favourite with the film, fashion and popular music industries, and other night owls, with a 24-hour bar and restaurant for the exclusive use of guests. Pastel decoration with antique armchairs in the bar and garden chairs in the marble-tiled dining-room give a fresh, light air. The sitting-room is a mixture of styles, with Victorian sofas, a large leather-top desk, parlour palms, and stripped french doors draped with brillant red livery. Bedrooms range from compact 'cabins' to spacious suites. Bathrooms are often small but have recently been refurbished.
Nearby Kensington Gardens; Kensington High Street.

22 Stanley Gardens, London W11 2NG
Tel (0171) 727 2777
Fax (0171) 792 9641
Location in residential area; nearest tube: Holland Park or Notting Hill Gate
Food & drink breakfast (in room); other meals available 24 hours a day
Prices B&B £90-£100; 'special' rooms £185-£220; meals widely variable
Rooms 17 double, 9 with bath; 5 single, all with shower; all rooms have central air heating, cable TV, phone, minibar, hairdrier, tea/coffee kit
Facilities dining-room, sitting-room, bar **Credit cards** AE, DC, MC, V **Children** welcome if well behaved **Disabled** lift/elevator **Pets** welcome if well behaved **Closed** Christmas and New Year
Proprietor John Ekperigin

The Fielding Hotel

The Fielding's guests come back time after time; they agree that finding another hotel of comparable price in such an enviable position (right in the heart of Covent Garden) would not be easy.

It is an 18thC building (named after the novelist, Henry Fielding, who lived in Broad Court and dispensed the law as a magistrate at Bow Street, next door). In a quiet pedestrian street, it has diamond-paned windows, flower-filled window boxes.and 19thC gas lamps to light the outside of the hotel at night. Bedrooms are decorated cottage-style and have pretty floral curtains and pine furnishings.
Nearby Royal Opera House, Covent Garden; West End.

4 Broad Court, Bow Street, London, WC2B 5QZ
Tel (0171) 836 8305
Fax (0171) 497 0064
Location in pedestrian zone opposite Royal Opera House; no private car parking
Food & drink breakfast; residential licence
Prices £42.50-£85 (breakfast not included)
Rooms 11 double (7 twin), 6 single; all with shower; all rooms have central heating, phone, TV
Facilities breakfast room, lobby/bar
Credit cards AE, DC, MC, V
Children not accepted
Disabled 5 ground-floor rooms
Pets not accepted
Closed Christmas
Manager Graham Chapman

The South-East

The Leonard

Yet another swanky town house hotel, designed to provide all the luxury and amenities of grand establishments, plus a homely, intimate atmosphere. Though expensive, the Leonard, opened in early 1996, has been brought to our attention by several correspondents who definitely did not feel skinned alive when they left. The hotel consists of four adjoining Grade II listed houses, similar in size but different in appearance. Decoration is very much that of a beautiful private home. Bedrooms are maintained to the highest standards, with all the latest accoutrements.

Nearby Planetarium, Madame Tussaud's, Oxford St and Bond St.

15 Seymour Street, London
W1H 5AA
Tel (0171) 935 2010
Fax (0171) 935 6700
Location West End; garage parking close by
Food & drink breakfast, light lunch and dinner; full room service; full licence
Prices B&B from £118.25-£200.50 **Rooms** 29; 9 double, 20 suites; some with butler's pantry or kitchen; all with bath; all rooms have central heating, phone, fax/modem line, TV, video, hi-fi, air-conditioning, minibar, safe, hairdrier **Facilities** sitting-room, Café Bar, conference room, exercise room, secretarial services
Credit cards AE, DC, MC, V
Children welcome
Disabled 1 specially adapted room **Pets** not accepted
Closed never
Manager Angela Stoppani

Fifehead Manor

This part-Medieval manor house has changed hands recently. We are told that there will be no material changes, but prices do seem to have increased considerably.

Our latest reporters liked the light and comfortable sitting-room and found the bedrooms and bathrooms 'large, individual and well decorated, but possibly lacking personality'. All overlook the attractive grounds. The interesting menu is stylishly presented. We look forward to further reports.

Nearby Museum of Army Flying; Salisbury; Stonehenge, 10 miles (16 km); Old Sarum.

Middle Wallop, Stockbridge, Hampshire SO20 8EG
Tel (01264) 781565
Fax (01264) 781400
Location 5 miles (8 km) SW of Andover on A343; in gardens with parking for 50 cars
Food & drink breakfast, lunch, dinner; full licence
Prices B&B £90-£130; dinner £22; bargain breaks; children sharing parents' room £12 (under 5 free)
Rooms 16 double, all with bath and shower; all rooms have central heating, TV, phone, radio, tea/coffee kit **Facilities** sitting-room, bar, 2 dining-rooms; croquet
Credit cards AE, DC, MC, V
Children welcome
Disabled access to 2 rooms
Pets welcome
Closed 1 week after Christmas
Manager Solomon Bader

The South-East

The Angel Hotel

We continue to receive praise from all quarters for the seamless conversion of this important mixed-period hostelry into a hotel full of style and panache. Behind a fine Georgian town-house façade you find an informal bar and brasserie, a small restaurant decked out in green and yellow, and bedrooms above, decorated with flair, each with a gleaming bathroom. Rooms range from a small double to the flamboyant Castle Suite. The inventive food is another draw. 'The exterior doesn't do it justice,' said our inspector who visited recently.

Nearby Cowdray ruins; Cowdray Park; Chichester, 12 miles (19 km).

North Street, Midhurst, West Sussex GU29 7DN
Tel (01730) 812421
Fax (01730) 815928
Location in centre of Midhurst on the A272/286, 11 miles (17 km) E of Petersfield
Food & drink breakfast, lunch, dinner; full licence
Prices B&B £47.50-£120; dinner from £21
Rooms 18 double, 3 single, 4 suites, all with bath; all rooms have central heating, TV, radio/alarm, phone, hairdrier, tea/coffee kit; trouser-press
Facilities lounge, bar, brasserie, restaurant, dining terrace, walled garden
Credit cards AE, DC, MC, V
Children welcome; dining in brasserie preferred
Pets not accepted
Disabled adapted ground-floor room
Closed never
Proprietors Nicholas Davies and Peter Crawford-Rolt

Park House

Park House has been a hotel for over 50 years, but has always retained the atmosphere of a private country house – thanks to the careful attention of Ioné O'Brien. Now Michael and Liza O'Brien have taken over the running of this 16thC farmhouse with Victorian additions, set in nine-acre gardens. The large, elegant public rooms include a drawing-room lined with books and ornaments, and a dining-room with polished tables. Bedrooms are individually furnished. Excellent English food. Our latest report describes it as 'a relaxing family home with plenty to do nearby'.

Nearby Petworth, 6 miles (10.5 km); Chichester, 12 miles (19 km).

Bepton, Nr Midhurst, West Sussex GU29
Tel (01730) 812880
Fax (01730) 815643
Location in countryside, on the B2226 and just N of village of Bepton, 3 miles (5 km) SSW of Midhurst; ample parking
Food & drink full breakfast, lunch, dinner; licenced
Prices B&B £49.50-£75; lunch from £10; dinner from £16.50
Rooms 12 double, 1 single, 1 family room; all with bath; all rooms have central heating, phone, TV, radio, hairdrier
Facilities dining-room, sitting-room, bar; swimming-pool, grass tennis courts, croquet, putting green, 9 hole pitch and putt course **Credit cards** AE, MC, V **Children** welcome **Disabled** ground-floor bedroom **Pets** not in dining-room **Closed** never **Proprietors** Michael and Liza O'Brien

The South-East

Country inn, Ringlestone

Ringlestone

Built in 1533, and originally used as a hospice for monks, the Ringlestone became an 'Ale House' around 1615, and now offers three comfortable rooms in the farmhouse opposite. The bar, which has several intimate dining areas, tasty food (pies a speciality) and over thirty English country wines, is affably run by Mike Millington-Buck, with daughter Michelle, and friendly team. At the back is a sloping garden and waterfall. Mike's passion for oak is evident everywhere – carved dressers, tables made from the timbers of an 18thC barge, and rustic furniture in cream-toned bedrooms.
Nearby Leeds Castle; Sissinghurst; Maidstone; Canterbury.

Ringlestone, nr Maidstone, Kent ME17 1NX
Tel (01622) 859900
Fax (01622) 859900
E-mail michelle@ringlestone.com
Website: http://www.ringlestone.com/ringlestone
Location in hamlet, off A20, between Harrietsham and Wormshill; garden, parking
Food & drink breakfast, buffet lunch, pub meals; full licence
Prices £39.50-£69, with light breakfast; English breakfast

£10, continental breakfast £7.50; lunch from £7.50; dinner from £20; special breaks
Rooms 3 double in self-contained farmhouse, all with bath; all rooms have central heating, phone, TV, hairdrier, minibar **Facilities** bars; sitting-room **Credit cards** AE, DC, MC, V **Children** welcome
Disabled bedrooms not suitable **Pets** not accepted **Closed** Christmas **Proprietor** Michael Millington-Buck

---

Town guest-house, Rye

The Old Vicarage ★

Paul and Julia Masters have built up a faithful following for this Tudor-Georgian house which has an excellent position – central but peaceful, next to St Mary's church. The bedrooms, temptingly supplied with home-made biscuits and fudge, are prettily decorated in Laura Ashley papers and fabrics. Breakfast is a highlight and includes local Ashbee sausages, freshly baked scones, home-made jams and marmalades, and tea from a Rwanda plantation. Maps and guidebooks abound for those interested in exploring. 'A gem for those who like small family-run places,' said our reporter.
Nearby Great Dixter, 6 miles (10 km); Ellen Terry Museum.

66 Church Square, Rye, East Sussex, TN31 7HF
Tel (01797) 222119
Fax (01797) 227466
Location on A259 near middle of town; with small walled garden, parking arrangements
Food & drink full breakfast, no licence
Prices B&B £22-£32
Rooms 6 double, one with bath, 4 with shower; one suite; all rooms have central heating,

TV, tea/coffee kit, hairdrier
Facilities sitting-room, dining-room, library
Credit cards not accepted
Children welcome over 8
Disabled not suitable
Pets not accepted
Closed Christmas
Proprietors Paul and Julia Masters

The South-East

Seaview Hotel & Restaurant

The Haywards relish providing a personal touch at Seaview (which is also the central pub of the village) from turning down the beds at night to squeezing fresh orange juice to serve along with early morning tea and coffee. Nicola (a former professional wine-taster) has built a high reputation for food and wine in the two smart restaurants (one traditional, the other a showcase for Nick's model ships). Fax and photocopying facilities for business guests. On the north shore, with ferry access from Portsmouth to Wootton/Ryde.
Nearby Flamingo Park, 1 mile (1.5 km); Bembridge Maritime Museum, 4 miles (6 km).

High Street, Seaview, Isle of Wight PO34 5EX
Tel (01983) 612711
Fax (01983) 613729
Location near the beach in seaside village 3 miles (5 km) E of Ryde; with car parking
Food & drink breakfast, lunch, dinner; pub meals; full licence
Prices B&B from £50; suite 130; dinner from £16
Rooms 14 double, 12 with bath, and 2 with shower; 2 suites both with bath; annexe; all have central heating, phone, TV, radio, hairdrier
Facilities 2 sitting-rooms (one non-smoking), 2 dining-rooms (one non-smoking), 2 bars
Credit cards AE, DC, MC, V
Children very welcome – special meals and baby-listening
Disabled 2 ground-floor bedrooms, but doors narrow
Pets welcome, if well behaved, except in public rooms
Closed restaurant, Sun dinner
Proprietors N and N Hayward

Brattle House

In their mainly Georgian, tile-hung and weatherboarded house, the Rawlinsons have created extremely comfortable accommodation. 'A family home which happily doubles as a guest house,' says our latest report. All is bright, spruce and pretty, with pine furniture, soft flowery patterns and white walls. The light, low-beamed sitting-room looks out over the garden, and in the dining-room candlelit dinners (bring your own wine) are served on the beautifully polished antique table, Maureen Rawlinson pays great attention to detail. Breakfast is hearty. No smoking.
Nearby steam railway; Sissinghurst 3 miles (5 km); Bodiam Castle.

Watermill Bridges, Tenterden, Kent TN30 6UL
Tel (01580) 763565
Location half a mile (1 km) W of town; in 11-acre garden, with car parking
Food & drink full breakfast, dinner; no licence
Prices B&B £31.50-£45; reduced rates for 4 nights; dinner £17.50
Rooms 3 double (one twin), all with shower; all rooms have central heating, radio, tea/coffee kit, hairdrier, bathrobes
Facilities sitting-room, dining-room, conservatory
Credit cards not accepted
Children welcome over 14
Disabled not suitable
Pets not accepted
Closed Christmas and New Year
Proprietors Maureen and Alan Rawlinson

Wales

Seaside hotel, Abersoch

Porth Tocyn

This whitewashed, slate-roofed establishment, looking out over the sea from the Lleyn peninsula towards Snowdonia, is a rare animal. The Fletcher-Brewers, who have owned it for over 50 years, call it a country house hotel; but it is not what most people would understand by the term. Porth Tocyn certainly contains as many antiques as the typical country house hotel and is run with as much skill and enthusiasm as the best of them. But the building – an amalgam of several old lead-miners' cottages, which has been much extended over the years – makes for a cosy, home-like atmosphere. And the seaside position has naturally encouraged the Fletcher-Brewers to cater well for children as well as parents keen to enjoy the hotel's civilised attractions. Chief among these is the excellent dinner-party-style food; don't go expecting to lose weight. Bedrooms have been kept low key and simply furnished, but are excellent value.

Nearby Plas Yn Rhiw 6 miles (10 km); Criccieth Castle 14 miles (23 km); Snowdonia within reach.

Bwlchtocyn, Abersoch, Pwllheli, Gwynedd LL53 7BU
Tel (01758) 713303
Fax (01758) 713538
Location 2.5 miles (4 km) S of Abersoch; in 25 acres of farm land and gardens with ample car parking
Food & drink breakfast, lunch, dinner, picnics; residential and restaurant licence
Prices B&B £34-£57.50; dinner £20.75-£27.75; reductions for longer stays
Rooms 13 double, 3 single, one family room, all with bath and shower; all rooms have central heating, TV, phone
Facilities cocktail bar, TV room, dining-room, 6 sitting-rooms, tennis, outdoor heated swimming-pool
Credit cards MC, V
Children welcome, but those under 7 usually take high tea instead of dinner
Disabled access easy – one step into hotel and 3 ground-floor bedrooms
Pets accepted by arrangement
Closed early Nov to week before Easter
Proprietors Fletcher-Brewer family

Wales

Country guest-house, Llanbrynmair

Barlings Barn

The only sounds to disturb the peace come from the sheep on the surrounding hillsides, and from the nearby brook. It is a rural idyll, with a garden full of roses and honeysuckle – a picturesque setting for the outdoor activities, such as the swimming-pool, which you can enjoy here.

It is, in fact, the perfect peace of the place that keeps it in these pages despite the Margolis's move towards a self-catering set-up. Home-made biscuits await your arrival in the two secluded 'Barnlets' adjacent to Felicity and Terry's Welsh farmhouse – one with an oak-beamed stone fireplace and wood-burning stove. The spring-fed heated swimming-pool is a flowery sun-trap; and sauna, sunbed and squash are all provided.

Nearby Riding, walking, fishing; Snowdonia; Aberdovey beach.

Llanbrynmair, Powys
SY19 7DY
Tel (01650) 521479
Fax (01650) 521520
Website http//www.telecentres.com/business/newtownbiz/barlingsbarn
Location 2 miles (3 km) NE of Llanbrynmair at end of private lane off road to Pandy; with garden, grounds and ample car parking
Food & drink home-cooked frozen meals
Prices £165-£760 per week; short off-season breaks from

£99
Rooms 2 'Barnlets', Sunnyside sleeps 2-6; Brookside sleeps 8-12; both have central heating, TV
Facilities heated swimming-pool, squash, sauna, sunbed; squash **Credit cards** not accepted **Children** very welcome **Disabled** Brookside has ground floor bedroom and facilities **Pets** accepted by arrangement **Closed** never **Proprietors** Terry and Felicity Margolis

Wales

Country hotel, Llandrillo

Tyddyn Llan

A firm favourite with readers since our first edition, this Georgian stone house has been decorated by the Kindreds with elegant flair, period antiques and fine paintings, creating a serene ambience. It is very much a home, despite the number of guests it can accommodate – there is a major extension to the building, cleverly complementary to the original, using slate, stone and cast-iron. We like it enough to give it a whole page in this new edition.

Our latest report glowed: 'No intrusive reception desk; spacious sitting-rooms furnished with style; dining-room shows great flair; bedrooms well equipped with original pieces of furniture; small but modern and very pleasing bathrooms; peaceful, comfortable stay, warm atmosphere provided by attentive hosts; great charm.'

The kitchen's already high reputation has been enhanced by the arrival of young chef, Jason Hornbuckle, who produces a new angle on Welsh country house food with his inventive and well-planned small menus using local quality ingredients.

The place is surrounded by large grounds, still needing work, but with real potential; the lawn is large enough to practice fly-casting; and the hotel has four miles of fishing on the Dee.

Nearby Bala Lake and Railway, 8 miles (13 km); Snowdonia.

Llandrillo, near Corwen, Denbighshire, LL21 0ST
Tel (01490) 440264
Fax (01490) 440414
E-mail tyddynllanhotel@compuserve.com
Location 5 miles (8 km) SW of Corwen off B4401; with ample car parking
Food & drink breakfast, lunch, tea, dinner; full licence
Prices B&B £49-£65; DB&B £76.50-£92.50; reductions for 2 nights or more, short breaks and for children sharing room
Rooms 10 double, 8 with bath, 2 with shower; all rooms have central heating, phone, TV, radio **Facilities** sitting-room, bar, restaurant; croquet, fishing **Credit cards** AE, DC, MC, V **Children** welcome
Disabled not suitable **Pets** dogs accepted by arrangement, and not in public rooms
Closed never **Proprietors** Bridget and Peter Kindred

Wales

St Tudno

The Blands are meticulous in attending to every detail of this award-winning seafront hotel, which they have been improving for 26 years now. The pretty rooms are each decorated differently in designer wallpapers and matching fabrics, and have found the balance between Victorian charm and modern facilities. A long list of thoughtful extras add to the sense of comfort, including complimentary wine. We continue to get favourable reports from readers.

The air-conditioned dining-room is light and inviting, with a profusion of plants and cane-backed chairs. The seasonal menu with daily changing *carte*, based on the best local ingredients, deserves serious study in the comfortable bar, and the cooking is right on target. All of this would be difficult to resist even without the bonus of the hotel's young and helpful staff.

Nearby Dry ski slope, 0.5 miles (1 km); Conwy Castle, 3 miles (5 km); Bodnant Gardens, 7 miles (11 km); Snowdonia.

Promenade, Llandudno, North Wales, LL30 2LP
Tel (01492) 874411
Fax (01492) 860407
Location on seafront opposite pier and promenade gardens; small garden and private parking for 12 cars; unrestricted street parking
Food & drink breakfast, lunch, dinner; residential and restaurant licence
Prices B&B £45-£95; dinner £32.50; reductions for children sharing parents' room; reduced DB&B rates for 2 nights or more
Rooms 15 double/twin, 13 with bath, 2 with shower; 1 suite; 2 single with bath; 4 family rooms, all with bath; all rooms have

central heating, satellite TV, phone, radio/alarm, fridge, tea/coffee kit, hairdrier
Facilities bar, 3 sitting-rooms, dining-room; covered heated swimming-pool
Credit cards AE, DC, MC, V
Children very welcome; baby-listening, cots, highchairs and high tea available (dinner not suitable for very young)
Disabled access fairly easy except for wheelchairs; lift/elevator to most bedrooms
Pets small well-behaved dogs accepted at proprietors' discretion
Closed never
Proprietors Martin and Janette Bland

Wales

Country rectory, Llansanffraid Glan Conwy

The Old Rectory

This pretty former Georgian rectory, home of the owners, enjoys an exceptional elevated position, standing in two and a half acres of flowery gardens with lovely sweeping views across the Conwy Estuary to Conwy Castle and Snowdonia beyond. Most of the bedrooms, two of which are in a separate building, share this view. The rooms have an old fashioned feel about them, with ponderous beds, mostly either half tester or four-poster, in walnut, mahogany and oak. Downstairs, is an elegant panelled drawing room with the Vaughan's collection of Victorian watercolours on the walls.

The couple's progression as hoteliers and particularly Wendy's as a chef has been remarkable. An ex-nurse with no culinary training whatsoever, she began by cooking for parties of visiting American tourists. As they started to take in bed-and-breakfast guests and then graduated to fully fledged hotel, so Wendy's culinary skills improved and they are now the possessors of a red M in Michelin as well as several other awards for food. Wendy still produces a delicious and imaginative three-course dinner each night unaided, except for help with the washing up and the vegetable chopping (done by Michael, who also oversees the wine list to complement her cuisine). Guests eat at separate mahogany, candle-lit tables dotted round the room. No smoking, except in coachhouse.
Nearby Bodnant Gardens, Betws-y-Coed, Llandudno.

Llansanffraid Glan Conwy,
Colwyn Bay, Conwy LL28 5LF
Tel (01492) 580611
Fax (01492) 584555
E-mail OldRect@aol.com
Website www.wales.com/oldrectory/
Location on A470 half a mile south of junction with A55; in 2.5 acres of grounds with ample car parking
Food & drink breakfast, dinner; full licence;
Prices B & B £49.50-£129;
dinner £29.50
Rooms 6 double, 5 with bath, 1 with shower; all rooms have central heating, phone, TV, radio, tea/coffee kit, ironing board, hairdrier **Facilities** sitting-room, dining- room; garden **Credit cards** MC, V
Children over 6 **Disabled** 2 ground floor rooms **Pets** in coachhouse only **Closed** 1 Dec-1 Feb **Proprietors** Michael and Wendy Vaughan

Wales

Ynyshir Hall

The Reens have been at Ynyshir Hall for some years now and, happily, seem to know what they are about. In that time they have upgraded the interior rooms and bedrooms considerably. Both are ex-teachers, Joan of geography, Rob of design and art – and his paintings now decorate the walls of the whole house. Given Rob's background, you might well expect the decoration of the hotel to be rather special, too – and you would not be disappointed. The colour schemes are adventurous, the patterns bold, the use of fabrics opulent, the attention to detail striking. The bedrooms are named after famous artists, and they are furnished accordingly.

The white-painted house dates from the 16th century, but is predominantly Georgian and Victorian. It stands in glorious landscaped gardens next to the Dovey estuary.

The award-winning food is adventurous but not over-complex – modern British – based on fresh local ingredients, especially fish, game, shellfish and Welsh lamb.

Nearby Llyfnant valley; Aberystwyth, 11 miles (18km).

Eglwysfach, Machynlleth, Powys SY20 8TA
Tel (01654) 781209
Fax (01654) 781366
Location 11 miles (18 km) NE of Aberystwyth, just off A487; in 12-acre grounds with ample car parking
Food & drink breakfast, lunch, dinner; residential and restaurant licence
Prices B&B £55-£90; meals from £32.50; reductions for 2 nights or more

Rooms 5 double, with bath; 3 suites; all rooms have central heating, phone, TV
Facilities dining-room, sitting-room, bar, conservatory
Credit cards AE, DC, MC, V
Children accepted over 9
Disabled access easy; one ground-floor room
Pets dogs accepted in one bedroom (£3 charge)
Closed never
Proprietors Rob and Joan Reen

Wales

Country house hotel, Reynoldston

Fairyhill

A recent inspection confirms that standards are being well maintained in this quiet and utterly civilized retreat situated in the heart of the Gower Peninsula and only about 25 minutes from the M4, since new owners took over in late 1993.

Set in 24 acres of grounds – with walled garden, orchard, trout stream and lake, and much of it still semi-wild – the three storey Georgian building has a series of spacious, newly furnished public rooms on the ground floor, leading to the dining-room.

Paul Davies, one of the proprietors, is the chef. He enjoys producing seasonal menus and makes excellent use of traditional local specialities such as Gower lobster and crab, Penclawdd cockles, Welsh lamb and laverbread. The extensive wine list, cellared in the old vaults of the house, includes five wines from Wales. Most bedrooms overlook the large park and woodland, and are comfortable and well-equipped.

More reports please.

Nearby Weobley Castle, 7 miles (11 km); scenic coast of Gower Peninsula; Swansea within reach.

Reynoldston, Gower, near Swansea, West Glamorgan SA3 1BS
Tel (01792) 390139
Fax (01792) 391358
Location 12 miles (19 km) W of Swansea, one mile (1.5 km) NW of village; in 24-acre park and woodland, with ample car parking
Food & Drink breakfast, lunch dinner; restaurant and residential licence
Prices B&B £60-£145; lunch from £14.50; dinner from £25
Rooms 8 double, all with bath; all rooms have central heating, colour TV, CD player, phone
Facilities sitting-room, bar, 2 dining-rooms, conference room; croquet
Credit cards AE, MC, V
Children accepted over 8
Disabled access easy to restaurant, but no ground-floor bedrooms
Pets not accepted
Closed 24-27 Dec
Proprietors P and J Camm, P Davies and A Hetherington

Wales

Manor house hotel, Three Cocks

Old Gwernyfed

Roger and Dawn Beetham ran this splendid Elizabethan manor house 'very quietly' after taking over the lease from Roger's parents in 1979; but in 1986 the opportunity arose to buy Old Gwernyfed outright, and the two of them have since set about making it 'the best personal small hotel around'.

Happily, the improvements so far have not interfered with the historic character of the place. Decoration is kept to a minimum and the slightly haphazard collection of grand old furniture goes on growing. The four newest bedrooms, created where the kitchens used to be, have the same high ceilings and sense of space of the larger of the old rooms (which range in size from very small to positively enormous). The public rooms are especially impressive – the oak-panelled sitting-room is overlooked by a minstrel's gallery, the dining-room has a vast fireplace with a wood-burning stove. Period music is played as a background to Dawn's original and satisfying dinners ('designed for people who have just walked half of Offa's Dyke' says our inspector), with some choice at beginning and end.

Nearby Brecon Beacons; Hay-on-Wye, 5 miles (8 km).

Felindre, Three Cocks, Brecon, Powys LD3 0SG
Tel (01497) 847376
Location 11 miles (18 km) NE of Brecon, off A438, in open countryside; in 13-acre grounds and gardens with ample car parking
Food & drink breakfast, dinner; packed lunch by arrangement; restaurant and residential licence
Prices B&B £30-£48; dinner £21; reductions for stays of 3 nights, and for children sharing room

Rooms 9 double, 7 with bath, one with shower; 2 single, one with bath; 3 family rooms, all with bath
Facilities dining-room, sitting-room, games room, bar; croquet
Credit cards not accepted
Children accepted if well behaved
Disabled access difficult
Pets accepted if well behaved, but not in public rooms
Closed Jan and Feb
Proprietors Dawn and Roger Beetham

Wales

Llanwenarth House

While the Weatherills have put tremendous efforts into rescuing this dignified house set in large grounds, they have at the same time taken great care to keep the personal touches. Llanwenarth House is still very much a family home, and guests dine as if at a dinner-party, in the splendid candlelit dining-room. Amanda, Cordon Bleu-trained, supervises the kitchen, where the emphasis is on home-grown and local ingredients. The bedrooms and public rooms (heavy on hunting memorabilia) are notably spacious and comfortable; many enjoy lovely views of the peaceful Usk valley.

Nearby Brecon Beacons National Park; Offa's Dyke path.

Govilon, Abergavenny, Monmouthshire, NP7 9SF
Tel (01873) 830289
Fax (01873) 832199
Location 4 miles (6 km) SW of Abergavenny, off A465; ample car parking
Food & drink breakfast, dinner; restaurant and residential licence
Prices B&B £37-£40; dinner £25.50; reductions for 2 nights or more
Rooms 5 double, 3 with bath, 2 with shower; all rooms have central heating, TV, radio, tea/coffee kit
Facilities sitting-room, dining-room; croquet
Credit cards not accepted
Children welcome over 10
Disabled access easy – one ground-floor bedroom
Pets dogs accepted if well behaved, but not in public rooms **Closed** Feb
Proprietors Bruce and Amanda Weatherill

Ty Mawr

New owners, the Westons, took over at this long, low 16thC house, a few years ago, so we welcome reports. It stands at right angles to the main street of a tiny village in deepest Carmarthenshire, with fine views of the surrounding wooded hillsides, dotted with sheep. Inside, public rooms are cosy and include an immaculate bar with rough stone walls and smart pine fittings, and a welcoming sitting-room with an open log fire. Bedrooms are comfortable and pleasantly rustic. The restaurant (beamed, stone-walled, has earned itself a good reputation. The emphasis is on regional specialities.

Nearby Brecon Beacons; Cardigan Bay within reach.

Brechfa, Dyfed SA32 7RA
Tel (01267) 202332
Fax (01267) 202437
Location 10 miles (16 km) NE of Carmarthen, on B4310, in village; with garden, and ample car parking
Food & drink full breakfast, dinner, light lunch; full licence
Prices B&B £42-£52; dinner from £23; bargain breaks
Rooms 4 double, 1 family room; all with bath; all rooms have central heating
Facilities sitting-room, bar, dining-room
Credit cards MC, V
Children welcome – cot available; play area
Disabled not suitable
Pets dogs welcome if well behaved **Closed** last week Nov; Christmas; end Jan
Proprietors Veronica and Roger Weston

Wales

Country house hotel, Dolgellau

Borthwnog Hall

Facing south, on the edge of the beautiful Mawddach estuary and surrounded by mature gardens, this elegant little Regency house enjoys a glorious position. It is an unusual hotel; there are only three rooms and the house is superbly furnished as only a home can be, but it is run on hotel lines – there is a civilized sitting-room for guests, with an open fire, and a proper dining-room with a wide choice of food and an award-winning wine list. The library has been turned into an art gallery, and is full of paintings, sculpture and pottery.

Nearby fishing, trekking, gold mine, narrow-gauge railways.

Bontddu, Dolgellau, Gwynedd LL40 2TT
Tel (01341) 430271
Fax (01341) 430682
E-mail borthwnoghall@enterprise.net
Website http://homepages.enterprise.net/borthwnoghall
Location beside estuary, outside village, 2 miles from junction of A470 and A496; in gardens with private parking
Food & drink breakfast, dinner; full licence
Prices B&B £27.50-£56; DB&B £45.50-£67.50; reductions for children, bargain breaks
Rooms 3 double (2 twin), all with bath or shower; all rooms have central heating, TV, phone, radio, alarm
Facilities sitting-room, dining-room, bar **Credit cards** AE, MC, V **Children** welcome
Disabled access restaurant only **Pets** accepted by arrangement **Closed** Christmas
Proprietors Derek and Vicki Hawes

Country house hotel, Dolgellau

Plas Dolmelynllyn

The father-and-daughter team of Jon Barkwith and Jo Reddicliffe have been running 'Dolly' with considerable style for over ten years now. Confident colour schemes are successfully teamed with Victorian antiques in some areas, more modern furnishings in others, to create a warmly comfortable atmosphere. Bedrooms are named after local rivers and individually decorated; many have splendid views. Jo's award-winning cooking is best described as 'imaginative modern British', with young guests, vegetarians and other diets catered for. Extensive wine cellar. A no smoking hotel.

Nearby fishing, walking, narrow-gauge railways; Snowdon.

Ganllwyd, Dolgellau, Gwynedd LL40 2HP
Tel (01341) 440273
Fax (01341) 440640
Location in countryside, on A470 5 miles (8 km) N of Dolgellau; in large grounds with private car parking
Food & drink breakfast, lunch by arrangement, tea, dinner; licenced
Prices B&B £50-£60; DB&B £65-£75 (2 days min)
Rooms 8 double, 2 single, all with bath and shower; all rooms have central heating, phone, radio, TV, hairdrier, tea/coffee kit
Facilities sitting-room, dining-room, conservatory bar; fishing **Credit cards** AE, DC, MC, V **Children** welcome over 8
Disabled not suitable **Pets** in 2 bedrooms (£5 per day) **Closed** Dec to Feb **Proprietors** Jon Barkwith and Jo Reddicliffe

Wales

George III

This 300-year-old inn, separated for a century from the nearby Mawddach estuary by a railway, now has access to the shore once again – and the bonus of space in the disused station a few yards away for some spacious, well-furnished bedrooms to add to those in the main building. The sitting-room has beams and an inglenook, while the main Welsh Dresser bar has wooden settles and oak tables; in summer the 'cellar' bar comes into play, suiting families particularly thanks to its children's menu, no smoking policy and outdoor seating overlooking the estuary. Reports please.
Nearby Fairbourne Railway, 6 miles (10 km); Snowdonia.

Penmaenpool, Dolgellau, Gwynedd LL40 1YD
Tel (01341) 422525
Fax (01341) 423565
Location 2 miles (3 km) W of Dolgellau on A493; on edge of Mawddach estuary, with ample car parking
Food & drink breakfast, morning coffee, lunch, dinner, snacks, afternoon tea; licence
Prices B&B £47-£50; dinner about £20; children sharing room £12.50; winter breaks

Rooms 12 double (4 twin), 11 with bath, 1 with shower; all rooms have central heating, TV, phone, tea/coffee kit, trouser press, hairdrier
Facilities sitting-room, 3 bars, dining-room; fishing; mountain bikes for hire **Credit cards** MC, V **Children** welcome **Disabled** access good in Lodge bedrooms **Pets** welcome if well behaved (£5 per night) **Closed** never **Proprietors** Julia and John Cartwright

Tregynon Country Farmhouse

The Heards' blissfully isolated retreat has matured nicely since its doors were opened in 1980. One bedroom is in the main 16thC stone farmhouse, the others in adjacent cottages; furnishing throughout is suitably cosy-rustic. Fires blaze in winter.

Jane learnt to cook at the knee of her French grandmother, and her food is a highlight: traditionally based, wholesome and imaginative, with proper care taken of vegetarians. There is a well rounded wine list. Children eat at tea-time, preserving adult peace at the dinner table. No smoking in the dining-room or bedrooms.
Nearby walks, wildlife, beaches.

Gwaun Valley, Fishguard, Pembrokeshire SA65 9TU
Tel (01239) 820531
Fax (01239) 820808
E-mail tregynon@uk-holidays.co.uk
Website http://www.uk-holidays.co.uk/tregynon
Location isolated in countryside - 7 miles (11 km) SE of Fishguard, 3 miles (5 km) S of Newport (get directions)
Food & drink breakfast, packed lunch, dinner; full licence

Prices B&B £31-£39; dinner £19.95-£25.45 **Rooms** 4 double (2 with four-posters), 2 family rooms, all with bath or shower; all have central heating, TV, phone, hairdrier, tea/coffee kit **Facilities** sitting-room, 2 dining-rooms, bar **Credit cards** MC, V **Children** under 8 welcome **Disabled** access possible **Pets** not accepted **Closed** 2 weeks in winter **Proprietors** Peter and Jane Heard

Wales

Whitegates

With magnificent views over St Brides Bay, this Welsh longhouse is right beside the Pembrokeshire coastal path and above the tiny village harbour and sandy beach. Three bedrooms have sea views as does the dining-room where local seafood, lamb and Welsh cheeses are on the four-course menu, on offer four days of the-week. The sitting-room has a cottagey look with comfortable sofas and easy chairs. Richard Llewelyn enjoys sharing his knowledge of local sights – and his own ostrich farm adds an exotic touch to the scenery. Self-catering cottages are also available.

Nearby Offshore islands reached by boat from coastal villages.

Little Haven, Haverfordwest, Pembrokeshire SA62 3LA
Tel (01437) 781552
Fax (01437) 781386
Location on the coast off the B431 road from Haverfordwest; ample parking
Food & drink full breakfast, dinner (available Sun, Mon, Wed and Fri)
Prices B&B £22-£25; cottages £90-£380; dinner £17 (4 courses, including glass of wine); gastronomic breaks

Rooms 3 double, 1 family room, all with bath; all rooms have central heating, tea/coffee kit, radio
Facilities dining-room, sitting-room with TV, outdoor heated swimming-pool
Credit cards MC, V
Children welcome
Disabled access difficult
Pets welcome
Closed never
Proprietors Richard and Marion Llewellin

The Pen-y-Gwryd Hotel

High up in the desolate heart of Snowdonia, this small coaching inn is a place of pilgrimage for mountaineers – the team which made the first ascent of Everest in 1953 came to Pen-y-Gwryd to train for the expedition (and still come back for reunions).

Mr and Mrs Pullee, whose family have owned the hotel for over 50 years, take pride in describing the hotel, its bedrooms, its food – even the Victorian bathrooms – as old-fashioned. For those hardy enough, there is an opportunity to try the natural swimming-pool after a sauna.

Nearby Snowdon Mountain Railway, 5 miles (8 km); Snowdonia.

Nant Gwynant, Gwynedd LL55 4NT
Tel (01286) 870211
Location 5 miles (8 km) SW of Llanberis, at junction of A498 and A4086, in isolated setting; garden, car parking
Food & drink full breakfast, bar lunch, tea, dinner; fully licenced
Prices B&B from £21; dinner from £16; reductions for 3 nights or more

Rooms 15 double, 5 with bath, 1 single; 1 family room with bath; all have central heating
Facilities sitting-room, bar, dining-room, games room
Credit cards not accepted
Children welcome
Disabled access easy
Pets well behaved dogs welcome **Closed** early Nov to New Year; weekdays Jan and Feb
Proprietors Mrs C B Briggs and Mr & Mrs B C Pullee

Wales

Country guest-house, Llandegley

The Ffaldau

We first came upon this listed 16thC house, sheltered by the Radnorshire hills, shortly after the Knotts opened for business in the summer of 1985. We were welcomed into the kitchen, where preparations for dinner were aromatically under way, with encouraging warmth and openness, and it is no surprise that the Ffaldau is now firmly on its feet. Oak beams, log fires and pretty country-style decorations give an inviting air. The bedrooms have been thoroughly revamped, as has the upstairs sitting-room. Readers commend the welcome and the 'superb', 'generous' food.
Nearby Llandrindod Wells, 4 miles (6 km).

Llandegley, Llandrindod Wells, Powys LD1 5UD
Tel & fax (01597) 851421
Location 4 miles (6 km) E of Llandrindod Wells on A44; ample car parking
Food & drink full breakfast, dinner; residential and restaurant licence
Prices B&B £20-£24; dinner from £10.50-£18
Rooms 4 double, 2 with bath, 2 with shower; all have tea/coffee kit, central heating, hairdrier
Facilities sitting-room, bar, dining-room
Credit cards MC, V
Children welcome over 10
Disabled access easy; one ground-floor bedroom
Pets dogs by arrangement
Closed never
Proprietors Leslie and Sylvia Knott

Country guest-house, Llanwrtyd Wells

Lasswade Country House

A three-storey Edwardian house standing in its own garden overlooking fields on the outskirts of Llanwrtyd Wells. Jack and Beryl Udall took over in 1993, and are delighted to arrange pony trekking, fishing or other local activities. There is a spacious sitting-room, with comfortable sofas; the individually styled bedrooms are light and airy, with well-kept bathrooms. In the new conservatory restaurant, diners can expect large helpings of mildly adventurous, mainly French/English dishes and a choice of 30 or so wines which are well described and fairly priced.
Nearby RSPB bird reserves, mountain walks; Brecon Beacons.

Station Road, Llanwrtyd Wells, Powys LD5 4RW
Tel (01591) 610515
Fax (01591) 610611
Location SE of middle of village, close to railway station; ample car parking
Food & drink breakfast, dinner; fully licensed
Prices B&B £29.50; DB&B £43.95; bargain breaks
Rooms 5 double (2 twin), 1 single, all with bath or shower; all rooms have central heating, colour TV, phone, radio, alarm, tea/coffee kit, hairdrier
Facilities sitting-room, dining-room, conservatory restaurant, sauna
Credit cards MC, V
Children by arrangement
Disabled access easy to dining-room and sitting-room only **Pets** accepted
Closed never **Proprietors** Jack and Beryl Udall

Wales

Penally Abbey

The setting is the key attraction of this Gothic country house, recently lavishly upgraded. It gives easy access to the lively little resort of Tenby, but stands secluded in its own extensive wooded gardens, complete with ruined chapel, and giving views of the splendid Pembrokeshire coastline; when the weather permits, you can even enjoy the views while taking breakfast on the terrace.

Food is freshly prepared, satisfying and eaten by candlelight in the elegant dining-room. Most of the bedrooms have four-poster beds, and antique furniture dotted around.

Nearby Tenby; Pembrokeshire coast.

Penally, near Tenby, Pembrokeshire, Dyfed SA70 7PY
Tel (01834) 843033
Fax (01834) 844714
Location in village 1.5 miles (2.5 km) SW of Tenby; with ample car parking
Food & drink breakfast, dinner; full licence
Prices B&B £50-£74; DB&B £74-£114; special breaks Nov-Apr
Rooms 12 double, one single; all with bath and shower; all rooms have central heating, TV, phone
Facilities sitting-room, dining-room, bar, billiards room; indoor pool
Credit cards AE, MC, V
Children accepted, if well behaved **Disabled** access possible: 2 ground-floor bedrooms in coach house
Pets not accepted **Closed** never **Proprietors** Mr and Mrs S T and E Warren

Penmaenuchaf Hall

Set in 21 acres of lawned and wooded grounds (which include a rose garden and water garden) overlooking Mawddach Estuary, this sturdy stone-built Victorian manor house was warmly recommended to us by a reader who describes leaving as 'very difficult'. 'The hotel is a dream, a real haven of peace and tranquillity, and when you do leave it's with a feeling of renewal. They really do look after you in every way possible.' The elegant interior features panelled walls, polished slate floors, log fires in winter, comfy sofas and armchairs and fresh flowers. Bedrooms are luxurious.

Nearby fishing, walking, Mawddach Estuary, Snowdonia.

Penmaenpool, Dolgellau, Gwynedd LL40 1YB
Tel (01341) 422129
Fax (01341) 422787
Location off the A493 Dolgellau-Tywyn road; ample car parking
Food & drink breakfast, lunch, dinner; fully licenced
Prices B&B £55-£110; dinner from £25
Rooms 14 double; all rooms have central heating, TV, clock/radio, tea/coffee kit, hairdrier; superior rooms have minibar **Facilities** morning room, library, hall, billiards room, 2 dining-rooms, bar; croquet lawn; fishing permits
Credit cards AE, DC, MC, V
Children babes-in-arms and children over 8 **Disabled** access easy for restaurant **Pets** not in bedrooms **Closed** never **Proprietors** Mark Watson and Lorraine Fielding

Wales

Minffordd

Recent visitors remark particularly on the relaxed pace of life at this former 17thC drovers' inn, set in the peaceful Dysynni Valley. Co-proprietor, Mark Warner, the chef, has made the dining-room the hub of the cosy ambience, thanks to his country recipes, freshly put together and cooked on the Aga. Besides central heating, there are real open fires in winter in the comfortable public rooms. There are also a sun room and a pleasant garden. The rambling building means that bedrooms come in all shapes and sizes.

Nearby Ascent of Cader Idris; Talyllyn Railway, 5 miles (8 km).

Talyllyn, Tywyn, Gwynedd LL36 9AJ
Tel (01654) 761665
Fax (01654) 761517
Location 8 miles (13 km) S of Dolgellau at junction of A487 and B4405; parking for 12 cars
Food & drink full breakfast, dinner; fully licenced
Prices DB&B £55-£65; reductions for 2 nights or more and for children sharing parents' room
Rooms 6 double (3 twin), 5 with bath and shower, one with shower; all rooms have central heating, phone, radio, tea/coffee kit, hairdrier
Facilities bar, sitting-room, dining-room
Credit cards MC, V
Children welcome over 3
Disabled access difficult
Pets not accepted
Closed Jan and Feb; also Nov, Dec except for weekends
Proprietors Mark Warner and Mary McQuillan

Three Cocks Hotel

There is no disputing the charm of this ivy-covered 15thC coaching inn, built around a tree (still in evidence in the kitchen) in the Welsh hills. The sitting-rooms have an 'olde worlde' feel; one is oak-panelled and towny, the other beamed and rustic. Bedrooms are small but quaint, with dark oak furniture and pale fabrics. But what makes the Three Cocks stand out is the Belgian influences over both the food and atmosphere – Marie-Jeanne and Michael used to live in Belgium. Game and shellfish regularly crop up on the menu and a large selection of Belgian beers is offered.

Nearby Brecon Beacons; Hay-on-Wye (second-hand book shops).

Three Cocks, nr Brecon, Powys, LD3 OSL
Tel Fax (01497) 847215
Fax (01497) 847339
Location in village, 11 miles (18 km) NE of Brecon on A438; with ample car parking
Food & drink breakfast, lunch (not Sun), dinner; full licence
Prices B&B £33.50; DB&B £52.50; bar snacks from £5; dinner £25; reductions for 2 nights, and children sharing parents' room
Rooms 7 double, 6 with bath, one with shower; all rooms have central heating
Facilities dining-room, breakfast room, 2 sitting-rooms, TV room
Credit cards MC, V
Children welcome; cot and high-chair
Disabled access difficult
Pets not accepted
Closed Dec to mid-Feb; restaurant only, Tue
Proprietors Michael and Marie-Jeanne Winstone

Wales

Stone Hall

The Watsons bought this white-painted stone manor house in 1982 and opened their doors as a hotel and restaurant at the end of 1984. For Francophile gastronomes, it is becoming something of a Mecca, thanks to the guiding hand of Martine Watson, who not only is French but also employs French chefs and waiters. The house, set in large, secluded grounds, retains its ancient character, with much stone and old oak in evidence. Bedrooms are notable mainly for spaciousness.

Nearby St David's Cathedral; Pembrokeshire coast within easy reach.

Welsh Hook, Wolf's Castle, Haverfordwest, Pembrokeshire SA62 5NS
Tel (01348) 840212
Fax (01348) 840815
Location in countryside 1.5 miles (2.5 km) W of A40, between Haverfordwest and Fishguard; ample car parking
Food & drink full breakfast, dinner; fully licenced
Prices B&B £35-£48; dinner £17-£23
Rooms 3 double, 2 with bath, one with shower; 2 single, one with bath, one with shower; all rooms have central heating, colour TV, tea/coffee kit
Facilities sitting-room, bar, 2 dining-rooms
Credit cards AE, DC, MC, V
Children welcome; special meal-times available
Disabled access difficult
Pets not accepted
Closed 2 weeks late Jan
Proprietors Alan and Martine Watson

Wolfscastle Country Hotel

Andrew Stirling is a qualified squash coach who has the luxury of a court he can call his own; but this welcoming country hotel has plenty of other, less specialized attractions, too.

The relaxed, unpretentious style of this well-run, much-extended Victorian house, now with a large landscaped patio area, has won many friends over the years and remains reassuringly the same. Staff at Wolfscastle are picked for their personality as much as for their skills. Comfortable, newly refurbished bedrooms. The wide-ranging menus use sound fresh ingredients.

Nearby Pembrokeshire coast; Preseli hills; Ramsay Island.

Wolf's Castle, Haverfordwest, Pembrokeshire SA62 5LZ
Tel (01437) 741225
Fax (01437) 741383
Location 8 miles (12 km) N of Haverfordwest on A40; with ample car parking
Food & drink full breakfast, bar lunch, dinner; restaurant and residential licence
Prices B&B £36.50-£47
Rooms 16 double, 4 single; all with bath; all rooms have central heating, phone, colour TV, radio/alarm, tea/coffee kit
Facilities sitting-room bar, dining-room, banqueting-suite; squash
Credit cards AE, MC, V
Children welcome
Disabled not suitable
Pets small dogs accepted by arrangement
Closed Christmas
Proprietor Andrew Stirling

Midlands

Country house hotel, Baslow

Cavendish

The Cavendish doesn't sound like a personal small hotel. But the smart name is not mere snobbery – it is the family name of the Duke of Devonshire, on whose glorious Chatsworth estate the hotel sits (and over which the bedrooms look). And neither the hotel's size nor its equipment interferes with its essential appeal as a polished but informal and enthusiastically run hotel – strictly speaking, an inn, as Eric Marsh is careful to point out, but for practical purposes a country house.

The solid stone building is plain and unassuming. Inside, all is grace and good taste; the welcoming entrance hall sets the tone – , striped sofas before an open fire, elegant antique tables standing on a brick-tile floor, while the walls act as a gallery for Eric Marsh's eclectic collection of over 300 pictures. The whole ground floor has recently been remodelled, and a café-style conservatory added. Bedrooms are consistently attractive and comfortable, but vary in size and character – older ones are more spacious.

The elegant restaurant claims to have a 'controversial' menu; it is certainly ambitious and highly priced, but it met the approval of recent guests who described the food as 'unsurpassed – we were spoilt to death!' The Garden Room is less formal.

Nearby Chatsworth, 1.5 miles (2.5 km); Haddon Hall, 4 miles (6 km); Peak District.

Baslow, Derbyshire DE45 1SP
Tel (01246) 582311
Fax (01246) 582312
Location 10 miles (16 km) W of Chesterfield on A619; in extensive gardens with ample car parking
Food & drink breakfast, lunch, dinner; full licence
Prices B&B £62.45-£98.20; dinner from £15-£37.75; extra bed or cot £7.50; winter weekend breaks

Rooms 23 double, all with bath and shower; all rooms have central heating, colour TV, phone, tea/coffee kit, clock radio, minibar, hairdrier
Facilities dining-room, bar, sitting-room, garden room; putting-green, fishing
Credit cards AE, DC, MC, V
Children welcome **Disabled** access difficult **Pets** not accepted **Closed** never
Proprietor Eric Marsh

Midlands

Country guest-house, Broad Campden

Malt House

It is easy to miss this 17thC Cotswold house (in fact a conversion of three cottages) in a tiny hamlet comprising little more than a church and a pub. Once found, the Malt House is delightful – with low beamed ceilings, antique furniture and leaded windows overlooking a dream garden, where the family cats potter contentedly about. 'Very pleasing, comfortable and quiet,' comments our latest reporter.

The bedrooms, most of which overlook the gardens, are individually decorated with antique furniture and include a room with a four-poster bed. Public rooms are comfortable, but small, with displays of fresh flowers and log fires in winter. The accommodation includes a pleasantly laid out garden suite with a private sitting-room and an entrance to the garden. Guests breakfast and dine in the beamed dining-room, complete with inglenook fireplace.

The Browns' son Julian, who is an experienced chef, cooks inspired evening meals using ingredients fresh from the kitchen gardens.

Nearby Batsford Park Arboretum, 3 miles (5 km); Sezincote Garden, 4.5 miles (7 km); Snowshill Manor, 5 miles (8 km); Stratford-upon-Avon, 12 miles (19.5 km); Cotswold villages; Cheltenham.

Broad Campden, Chipping Campden, Gloucestershire GL55 6UU
Tel (01386) 840295
Fax (01386) 841334
Location one mile (1.5 km) SE of Chipping Campden just outside village; in 4.5 acre paddocks, orchard and garden; ample car parking
Food & drink full breakfast, dinner; restaurant licence
Prices B&B from £47.50-£92.50; suite £97.50; dinner from £25.50
Rooms 7 double, 4 with bath; one single; one suite/family room; all rooms have central heating, TV, radio, tea/coffee kit **Facilities** 2 sitting-rooms, dining-room; croquet
Credit cards AE, DC, MC, V
Children welcome if well behaved; high tea provided
Disabled access difficult
Pets accepted **Closed** Christmas **Proprietors** Nick and Jean Brown

Midlands

Country hotel, Broadway

Collin House

Tucked well away from commercialized Broadway in two acres of orchards and country gardens, this 16thC stone manor house is a haven of peace. The bar is a warm, agreeable place to sit, with oak beams, gleaming copper and comfortable armchairs grouped around an imposing inglenook fireplace, where log fires blaze on cool evenings. Another sitting-room features a fine old stone fireplace and ancient mullion window overlooking the gardens.

Keith and Tricia Ferguson took over in 1998 and set about upgrading the bathrooms and bedrooms. Two rooms have four-poster beds, and all are prettily furnished in traditional style, and like the rest of the house, full of interesting items. The extensive gardens come into their own in fine weather. Appetizing 'Cotswold Suppers' can be taken in the bar area, while the candlelit dining-room serves more formal three-course dinners.

Collin House is warmly praised: 'It far exceeded our needs and expectations'; 'Our favourite small hotel'; 'Graceful service with smiles all round. . .this was our first weekend without the childen – *just* what we were looking for', write several appreciative visitors.

Nearby Snowshill Manor, 2.5 miles (4 km); Batsford Park Arboretum, 6 miles (10 km); Sudeley Castle, 6 miles (10 km).

Collin Lane, Broadway,
Worcestershire WR1 7PB
Tel (01386) 858354
Fax (01386) 858697
Location one mile (1.5 km)
NW of Broadway, off A44; in
spacious grounds with ample
private car parking
Food & drink full breakfast,
lunch, dinner; restaurant and
residential licence
Prices B&B £44-£68; dinner
£26; half-board reductions for
2 nights or more
Rooms 6 double, 5 with bath,
one with shower; one single,
with shower; all rooms have
central heating, tea/coffee kit,
TV, hairdrier
Facilities sitting-room, bar,
dining-room; croquet
Credit cards MC, V
Children welcome; not in
dining-room under 5
Disabled no special facilities
Pets not accepted
Closed Christmas
Proprietor Keith and Tricia
Ferguson

Midlands

Inn, Burford

The Lamb

If you want some respite from Burford's summer throng, you won't do better than the Lamb, only a few yards behind the High Street, but a veritable haven of tranquillity – particularly in the pretty walled garden.

Inside the creeper-clad stone cottages, you won't be surprised to find traditional pub trappings (after all, the Lamb has been an inn since the 15thC), but you may be surprised to discover 15 spacious beamed bedrooms, decorated with floral fabrics and antiques. All are different – 'Shepherds', for example, has a vast antique four-poster bed and a little attic-like bathroom, 'Malt' (in what was once the neighbouring brewery) has a smart brass bed and large stone mullion windows.

The hotel is run by Caroline and Richard De Wolf, with the help of Caroline's mother Bunty. It's very much a family enterprise, although they employ four chefs (one French) to produce the impressive-sounding, daily-changing meals. These are served in the dining-room, looking on to the geranium-filled patio. Coffee can be taken in here, or in the sitting-room or TV room, both of which have comfortable chairs and sofas grouped around open fires. The Lamb manages to combine the convivial atmosphere of a pub with that of a comfortable hotel.

Nearby Minster Lovell Hall, 5 miles (8 km); Cotswold villages.

Sheep Street, Burford
OX18 4LR
Tel (01993) 823155
Fax (01993) 822228
Location in village, with car parking for 6 in courtyard
Food & drink breakfast, lunch, dinner; full licence
Prices B&B £45-£55; bar meals about £7.95; restaurant meals (3-course) £24; midweek and weekend breaks
Rooms 15 double (3 twin), all with bath or shower; all rooms have central heating; all rooms have hairdrier, TV, phone
Facilities bar, 3 sitting-rooms, dining-room
Credit cards MC, V
Children welcome; baby listening service
Disabled 3 ground-floor bedrooms
Pets dogs in room by prior arrangement
Closed 25 and 26 December
Proprietors Mr and Mrs R M De Wolf

Midlands

Town hotel, Chipping Campden

Cotswold House

Recent visitors write: 'We had a fine dinner here. . .service very attentive', and intend to return. Another reporter says, *'The* place to stay in popular Chipping Camden: beautiful house, lovely garden, plenty of personality, not expensive, but highly polished and clean as a pin.' Set in a fine street, the building, dating to 1650, was meticulously renovated in the late 1980s with great attention to detail. Using local craftsmen, Christopher and Louise Forbes restored the magnificent spiral staircase to its former glory and filled the public rooms with antiques, collector's items and hand-painted murals. There are two dining-rooms: the Forbes Brasserie (with courtyard), also used for afternoon cream teas, and the Gar-den Room Restaurant, the 'grand' dining-room (marble pillars, classy fabrics, French windows overlooking the garden) where interesting *à la carte* dinners are served – often with piano accompaniment. Sitting-rooms are large and airy, decorated in Regency style.

Each of the 15 bedrooms has a different theme, carried through to the last detail; the Military room is full of regimental souvenirs, the Indian room has dome-shaped mirrors and bedheads, Aunt Lizzie's is romantically lacy, and the Colonial Room, with four-poster bed, has all the trappings of an American residence at the turn of the century. All rooms have impeccable bathrooms.

Nearby Broadway, 4 miles (6.5 km); Stratford on Avon, 10 miles.

The Square, Chipping Campden, Gloucestershire, GL55 6AN
Tel (01386) 840330
Fax (01386) 840310
E-mail reception@Cotswold-house.demon.co.uk
Location in main street of town; parking for 12 cars
Food & drink full breakfast, lunch, dinner; full licence
Prices B&B £55-£85; lunch around £12, Sun lunch £17; dinner £22-£30; weekend and midweek breaks
Rooms 12 double, (one 4-poster); 3 single; all with bath; all rooms have central heating, phone, satellite TV, hairdrier, radio **Facilities** 2 sitting-rooms, bar; croquet **Credit cards** AE, DC, MC, V **Children** accepted over 6 **Disabled** access difficult
Pets not accepted
Closed Christmas
Proprietors Christopher and Louise Forbes

Midlands

Country hotel, Corse Lawn

Corse Lawn House

This tall, red-brick Queen Anne house, set back across common land from what is now a minor road, must have been one of the most refined coaching inns of its day. Should you arrive in traditional style, you could still drive your coach-and-four down the slipway into the large pond in front of the house, to cool the horses and wash the carriage.

The Hines have been here since the late 1970s, first running the house purely as a restaurant, later opening up four rooms and in recent years adding various extensions (carefully designed to blend with the original building) to provide more and more bedrooms as well as more space for drinking, eating and sitting. The Falstaffian Denis Hine – a member of the famous French Cognac family – and son Giles extend a warm welcome to guests, while Baba Hine cooks. Her repertoire is an eclectic mix of English and French, modern and provincial dishes, all carefully prepared and served in substantial portions; there are fixed-price menus (with a vegetarian alternative) at both lunch and dinner as well as a *carte*, all notably good value.

Bedrooms are large, with a mixture of antique and modern furnishings and the atmosphere of the house is calm and relaxing. Breakfasts are a home-made feast. A recent visitor was enchanted.
Nearby Tewkesbury Abbey, 5 miles (8 km); Malvern Hills.

Corse Lawn, Gloucestershire GL19 4LZ
Tel (01452) 780771
Fax (01452) 780840
Location 5 miles (8 km) W of Tewkesbury on B4211; in 12-acre grounds with ample car parking
Food & drink full breakfast, lunch, tea, dinner; full licence
Prices B&B £50-£135; lunch £16.95; dinner £24.50
Rooms 19 double (2 suites), all with bath and shower; all rooms have central heating, colour TV, phone, tea/coffee kit, hairdrier, trouser-press
Facilities 3 sitting-rooms, bar, restaurant, 2 meeting rooms; croquet, tennis, swimming-pool **Credit cards** AE, DC, MC, V **Children** welcome if well behaved **Disabled** access easy to public rooms and 5 ground-floor bedrooms **Pets** dogs allowed in bedrooms **Closed** 24-26 Dec **Proprietors** Denis, Baba and Giles Hine

Midlands

Manor house hotel, Flitwick

Flitwick Manor

A recent visitor was favourably impressed with his alert and friendly welcome, despite arriving well after midnight.

Built between the 17th and 19th centuries, and converted to a hotel in 1984, this red-brick manor stands at the end of an authentically crunchy, tree-lined drive. The house overlooks parkland that extends far beyond its own substantial gardens. The public rooms are all highly individual: the mellow panelled morning room; the library with ornamental plaster; the recently refurbished dining-room in elegant Regency style; the Gothic-style music room. Bedrooms are spacious and beautifully furnished in varying traditional styles, with many antique pieces.

The imaginative food, prepared by award-winning chef, Richard Salt, is described as 'Modern English'. There are fixed-price menus and vegetarian options. All in all, an oasis in the Bedfordshire wasteland. You can even get married here – the hotel has recently acquired a civil marriage licence. There has been a recent change of management so we welcome further reports.

Nearby Woburn Abbey, 4.5 miles (7 km); Chilterns; golf.

Church Road, Flitwick, Bedfordshire MK45 1AE
Tel (01525) 712242
Fax (01525) 718753
Location 2 miles (3 km) S of Ampthill, on S side of village, close to A5120; in 6.5-acre grounds with ample car parking
Food & drink breakfast, lunch, dinner; full licence
Prices B&B £75-£145; lunch £24.50; dinner from £37.50;
Rooms 13 double, 11 with bath, 2 with shower; 4 single, all with bath; all rooms have central heating, satellite TV, phone, radio, hairdrier
Facilities dining-room, library, morning-room, music room; croquet, putting, tennis, fishing
Credit cards AE, DC, MC, V
Children welcome
Disabled not suitable
Pets by arrangement
Closed never
Manager Tim Howard

Country house, Kemerton

Upper Court

Kemerton is a pretty village on Bredon Hill, an outcrop of the Cotswolds, and on the edge of the Vale of Evesham. Its stunning Georgian manor house acts as a home, a shop and a hotel for its friendly owners, Bill and Diane Herford, and their children. The interior is filled with fine furniture and *objets d'art*, some of it stock from their antiques business, and some of it for sale.

Bedrooms are in the grand country-house style, three with romantic four-posters. In the lovely, rather wild grounds (open under the National Gardens Scheme) can be found the ruins of a thousand-year-old watermill and a huge lake (complete with two islands) on which guests may row and fly-fish for trout in season. As to food, dinner (by prior arrangement) is served in the gracious candlelit dining-room around a communal table; their own or locally grown vegetables feature on the four-course menu.

As well as the bedrooms in the main house, more accommodation is available in the adjoining cottages and the coach-house in the courtyards, which are self-catering and can also have meals delivered to them.

Nearby Cotswold villages; Malvern Hills; Tewkesbury Abbey, 3 miles (5 km)

Kemerton, near Tewkesbury, Gloucestershire GL20 7HY **Tel** (01386) 725351 **Location** 4 miles (6.5 km) NE of M5, exit 9, 1 mile (2.5 km) E of Bredon; from Bredon turn right at war memorial in Kemerton; house is behind parish church; in 15-acre grounds; ample car parking **Food & drink** full breakfast, dinner by arrangement **Prices** B&B £25-£55; dinner £27

Rooms 3 double, 2 twin, all with bath; all rooms have central heating, TV, tea/coffee kit, hairdrier **Facilities** drawing-room, smoking-room, dining-room; gardens, lake, heated outdoor swimming-pool, tennis court **Credit cards** MC, V **Children** welcome **Disabled** 2 easy access ground floor rooms **Pets** accepted by arrangement **Closed** Christmas **Proprietors** Bill, Diana and Hamish Herford

Midlands

Village guest-house and restaurant, Kingham

Conygree Gate

This is one to watch. If youth, enthusiasm and sheer determination can win through, then Judy Krasker will surely make a success of this fine old Cotswold stone house. A graphic designer by training, she and her husband took over a somewhat forlorn bed and breakfast operation in early 1997, and immediately set about establishing a restaurant of repute. The rather soulless dining room was given a facelift and a talented young chef eager to prove himself, Andrew Foster, was engaged. In late 1997 the restaurant opened to non-residents as well as residents: reports welcome. As for the bizarrely decorated rooms, Judy is painting, papering and furnishing them as and when funds allow; wherever she has, she displays flair, originality and a sure sense of colour. She has much to achieve, however; bathrooms in particular are basic, and there are few extras in the bedrooms. A charming letter left in each bedroom explains the situation, asking for comments and ideas, but assures clients that 'the way we treat our guests is of the highest possible standard at all times'.

Guests warm to her openess, and to the challenge before her, and she already has a high percentage of returnees. We wish her luck.

Nearby Stow-on-the Wold, 5 miles (8 km); Burford 10 miles (16km); Cotswold villages.

Kingham, Oxfordshire OX7 6YA
Tel (01608) 658389
Location in village centre, 5 miles (8 km) E of Stow-on-the-Wold; ample parking
Food & drink full breakfast, dinner; residential and restaurant licence
Prices B&B £27.50-£37.50; dinner £20
Rooms 5 double, 3 twin, 1 single, 7 with shower, 2 with bath; all rooms have central heating, TV, tea/coffee kit, hairdrier
Facilities 2 sitting rooms, dining room
Credit cards MC, V
Children babies and children over 10 welcome
Disabled no special facilities, but 3 rooms (with steps) on ground floor
Pets accepted **Closed** never
Proprietor Judy Krasker

Midlands

Country guest house, Ledbury

Grove House

Although Grove House dates back to the 15th century it has the appearance of a Georgian farm manor-house, complete with courtyard, red-brick outhouses and stables. By keeping the number of rooms down to three, the Rosses have preserved entirely the atmosphere of a private home.

The origins of the house are more evident inside, with timber framing in the walls and red oak panelling in the dining-room, where logs are burned in winter. The bedrooms are large, comfortable and carefully furnished with antiques – two with four-posters – and our anonymous inspector records with great delight that hot water bottles are slipped between the crisp cotton sheets in the late evening. There are fresh cut flowers, and towels are not stinted. Guests have the use of a large, separate sitting-room.

Ellen Ross is an excellent cook who aims higher than is usual in such small establishments, aided by the produce of her own large vegetable garden. After help-yourself drinks in the sitting-room, dinner is served at a single long table. It is essential to book in advance.

Nearby Eastnor Castle, 1.5 miles (2.5 km); Malvern Hills.

Bromsberrow Heath, Ledbury, Herefordshire HR8 1PE
Tel (01531) 650584
Location 3 miles (5 km) S of Ledbury off A417, close to M50; ample car parking
Food & drink full breakfast, dinner; no licence
Prices B&B £34-£49; dinner £20
Rooms 3 double, all with bath, one also with shower; all rooms have central heating,
TV, tea kit, radio, hairdrier
Facilities sitting-room, dining-room; tennis, riding (by arrangement), outdoor swimming-pool
Credit cards not accepted
Children accepted
Disabled not suitable
Pets can stay in car
Closed 17 Dec to 4 Jan
Proprietors Michael and Ellen Ross

Midlands

Village guest-house, Leonard Stanley

Grey Cottage

This stone-built cottage, owned by Andrew and Roesmary Reeves, dates from 1824 and is spotless and pleasingly furnished. During renovation, original stonework and a tessellated hall floor were laid bare. Theirs is a very private guest-house with a cosy, cottagey atmosphere; there is no roadside advertisement and advance bookings only are accepted.

Generous home cooking includes such dishes as poached sea trout, followed by baked pineapple Alaska. The Reeves often join their guests for after-dinner coffee. An evidently discriminating New York couple give Grey Cottage a rave review: 'Even more than your guide promised. Beautiful garden with a 100-foot Wellingtonia, planted almost 150 years ago. Furnished with appropriate and interesting pieces. . .yet they have made changes that increase visitors' comfort: firm beds, reliable hot water, heated towel rails and fresh fruit.

'The food is fresh, of high quality, and abundant. The Reeves are capable, charming and dedicated – but not intrusive. Unfortunately, most tourists are preoccupied with location, and end up paying more for accommodation nearer the principal sights hereabouts – but actually getting far less.'

Nearby Cotswold villages; Owlpen Manor, 5 miles (8 km); Gloucester Cathedral, 10 miles (16 km); Tetbury, 12 miles (20 km).

Leonard Stanley, Stonehouse, Gloucestershire GL10 3LU
Tel (01453) 822515
Location 4 miles (6.5 km) SW of Stroud, 1 mile (2.5 km) off A419 between Leonard Stanley and King Stanley; ample private car parking
Food & drink full breakfast, dinner by arrangement
Prices B&B £32-£55
Rooms 1 double, 1 twin, 1 single, two with bath, one with shower; all rooms have central heating, TV, radio, hairdrier, trouser-press
Facilities sitting-room, garden room, dining-room; garden
Credit cards not accepted
Children by arrangement
Disabled not suitable
Pets dogs not accepted
Closed occasional holidays
Proprietors Andrew and Rosemary Reeves

Midlands

Town guest-house, Lincoln

D'Isney Place

Since moving to this delightful red-brick Georgian house, on a bustling street a few yards from Lincoln Cathedral, David and Judy Payne (he a property developer, she an ex-antique dealer) have been continually improving and adding to it. A few years ago they converted the former billiard room into a family suite; now they have a fully-equipped cottage for longer-staying guests.

For the purposes of this guide, D'Isney Place, named after its 15thC founder John D'Isney, is on the large side. And unfortunately it has no public rooms or restaurant – though there are plenty of respectable ones within walking distance. But we continue to recommend it because of the comfortable, stylish bedrooms, the well co-ordinated decorations and fabrics, the breakfast (cooked to order, served on bone china and delivered to the rooms along with the morning newspaper) and, last but certainly not least, the impressive walled garden which incorporates a 700-year old tower from the old cathedral close wall.

Nearby Cathedral, Bishop's Palace, Usher Gallery.

Eastgate, Lincoln,
Lincolnshire LN2 4AA
Tel (01522) 538881
Fax (01522) 511321
Location in middle of city, just E of cathedral; with large walled garden and adequate car parking
Food & drink full breakfast, snacks at night; no licence
Prices B&B £36-£68; self-catering cottage £325 per week; weekend breaks £58 per night
Rooms 16 double (3 twin), all with bath or shower (3 with spa bath); 1 single, with bath;
family rooms available; all rooms have central heating, colour TV, radio, phone, tea/coffee kit; some rooms have hairdrier.
Facilities none
Credit cards AE, DC, MC, V
Children welcome; cots available
Disabled access good – wheelchair ramp and wide doors; ground-floor bedrooms
Pets welcome
Closed never
Proprietors David and Judy Payne

Midlands

Country hotel, Little Malvern

Holdfast Cottage

'Cottage' seems to be stretching things a bit – and yet, despite its size, this Victorian farmhouse does have the cosy intimacy of a cottage, and Stephen and Jane Knowles create an atmosphere of friendly informality.

Inside, low oak beams and a polished flagstone floor in the hall conform to cottage requirement; beyond there, headroom improves – though flowery decoration emphasizes the cottage status. Bedrooms are light and airy, with carefully co-ordinated fabrics and papers; some bathrooms are small. Outside, the veranda with its wisteria keeps the scale of the house down. The garden – scarcely cottage-style – adds enormously to the overall appeal of the place, with its lawns, shrubberies, fruit trees and delightful 'wilderness'. Beyond is open farmland with specatular views of the Malvern Hills.

The daily-changing *carte* is based on continental as well as traditional English dishes, employing the best local produce.

Nearby Eastnor Castle, 4 miles (6 km); Worcester, Hereford and Gloucester all within easy reach.

Little Malvern, near Malvern, Hereford and Worcester WR13 6NA
Tel (01684) 310288
Location 4 miles (6.5 km) S of Great Malvern on A4104; with ample car parking
Food & drink full breakfast, dinner; residential and restaurant licence
Prices B&B £39-£42.50; dinner £18; bargain breaks
Rooms 7 double, all with bath; 1 single with shower; all rooms have central heating, tea/coffee kit, colour TV, radio/alarm, phone, hairdrier, electric blanket
Facilities sitting-room, bar, dining-room, conservatory; croquet
Credit cards MC, V
Children welcome
Disabled access difficult
Pets allowed indoors
Closed first 2 weeks in Jan
Proprietors Stephen and Jane Knowles

Midlands

Riber Hall

Twenty-seven years ago, Alex Biggin rescued this peaceful, sturdy Elizabethan manor from the verge of dereliction, furnished it sympathetically, and opened it as a restaurant to the applause of local gourmets, who are not spoilt for choice of ambitious and competent French cooking. The bedrooms came later – created in outbuildings across an open courtyard and ranging from the merely charming and comfortable to the huge and delightful, with deep armchairs. Exposed timbers, stone walling, and antique four-posters are the norm, and all the thoughtful trimmings you could wish for are on hand.

The spacious, new main dining-room, The Garden Room, has mullioned windows and is furnished with antiques. Wedgewood bone china, and exclusively designed cut glass, adorns the dining table. Breakfast is taken in the traditional old dining-room and the recent addition of a new sitting-room has increased the area available for relaxation in the public rooms.

A romantic and cosy pastime at Riber is simply to sit by an open fire on a stormy winter evening – umbrellas provided for crossing the courtyard. In the morning you can enjoy the delicious seclusion of the luxuriant walled garden and orchard.

Nearby Chatsworth House, Haddon Hall, all at 7 miles (11 km); Calke Abbey; Carsington Water.

Matlock, Derbyshire, DE4 5JU
Tel (01629) 582795
Fax (01629) 580475
Location 2 miles (3 km) SE of Matlock by A615 (20 minutes from exit 28, M1); take minor road S at Tansley; in extensive grounds with adequate car parking in courtyard
Food & drink breakfast, lunch, dinner; restaurant and residential licence
Prices B&B £57.50-£89.75; dinner £26; 2-day breaks Oct-Apr
Rooms 11 double, all with bath and shower (5 with whirlpools), no twin beds, most antique four-posters; all rooms have central heating, minibar, colour TV, hairdrier, tea/coffee kit, trouser-press
Facilities sitting-room with bar service, conservatory, dining- room; tennis court, tennis trainer ball machine
Credit cards AE, DC, MC, V
Children not under 10
Disabled not suitable
Closed never
Proprietor Alex Biggin

Midlands

Town hotel, Oxford

Bath Place

It came as a relief, a few years ago, to find at last an entry for downtown Oxford. Bath Place is a tight group of carefully restored 17thC cottages, opened as a hotel in 1989 and about as centrally placed as you could wish. It does not have much in the way of sitting-space, but for sightseers that is not likely to matter greatly, and there are compensations: well equipped and tasteful bedrooms, a bar, a restaurant, and – most important – adventurous modern cooking by chef Jeremy Blake O'Connor, who has made quite a name for himself in the area.

Following our inspector's report, we promoted Bath Place to a long entry in 1997. 'People who are interested in spas, high-pressure showers and trouser-presses would be disappointed. There are narrow stairways, quaintly uneven floors and ceilings. Rooms vary in character, some low-ceilinged with small-paned windows and some are more modern. All are prettily furnished in country cottage style, with period pieces. A snug little bar has just enough room for a few large, old armchairs. The restaurant is low-ceilinged and oak-beamed, with an intimate atmosphere in which to enjoy the truly exceptional contemporary cooking. A quaint hotel, full of character.' Another more recent visitor was less enchanted; we hope Bath Place is not becoming complacent. More reports please.
Nearby Sheldonian Theatre; Oxford colleges.

4-5 Bath Place, Holywell St, Oxford OX1 3SU
Tel (01865) 791812
Fax (01865) 791834
Location in small mews off Holywell St in heart of city; with parking for 6 cars
Food & drink breakfast, lunch, dinner;
Prices B&B £45-£125; lunch from £14-£29.50, £23.50 on Sunday; dinner £21-£36.50
Rooms 12 double, 7 with bath, 4 with shower, 1 with bath and shower; all rooms have central heating, phone, TV, minibar, radio
Facilities dining-room, bar, sitting-area
Credit cards AE, MC, V
Children accepted
Disabled no special facilities
Pets by arrangement
Closed never
Proprietors Yolanda and Kathleen Fawsitt

Midlands

Country house, Painswick

Painswick Hotel

This distinctly upmarket Georgian rectory is tucked away in the back lanes of prosperous Painswick. The graceful proportions of the rooms – beautifully and expensively furnished with an elegant mix of classy reproductions, antiques and well chosen objects, the serenity of the gardens, and the fine views of the westerly Cotswold scarp, all contribute to the effect.

A recent inspection revealed that Painswick manages, despite its class, to retain the feel of a friendly, family-run establishment. It is in a beautiful Cotswold village, and some of the better rooms, had the best views of any our inspector had experienced in several weeks on the road. The panelled dining-room is 'elegant rather than cosy', and the food very acceptable, making good use of Gloucestershire produce, including locally reared lamb and home-smoked salmon. A sea water fish tank provides fresh seafood and the cheese board includes local farmhouse cheeses, some really unusual.

Painswick was taken over by new owners, Gareth and Helen Pugh, in 1998. We welcome reports.

Nearby Cotswold villages; Gloucester 5 miles (8 km).

Kemps Lane, Painswick, Gloucestershire GL6 6YB
Tel (01452) 812160
Fax (01452) 814059
Location near middle of village, 3 miles (5 km) N of Stroud on A46; with car parking in front of hotel
Food & drink breakfast, dinner, Sun lunch; full licence
Prices B&B £52.50-£75; Sun lunch £14.75; dinner £24.50; reductions for children sharing parents' room
Rooms 14 double (3 twin), all with bath; 2 single, 1 with bath, 1 with shower; 3 family rooms, all with bath; all rooms have central heating, phone, TV, radio, tea/coffee kit
Facilities sitting-room, 2 dining-rooms, bar; croquet
Credit Cards AE, MC, V
Children welcome; cots, high chairs, baby-listening devices available **Pets** only by prior arrangement **Disabled** access difficult **Closed** never
Proprietor Gareth and Helen Pugh

Midlands

Country hotel, Paulerspury

Vine House

This old farmhouse in a tiny Northamptonshire village, remains a very welcome presence in an area where good hotels are thin on the ground. It was taken over in 1991 by Julie and Marcus Springett.

The kitchen, under the supervision of Marcus, remains at the heart of the hotel and its success. As before, everything possible is home-made, including the bread and preserves at breakfast. There are fixed-price menus of three courses for lunch and dinner. One visitor described the cooking as elaborate and highly competent. Another writes to commend the 'freshness and interest of the dishes'. The dining-room, with its white linen against warm peach walls, is a fair size – but the bar and sitting-room are rather small. We understand that extensive redecoration has taken place recently.

The hotel's six spotless bedrooms are all individually decorated in country style, and named after grape varieties. Back rooms overlook the walled garden and outbuildings – one of them is decidedly small, in sharp contrast to the rest. The shower rooms are also on the small side, but there is plenty of piping-hot water.

Nearby Silverstone, 5 miles (8 km); Buckingham, 9 miles (14 km).

100 High Street, Paulerspury, Towcester, Northamptonshire NN12 7NA
Tel (01327) 811267
Fax (01327) 811309
Location 3 miles (5 km) SE of Towcester, in village off A5; with ample car parking
Food & drink full breakfast, lunch, dinner; restaurant and residential licence
Prices B&B £34.50-£49; lunch £21; dinner £24.95
Rooms 5 double (1 twin), 4 with shower, one with bath; one single, with shower; all have central heating, TV, radio/ alarm, phone, tea/ coffee kit
Facilities sitting-room, bar, dining-room **Credit cards** MC, V **Children** welcome
Disabled access easy to public rooms only **Pets** not accepted
Closed restaurant, Sun, Mon to Wed at lunch-time
Proprietors Julie and Marcus Springett

Inn, Shipton-under-Wychwood

The Shaven Crown

The Shaven Crown, as its name suggests, has monastic origins; it was built in 1384 as a hospice to nearby Bruern Abbey, and many of the original features remain intact – most impressively the medieval hall, with its beautiful double-collar braced roof and stone walls decorated with tapestries and wrought ironwork.The hall forms one side of the courtyard garden, which is decked with flowers and parasols, and on a sunny day is a lovely place to enjoy wholesome pub lunches. Some of the bedrooms overlook the courtyard, others are at the front of the house and suffer from road noise – though this is unlikely to be a problem at night.

Robert and Jane Burpitt who moved south to take over The Shaven Crown after running a hotel in Dumfrieshire for ten years, have begun the refurbishment they promised. Rooms are decorated sympathetically, leaving the low ceilings, uneven floor-boards, exposed beams and open fireplaces intact, and are furnished with antiques and Jacobean furniture.

Dinner is taken in the oak-beamed dining-room which leads off the hall. The menu offers plenty of choice and changes with the seasons – it is not elaborate, but the food is interesting and competently cooked. And if you still have the energy after 4 or 5 courses, you can join the locals in the narrow chapel-like bar, or adjourn to the hall, which doubles as a sitting-room.

Nearby North Leigh Roman Villa, 6 miles (10 km).

Shipton-under-Wychwood,
Oxfordshire OX7 6BA
Tel (01993) 830330
Fax (01993) 832136
Location in middle of village;
ample car parking
Food & drink full breakfast,
lunch, dinner; full licence
Prices B&B £36-£53; dinner
from £16.95-£21; bargain
breaks Nov to Apr
Rooms 7 double, with bath;
one single, with bath; one

family room, with bath; all
rooms have central heating,
TV, tea/coffee kit
Facilities restaurant, bar,
medieval hall; bowling green
Credit cards AE, MC, V
Children welcome
Disabled good access – one
ground-floor bedroom
Pets allowed in bedrooms, not
in public rooms
Closed never **Proprietors**
Robert and Jane Burpitt

Midlands

Country house hotel, Tetbury

Calcot Manor

This 15thC Cotswold farmhouse has been functioning as a hotel since 1984. Richard Ball took over Calcot Manor from his parents when they retired, and with a team of dedicated staff continues to provide the highest standards of comfort and service while preserving a calm and relaxed atmosphere. The lovely old house itself was a sound choice – its rooms are spacious and elegant without being grand – and the setting amid lawns and old barns, surrounded by rolling countryside, is all you could ask for.

Furnishings and decorations are carefully harmonious, with rich fabrics and pastel colours throughout. A recently converted cottage now provides nine family suites, designed specifically for parents travelling with young children. For their entertainment, there's an indoor playroom.

Michael Croft is head chef of both the dining-room and the adjoining Gumstool Inn, which is more informal and moderately priced.

Nearby Chavenage, 1.5 miles (2.5 km); Owlpen Manor, 3 miles (5 km); Westonbirt Arboretum, 4 miles (6 km); Slimbridge, 6 miles (10 km).

Near Tetbury, Gloucestershire GL8 8YJ
Tel (01666) 890391
Fax (01666) 890394
Location 3 miles (5 km) W of Tetbury on A4135; in 4-acre grounds with ample car parking (2 under cover)
Food & drink full breakfast, lunch, dinner; residential and restaurant licence
Prices B&B £55-£100; dinner £22-£28; Gumstool £10-£18
Rooms 16 double, all with bath and shower (6 with spa bath); 5 family suites; all rooms have central heating, colour TV, phone, radio, hairdrier
Facilities 2 sitting-rooms, dining-room; heated outdoor swimming-pool, croquet, 2 all-weather tennis courts; playroom **Credit cards** AE, DC, MC, V **Children** welcome; baby- listening
Disabled access good to all ground-floor public rooms; 4 ground-floor bedrooms
Pets not accepted
Closed never
Proprietor Richard Ball

Midlands

Halewell

Elizabeth Carey-Wilson opened her lovely Cotswold-stone house to guests in the early 1980s, and has managed to keep the atmosphere of a gracious family home entirely intact. The house, part of it an early 15thC monastery, forms a picture-postcard group around a courtyard. Breakfast is whenever you will after 9 o'clock; dinner is by arrangement – usually a roast or a grill – and is served at a single table at a set time (couples are split). We visited in 1996 and were impressed enough to promote Halewell to a long entry. 'Set in beautiful scenery among hills,' writes our inspector – right off the main tourist routes, though near enough to all of them. 'The garden is glorious – elegant around the house but extensive and informal as it descentds to a newly built heated pool and the river.

The house is nothing short of stunning; with beautiful beamed ceilings and abundant original features, such as wide oak floor-boards and a minstrel gallery. Bedrooms are furnished as in a private house, including the adjoining childrens' rooms, full of toys and pleasant old childrens' furniture. 'It would be hard to find a Coswold stone house, or a hostess, with as much character. Elizabeth Carey-Wilson treats her guests as friends invited to a private house party' – and is very much in charge of proceedings.
Nearby Chedworth Roman Villa, 3.5 miles (5.5 km).

Withington, near Cheltenham, Gloucestershire GL54 4BN
Tel (01242) 890238
Fax (01242) 890332
Location 8 miles (13 km) SE of Cheltenham S of A40, on edge of village; car parking
Food & drink full breakfast, dinner; residential licence
Prices B&B £43.50-£70; dinner £25; reductions for children in family suites
Rooms 6 double, all with bath, some also with shower; all have central heating, colour TV, radio, tea/coffee kit
Facilities guest sitting-room, breakfast room, dining-room; heated outdoor swimmmg-pool (summer), trout lake
Credit cards AE, MC, V
Children by arrangement
Disabled ground-floor suite
Pets accepted by arrangement
Closed never **Proprietor** Elizabeth Carey-Wilson

Midlands

Town hotel, Woodstock

Feathers

An amalgam of four tall 17thC town houses of mellow red brick, now an exceptionally civilized town hotel. One visitor was full of praise for the way the staff managed to make a weekend 'entirely relaxing, without intruding in the way that hotel staff so often do'.

'The upstairs drawing-room (with library and open fire) has the relaxed atmosphere of a well-kept English country home rather than a hotel, with antiques, fine fabrics, an abundance of fresh flowers and a refreshing absence of the ubiquitous Olde Worlde. There is also a cosy study for reading the papers or drinking tea.' If you want fresh air, there is a pleasant courtyard garden and bar. Bedrooms are spacious (on the whole) and beautifully decorated, comfortable yet still with the understated elegance that pervades the whole hotel. Five further bedrooms are to be found in the newly renovated building next door. The elegant panelled dining-room serves excellent food from Mark Treasure's interesting contemporary menu. A recent Swiss visitor was impressed by both the food and service in the 'lively' restaurant.

Technically, this has all the trappings of a smart business hotel – but don't be put off by that because it has character and a very home-like atmosphere.

Nearby Blenheim Palace; Oxford, 7 miles (11 km).

Market Street, Woodstock, Oxfordshire OX20 1SX
Tel (01993) 812291
Fax (01993) 813158
Location in middle of town; with courtyard garden and limited private car parking
Food & drink breakfast, lunch, dinner; full licence
Prices B&B £52.50-£156; dinner from £30; 7-course menu £44
Rooms 22, 17 double with bath; 4 suites with bath; one single with shower; all rooms have central heating, colour TV, phone, radio
Facilities bar, 2 sitting-rooms, dining-room, restaurant; conservatory
Credit cards AE, DC, V
Children welcome
Disabled access difficult
Pets accepted by arrangement
Closed never
Manager Martin Godward

Midlands

The Old Vicarage

When Peter Iles and his wife, Christine, decided to convert this substantial red-brick vicarage, which stands in two acres of mature grounds, into a small hotel in 1981, they made every effort to retain the Edwardian character of the place – restoring original wood block floors, discreetly adding bathrooms to bedrooms, furnishing the rooms with handsome Victorian and Edwardian pieces, carefully converting the coach house to four 'luxury' bedrooms (one of which, 'Leighton', has been specially designed for disabled guests). Readers have praised the large, comfortable bedrooms, named after Shropshire villages and decorated in subtle colours, with matching bathrobes and soaps.

Attention to detail extends to the sitting-rooms (one is the conservatory, with glorious views of the Worfe valley) and the three dining-rooms. The award-winning food (a daily changing menu with several choices and impressive cheeseboard) is English-based, ambitious and not cheap, served at polished tables by cheerful staff. Peter has a reasonably extensive wine cellar. The dining-room is strictly non-smoking, as are the bedrooms.

Nearby Ludlow, Severn Valley Railway, Ironbridge Gorge Museum.

Worfield, near Bridgnorth, Shropshire WV15 5JZ
Tel (01746) 716497
Fax (01746) 716552
Location in village, 8 miles (12 km) W of Wolverhampton, 1 mile off A454 , 8 miles (12 km) S of junction 4 of M54; ample car parking
Food & drink breakfast, lunch, dinner; residential and restaurant licence
Prices B&B £53.75-£100; Sunday lunch £17.50; dinner £25-£34.50; reductions for children; leisure breaks

Rooms 14 double, 12 with bath, 2 with shower; one family room with bath; all have central heating, phone, TV, minibar, radio, hairdrier, tea/coffee kit, trouser-press
Facilities 3 dining-rooms, 2 sitting-rooms, one with bar
Credit cards AE, DC, MC, V
Children welcome; baby listening **Disabled** access good; one ground-floor bedroom **Pets** accepted; not in public rooms **Closed** Christmas **Proprietors** Peter and Christine Iles

Midlands

Riverside

Nestling in a Peak District village, this Georgian L-shaped house, stone-built and ivy-clad, is in its own secluded grounds, bordered by the river Wye. It has been a hotel and in this guide since the early 1980s, and was recently acquired by the Thornton chocolate family, with Sonia Banks (formerly of Flitwick Manor, page 125) in place as manager. Bedrooms, which vary widely in size, are richly decorated with fabrics and antiques. An ambitious menu is served in the spacious dining-room; lighter meals can be taken in the conservatory. We welcome reports on the extensive refurbishment.

Nearby Chatsworth and Haddon Hall, 4 miles (6 km); Bakewell.

Fennel Street, Ashford-in-the-Water, Bakewell, Derbyshire DE4 1QF
Tel (01629) 814275
Fax (01629) 812873
Location 2 miles (3 km) NW of Bakewell off A6, at top of village main street; parking
Food & drink full breakfast, lunch, dinner; full licence
Prices B&B £55.75; DB&B from £175 for 2-day break
Rooms 10 double, 5 twin, 13 with bath, 2 with shower; all rooms have central heating, TV, radio/alarm, tea/coffee kit, phone, bathrobe
Facilities sitting-room, cocktail bar, 2 dining-rooms, croquet
Credit cards AE, MC, V
Children welcome over 8
Disabled access easy to public rooms; ground-floor bedrooms
Pets not accepted
Closed never
Proprietor Penelope Thornton

Bibury Court

The location is the main appeal of this beautiful Jacobean mansion. It is in an idyllic setting with seven acres to explore and bordered by a trout-filled river (rods available). In the orchard garden wall a door leads into the churchyard of St Mary's, a little church with a notable stained glass window. Bedrooms may not be luxurious but they are atmospheric (six with four-posters). Breakfast is served in a stylish conservatory; public rooms are wood panelled, with antique furniture and displays of old china. Dishes of temptingly combined ingredients from head chef, Tom Bridgeman.

Nearby Arlington Row, Arlington Mill museum, trout hatchery.

Bibury, Cirencester, Gloucestershire GL7 5NT
Tel (01285) 740337
Fax (10285) 740660
Location in village on B4425, 6 miles (10 km) NE of Cirencester; garden; parking
Food & drink breakfast, lunch, dinner; full licence
Prices B&B £45-£79; suite £135; lunch from £7; Sun lunch £7; dinner £20-£25; special breaks from £140
Rooms 16 double; 2 singles; 1 suite; all with bath; all have central heating, phone, hairdrier, TV, tea/coffee kit
Facilities sitting-room, dining-room, bar; fishing, croquet
Credit Cards AE, DC, MC, V
Children welcome **Pets** accepted in bedrooms (£3 charge per dog) **Disabled** access difficult **Closed** Christmas
Proprietors Miss P J Collier, Mr and Mrs A Johnston

Midlands

Country house hotel, Bromsgrove

Grafton Manor

The old red-brick manor house is very much a family affair, with father John and twins Nicola and Simon in the kitchen, and elder son Stephen running the front of house. They opened as a restaurant in 1980, and the four-course dinners are still the best for miles around. Bedrooms are well furnished and thoroughly equipped. The heart of the house is the lofty old Great Parlour, now the bar/sitting-room. Large formal herb garden and in summer months, a glorious checkerboard of sunflowers. Our inspector thinks that recent publicity about traffic noise is overstressed.
Nearby Hagley Hall, 6 miles (10 km).

Grafton Lane, Bromsgrove, Hereford and Worcester B61 7HA
Tel (01527) 579007
Fax (01527) 575221
Location 2 miles (3 km) SW of Bromsgrove off B4091; 11-acre gardens; ample car parking
Food & drink breakfast, lunch, dinner; residential licence
Prices B&B £52.50-£150; dinner £31.50
Rooms 6 double (2 twins), one single, two suites; all with bath; all rooms have central heating, coal gas fires, TV radio/alarm, hairdrier, phone
Facilities sitting-room/bar, dining-room; croquet
Credit cards AE, DC, MC, V
Children welcome if well behaved
Disabled access
Pets not accepted; kennels can be provided **Closed** never
Proprietors Morris family

Town house hotel, Burford

Burford House

Burford House used to be in this guide under its old name of Andrews Hotel. Over the past three years, its new owners Simon and Jane Henty, have increased the level of comfort and brought a more personal touch. They have put fresh flowers, books and magazines in the bedrooms, and personal possessions amongst the existing furniture, and run the place with a very 'hands on' approach. The 15thC Cotswold stone and timbered building positively gleams with care and attention, and upstairs there are 7 smartly decorated, dark beamed bedrooms; four have four-posters.
Nearby Cotswold villages.

High Street, Burford, Oxfordshire OX18 4QA
Tel (01993) 823151
Fax (01993) 823240
Location in middle of Burford; no private parking
Food & drink full breakfast, light lunch, afternoon teas; residential licence
Prices B&B £40-£95; winter reductions for 2 nights plus
Rooms 7 double, all with bath; all rooms have central heating, phone, colour TV
Facilities breakfast room, sitting-room; courtyard garden
Credit cards AE, MC, V
Children welcome
Disabled one ground-floor room
Pets not accepted
Closed never
Proprietors Jane and Simon Henty

Midlands

Brockencote Hall

The present Brockencote Hall is of Victorian origin and more or less Georgian in style, but it lies at the heart of a 300-year-old estate that provides a grand setting of mature and varied trees. The Anglo-French Petitjeans, trained hoteliers both, opened it as a hotel in 1986, having renovated and furnished it with great taste and style. The pine- and maple-panelled library is particularly welcoming. Bedrooms are splendidly spacious, all of them with carefully coordinated colour schemes. The cooking is appropriately ambitious.

Nearby walks in grounds; Worcester, 15 miles (24 km).

Chaddesley Corbett, nr Kidderminster, Hereford & Worcester DY10 4PY
Tel (01562) 777876
Fax (01562) 777872
Location in countryside, on A448 4 miles (6 km) SE of Kidderminster; in large grounds; ample car parking
Food & drink breakfast, lunch dinner; full licence
Prices B&B £62.50-£112; DB&B £83.50-£136.50
Rooms 13 double, (4 twin), all with bath; all rooms have central heating, phone, radio, TV
Facilities sitting-room, dining-room, library, conservatory; croquet
Credit cards AE, DC, MC, V
Children welcome if well behaved **Disabled** one adapted bedroom **Pets** not welcome
Closed never
Proprietors Joseph and Alison Petitjean

The Plough

Recent owners, John and Rosemary Hodges have implemented the improvements they promised when they took over this glossy little inn a few years ago. The building is a mellow Cotswold-stone manor-house, which they have upgraded and redecorated – not surprisingly, some of the rooms are on the small side, though some bathrooms include whirlpool baths. There is no sitting-room apart from the bar/lounge. There is a comfortable and relaxing ambience and a welcoming atmosphere added by the staff. The food is sophisticated.

Nearby Cotswolds; Oxford, 25 miles (40 km).

Bourton Road, Clanfield, Oxfordshire OX8 2RB
Tel (01367) 810222
Fax (01367) 810596
Location in village 4 miles (6 km) N of Faringdon; with garden and private car parking
Food & drink breakfast, lunch dinner; restaurant and full licence
Prices B&B £47.50-£65; dinner from £32.50
Rooms 6 double, all with bath or shower; all rooms have central heating, phone, TV, hairdrier, trouser-press
Facilities dining-room, bar/lounge, private dining-room **Credit cards** AE, DC, MC, V **Children** preferred over 12 **Disabled** access difficult
Pets not accepted
Closed 27-29 Dec
Proprietors John and Rosemary Hodges

Midlands

Tudor Farmhouse

A lovely 14thC stone farmhouse, prettily decorated and neatly furnished – with new owners and an injection of fresh fabrics and decoration recently. A fine oak staircase spirals up to the rooms in the main house, which include two four-posters. Three rooms are in converted cider makers' cottages across the courtyard behind; two new family suites share a 'Japanese-style' garden. The sitting- and dining-rooms have exposed stone and beams. There is a set-price dinner menu of four courses that changes regularly. Breakfast is a minor feast. When we inspected we liked the place for what it is.

Nearby Monmouth, 5 miles (8 km); Forest of Dean; Wye valley.

Clearwell, near Coleford
Gloucestershire GL16 8JS
Tel (01594) 833046
Fax (01594) 837093
Location 5 miles (8 km) SE of Monmouth on B4231; parking for 15 cars
Food & drink full breakfast, dinner; residential and restaurant licence
Prices B&B £30-£45; dinner from £19.50; short breaks
Rooms 8 double, 4 family suites, all with bath or shower; all rooms have central heating, TV, tea/coffee kit, phone, hairdrier
Facilities sitting- room/bar, dining-room, conservatory
Credit cards AE, MC, V
Children welcome
Disabled access easy
Pets accepted in cottage annexe **Closed** Christmas
Proprietors Colin and Linda Gray

Cleeve Hill

'Ideal for a few relaxing days in the Cotswolds. The views from the bedroom and breakfast room were breathtaking, and the bedroom was very comfortable, tastefully decorated. Most important was the friendly, helpful attitude of John and Marian Enstone – always available, but melting unobtrusively into the background when not required.' This report from an experienced 'scout' leaves little to add, and it's not the only favourable one we've had recently. The house, near the summit of Cleeve Hill, is Edwardian in style, refurbished entirely since they bought it in 1991. No smoking.

Nearby Cheltenham; Sudeley Castle, 2 miles (6 km).

Cleeve Hill, Cheltenham, Gloucestershire GL52 3PR
Tel (01242) 672052
Fax (01242) 679969
Location in countryside, on B4632, 2 miles (6 km) NE of Cheltenham; with terraced garden and parking for 12 cars
Food & drink breakfast; residential licence
Prices B&B £30-£40; reductions for children sharing parents' room
Rooms 7 double (2 twin), one single, one family room, all with bath and/or shower; all rooms have central heating, TV, phone, radio, hairdrier
Facilities sitting-room with bar, dining-room **Credit cards** AE, MC, V **Children** accepted over 8 **Disabled** access difficult
Pets not accepted
Closed Christmas
Proprietors John and Marian Enstone

Midlands

The Marsh

The Marsh hovers in status between the home that takes guests and the proper hotel. It is tipped into the latter category by the polished approach of the enthusiastic Gillelands, and the fact that the place operates as a restaurant. Jacqueline's three-course menus have acquired a reputation. But the real appeal is the house: a 14thC timbered and stone-floored marvel, with richly decorated bedrooms, a Medieval great hall in authentic colours of vivid yellow, green, red and blue, and a splendid fragrant garden with stream and lily-pond. Our latest reporter could not fault it.

Nearby Eye Manor, 2.5 miles (4 km).

Eyton, Leominster,
Herefordshire HR6 0AG
Tel (01568) 613952
E-mail meg@the marsh.kc3ltd.co.uk
Location 2 miles (3km) NW of Leominster, 1.5 miles (2 km) W of B4361; in 1.5-acre gardens with car parking
Food & drink breakfast, Sunday lunch, dinner; residential and restaurant licence
Prices B&B £60-£80; lunch, dinner £24.50
Rooms 4 double (one twin), all with bath; all have radio, central heating, phone, TV, hairdrier
Facilities dining-room, bar, sitting-room
Credit cards AE, DC, MC, V
Children accepted over 12
Disabled access possible
Pets not accepted
Closed last three weeks of Jan
Proprietors Martin and Jacqueline Gilleland

The Green Man

This substantial old timber-framed inn successfully plays the dual roles of popular country pub and small hotel. Bedrooms vary widely: the four-poster room, with its exposed beams, is snugly traditional; others, which have been modernized, are light and airy. A ground-floor bedroom across the courtyard is convenient for the disabled or elderly. There is not much sitting space apart from the oak-beamed bars, but the large lawned garden has tables and benches. Modest but tasty food is served both in the bars and in the smartly converted barn which forms the dining-room.

Nearby Ross-on-Wye, 3 miles (5 km); Hereford.

Fownhope, near Hereford, Hereford and Worcester HR1 4PE
Tel (01432) 860243
Fax (01432) 860207
Location 8 miles SE of Hereford on B4224, in village; ample car parking
Food & drink full breakfast, bar or packed lunch, tea, dinner, snacks; full licence
Prices B&B £27.50-£34.50; special reductions and for children sharing parents' room
Rooms 12 double, 4 with bath; 3 family rooms, 2 with bath; all with shower; all rooms have central heating, tea/coffee kit, satellite TV, trouser-press
Facilities 2 bars, dining-room, sitting-room **Credit cards** AE, DC, MC, V **Children** welcome; cots, high-chairs **Disabled** access easy **Pets** welcome
Closed never **Proprietors** Arthur and Margaret Williams

Midlands

Wind in the Willows

The whimsical name honours not Kenneth Grahame's classic but a tree in the garden. Peter and Anne Marsh – who are the brother and mother of Eric Marsh of the Cavendish at Baslow (see page 115) – spent six years upgrading their Victorian guest-house before launching it under the new name in 1987.

They have recently completed major reburbishments to the bedrooms and a meeting room. The Erika Louise room has a magnificent Victorian half tester and a splendid period-style bathroom. Toad Hall is more masculine in style, with lovely views.

Nearby Peak District.

Derbyshire Level, Glossop, Derbyshire SK13 9PT
Tel (01457) 868001
Fax (01457) 853354
Location 1 mile (1.5 km) E of Glossop off A57; with parking for 12 cars
Food & drink full breakfast, dinner; restaurant licence
Prices B&B £35-£78; dinner £17.50
Rooms 12 double, 6 with bath and shower, 6 with shower; all rooms have central heating, phone, clock, radio/alarm, tea/coffee kit, hairdrier, trouser-press, TV
Facilities sitting-room/bar, study, dining-room, boardroom **Credit cards** AE, DC, MC, V **Children** not discouraged **Disabled** access difficult to bedrooms **Pets** by arrangement **Closed** never
Proprietors Peter Marsh and Anne Marsh

Lamb Inn

Richard and Kate Cleverly's inn is not luxurious, but it epitomizes what this guide is about – they run it with energy, verve and good humour; the features of the 300-year-old inn have been retained using original stone and beams, and two further suites have been created in the delightful garden; respectable beers such as Wadworths 6X, Tanglefoot and Flowers IPA are on tap; the furniture is comfortable; the bedrooms are well equipped and prettily decorated (two with four-posters); food is home-cooked, and it is very reasonably priced. A recent inspector agreed with all of this.

Nearby Stow-on-the-Wold, 5 miles (8 km); Burford, 6 miles.

Great Rissington, Bourton- on-the-Water, Gloucestershire GL54 2LJ
Tel (01451) 820388
Location 4 miles (6 km) SE of Bourton-on-the-Water, 3 miles (5 km) N of A40; in gardens with ample car parking
Food & drink full breakfast, light (or packed) lunch, dinner; full licence
Prices B&B £25-£38; dinner from £10.50; bargain breaks
Rooms 12 double, 5 with bath, 6 with shower; 6 suites; all rooms have central heating
Facilities sitting-room with TV
Credit cards AE, MC, V
Children welcome, but not in bar **Disabled** not suitable
Pets dogs welcome in bedrooms if well behaved
Closed Christmas Day and Boxing Day
Proprietors Richard and Kate Cleverly

Midlands

Penrhos Court

A discriminating visitor observes: 'This has more personality than most.' It's a notably eccentric building, built over three different periods and with all their features restored, hence a great Medieval Cruck hall together with an Elizabethan wing. Rooms are all different, decorated and furnished to a high standard – 'bold and tasteful fabrics'.

Daphne Lambert is a believer in organic produce and inventive vegetarian/vegan cooking (Soil Association guaranteed). She also makes allowances for meat eaters.

Nearby Offa's Dyke Path; Hergest Croft Garden 3 miles (5 km).

Kington, Herefordshire
HR5 3LH
Tel (01544) 230720
Fax (01544) 230754
Location one mile (2 km) E of Kington on A44; with 6-acre grounds and ample car parking
Food & drink breakfast, lunch (by prior arrangement), dinner; full licence
Prices B&B £37.50-£55; dinner (four courses) £28.50
Rooms 12 double (3 twin), 4 family rooms, all with bath; all rooms have central heating, phone, satellite TV, radio, hairdrier
Facilities 3 dining-rooms, 2 sitting-rooms, bar
Credit cards AE
Children welcome
Disabled access easy
Pets not accepted
Closed never
Proprietors Martin Griffiths and Daphne Lambert

The Lansdowne

A creeper-covered Regency house in the heart of Leamington – 'just as well there is double-glazing,' says our reporter, who liked it not for its location but its food. David Allen (Swiss-trained chef) and his wife Gillian concentrate on quality and value – dishes include buckwheat blinis with herring and sour cream or Barbary duck with honey and balsamic sauce. The Allens have combined home with hotel; public rooms are elegant, bedrooms cosy with pine furniture and pretty fabrics. Readers comment on the friendly atmosphere. Our reporter thought the Allens charming.

Nearby Warwick Castle, 2 miles (3 km).

Clarendon Street, Leamington Spa, Warwickshire CV32 4PF
Tel (01926) 450505
Location in middle of town near A425 Warwick road; with private car parking
Food & drink full breakfast, dinner, snacks; restaurant licence
Prices B&B £19.95-£54.95; dinner from £14.95; reductions for children; 2-day breaks
Rooms 9 double, 4 single, one family room, all with bath or shower; all rooms have central heating, phone, TV, radio, tea/coffee kit, hairdrier
Facilities dining-room, sitting-room, bar; discount tickets for Warwick Castle **Credit cards** MC, V **Children** welcome over 5 **Disabled** access good; 2 ground-floor bedrooms
Pets by arrangement
Closed never **Proprietors** David and Gillian Allen

Midlands

The Cottage in the Wood

Three buildings form this glossy little hotel. There are bedrooms in all three, taking the hotel over our usual size limit; but the smartly furnished Georgian dower house at its heart is intimate, calm and comfortable. A short stroll away is the Coach House, where rooms are smaller but have the best views (binoculars provided), and Beech Cottage with four cottage-style bedrooms, The setting is the key – superb vistas across the Severn Valley to the Cotswolds. Ideal for walkers. Free squash, and video hire from the hotel's extensive library.

Nearby Malvern Hills; Eastnor Castle, 5 miles (8 km).

Holywell Road, Malvern Wells, Hereford and Worcester WR14 4LG
Tel (01684) 575859
Fax (01684) 560662
Location 2 miles (3 km) S of Great Malvern off A449; ample car parking
Food & drink full breakfast, lunch, tea (Sat, Sun), dinner; full licence
Prices B&B £45-£82; dinner about £27; special breaks
Rooms 20 double, all with bath, 16 also with shower; all have central heating, phone, TV, tea/coffee kit, hairdrier
Facilities sitting-room, bar, dining-room, conference suite
Credit cards AE, MC, V
Children welcome; cots
Disabled not ideal; ground-floor rooms in annexe
Pets accepted (not main building)
Closed never
Proprietors John and Sue Pattin and family

Beetle and Wedge

This larger Victorian inn is in a superb position on the Thames. Public rooms have been tastefully decorated by Kate and Richard Smith and bedrooms are spacious and individually furnished; bathrooms have large cast iron baths.

The Boathouse offers à la carte meals in a brasserie-style setting; the Dining Room, in a conservatory, serves such dishes as fillet of halibut with mussels and fennel. Lunch is also served outside in The Watergarden in summer. Enthusiastically endorsed by readers' letters.

Nearby Thames valley; Oxford.

Moulsford-on-Thames, Oxford OX10 9JF
Tel (01491) 651381
Fax (01491) 651376
Location 2 miles (3 km) N of Goring on A329; car parking
Food & drink full breakfast, lunch, dinner; full licence
Prices B&B £60-£110; meals from £27.50; reductions for 2 nights or more; children sharing parents' room
Rooms 10 double, all with bath (one suite); all rooms have central heating, phone, TV, radio, hairdrier, tea/coffee kit **Facilities** 2 restaurants, sitting-room, private room **Credit cards** AE, DC, MC, V **Children** accepted **Disabled** access easy; ground-floor rooms and adapted toilets **Pets** by arrangement only **Closed** restaurant only, Sun evening, Mon **Proprietors** Richard and Kate Smith

Midlands

Hundred House

We inspected in late 1997 and appreciated the unusual, occasionally eccentric decoration. Henry and Sylvia Phillips rescued the derelict building in 1986. There is a cottagey air to the Medieval building, thanks to patchwork quilts in the cosy bedrooms and ubiquitous drying herb bunches. Sylvia grows 50 varieties of herbs in the aromatic garden.

The innovative cooking is done by their son, Stuart, who trained in France. It is served by friendly staff in the bar-cum-restaurant area.

Nearby Ironbridge Gorge museums; Weston Park; the Long Mynd.

Norton, near Shifnal, Shropshire TF11 9EE
Tel (01952) 730353
Fax (01952) 730355
Location on A442 Bridgnorth to Telford road, 4 miles (6 km) from Telford; parking
Food & drink full breakfast; dinner in restaurant; residential licence
Prices £69-£110; dinner from £25; bargain breaks
Rooms 10 double (can be twin), all with bath and shower; all rooms have central heating, TV, hairdrier, phone, radio alarm, tea/coffee kit, iron and ironing board
Facilities sitting-room, bar, restaurant
Credit cards AE, MC, V
Children accepted
Disabled access limited
Pets well-behaved dogs in bedrooms
Closed never
Proprietors Henry, Sylvia, David and Stuart Phillips

Manor Hill House

During the week Manor Hill House is popular with businessmen who appreciate its relaxed atmosphere and home comforts, especially in the huge, farmhouse-style 'family room' where guests breakfast at a massive pine table while Mrs Grove cooks at the Aga. Quite often they return with their wives for weekend breaks, to show them the amazing interior of this restored Victorian manor: pure Victoriana from top to toe, from the ornate beds in the pretty bedrooms to the dim lighting in the hall which hardly pierces the gloom.

Nearby Cirencester; Avebury; Stonehenge; Cotswold villages.

Purton, Swindon, Wiltshire SN5 9EG
Tel (01793) 772311
Location in village, 4 miles (6,5 km) W of Swindon; house signposted from road (no sign on door); parking
Food & drink full breakfast; dinner by arrangement
Prices B&B £21-£32; dinner £12.50
Rooms 3 double, 1 twin, 2 single, 3 with bath, 3 with shower; all rooms have central heating, TV
Facilities 2 sitting rooms, study, kitchen/breakfast room, conservatory
Credit cards not accepted
Children welcome
Disabled not suitable
Pets not accepted
Closed Christmas
Proprietors Barbara and Richard Gore

Midlands

Country guest-house, Stinchcombe

Drakestone House

Our most recent reporter writes: 'magnificent Edwardian house; beautiful landscaped gardens. For anyone wanting a taste of by-gone elegance, this is the place without a doubt.' However, please note that the facilities are of a normal B&B, and you must provide your own wine at dinner, which is by prior arrangement. There's a warm welcome from Hugh and Crystal St John-Mildmay, whose family home this is. They serve breakfast before a log fire on chilly days, and trays of tea in the friendly sitting-room.
Nearby Slimbridge Wildfowl Trust, 4 miles (6 km); Owlpen Manor, 4 miles (6 km); Berkeley Castle, 4 miles (6 km); Cotswold villages

Stinchcombe, near Dursley, Gloucestershire GL11 6AS
Tel (01453) 542140
Location 3 miles (5 km) NW of Dursley, off B4060; ample car parking in courtyard
Food & drink full breakfast; dinner by prior arrangement; no licence, take your own wine
Prices B&B £28; dinner £17.50; reduction for children
Rooms 3 double, one with shower; all rooms have central heating

Facilities sitting-room, dining-room
Credit cards not accepted
Children welcome
Disabled access difficult
Pets not allowed in house
Closed Nov to Mar
Proprietors Hugh and Crystal St John-Mildmay

Town hotel, Uppingham

The Lake Isle

David and Clare Whitfield have gradually added more bedrooms to this rustic restaurant (once a hairdresser's) in the heart of Uppingham. Bedrooms (fresh fruit and sherry provided) are named after French wine regions, and vary in size and style, from the bright and comfortable in a building at the rear, to the small and cosy in an adjacent cottage. There is an inviting first-floor sitting-room, with armchairs and an upright bench in front of a log fire. Meals are served at pine tables in the original shop: delicious French food, loaves of home-made bread, an excellent wine list.
Nearby Rockingham Castle, 6 miles (10 km); Rutland Water.

High Street East, Uppingham, Leicestershire LE15 9PZ
Tel & **Fax** (01572) 822951
Location in middle of town, close to A6003 London road; with small walled garden and parking for 6 cars
Food & drink full breakfast, lunch, dinner; full licence
Prices B&B £32.50-£62; lunch £13.50; dinner £22.50-£26.50
Rooms 11 double, 7 with bath, 2 with whirlpool, 2 with shower; one single with shower; 2 cottage suites; all have radio, central heating, phone, TV, hairdrier
Facilities dining-room, sitting-room, bar **Credit cards** AE, DC, MC, V **Children** accepted
Disabled no special facilities
Pets well-behaved dogs in bedrooms only **Closed** never; restaurant only Mon lunch
Proprietors David and Claire Whitfield

Midlands

Old Beams

The kitchen is at the heart of Old Beams. Chef and owner Nigel Wallis describes his food as 'modern English with a French classic lean' and stresses presentation and freshness – bread is baked twice a day. The lively Ann Wallis presides with their son, Simon, over the restaurant – choose between the oak-panelled dining-room in the 18thC main house and the conservatory extension, with its fantasy murals. Most of the compact but stylish bedrooms are in 'Les Chambres' across the road; each is named after a local pottery company – complete with the appropriate china, of course.

Nearby Chatsworth House; the Potteries; Alton Towers.

Waterhouses, Staffs ST10 3HW
Tel (01538) 308254
Fax (01538) 308157
Location in middle of village, on A523 7 miles (11 km) NW of Ashbourne; with gardens and parking for 25 cars
Food & drink breakfast, lunch, dinner; restaurant licence
Prices B&B £37.50-£72; lunch £21; dinner *à la carte*
Rooms 5 double, all with bath; all rooms have central heating, phone, TV, radio

Facilities dining-room, conservatory, bar area; fishing; no smoking allowed
Credit cards AE, DC, MC, V
Children accepted
Disabled access good; ground-floor rooms
Pets not accepted
Closed restaurant only Sun eve, Mon; Sat and Tue lunch
Proprietors Nigel and Ann Wallis

Holmwood

For many years Roberto and Christina Gramellini ran an excellent guest house in York. In 1995 they moved to a beautiful Queen Anne house in the heart of Woodstock, where they let just two rooms, or rather suites. Decorated with Sanderson fabrics and wallpapers, they each have their own sitting-room and large bathroom with separate shower cubicle. One bedroom has a queen-size bed, the other a king-size which can become two singles. The Gramellinis have completely renovated the house, which is built of Cotswold stone, with a lovely oak staircase. Excellent breakfast.

Nearby Blenheim Palace; Oxford 7 miles (11 km); Cotswolds.

6 High Street, Woodstock, Oxfordshire OX20 1TF
Tel (01993) 812266
Fax (01993) 813233
E-mail cristina@ holm-wood.demon.co.uk
Location in centre of town; public car park behind house, or on street
Food & drink breakfast
Prices B&B £32.50-£50
Rooms 2 suites both with bath; rooms have central heating with individual thermostats, TV, tea/coffee kit, hairdrier
Facilities dining-room; walled garden. No smoking.
Credit cards not accepted
Children not accepted
Disabled not suitable
Pets not accepted
Closed Jan
Proprietors Roberto and Christina Gramellini

East Anglia and Region

Town hotel, Bury St Edmunds

Twelve Angel Hill

'Gets away with trouser-presses without being boring,' says our latest highly satisfied inspector. Twelve Angel Hill occupies a house in a mellow brick terrace, close to the cathedral. It is Georgian to the front but Tudor behind, and opened as a hotel in 1988 after being thoroughly renovated. The spacious bedrooms are light, generously proportioned, in superb condition and beautifully furnished, with antiques and sympathetic reproductions, and have bold floral decoration and fabrics.

'The Clarkes have made the most of the original features of the house, and have evidently thought carefully about the comfort of their guests: witness the charming window seat scattered with cushions overlooking the Italian walled garden; a fine four-poster bed with canopy; an intimate oak-panelled bar; the light, pleasant drawing-room overlooking Angel Hill (not noisy, since it's double-glazed). It all has the feel of a private house yet manages to include all the sleeping facilities of a hotel. Breakfast is by all accounts well above the average.'

Totally no-smoking. Dinner can be arranged at one of the many local restaurants. The Clarkes are charming hosts and our inspector saw much evidence that their guests were highly impressed.

Nearby Cathedral, museums, Abbey Gardens.

12 Angel Hill, Bury St Edmunds, Suffolk IP33 1UZ
Tel (01284) 704088
Fax (01284) 725549
Location on Angel Hill, 100 metres from cathedral; with patio garden and car parking
Food & drink full breakfast; full licence
Prices B&B £35-£60
Rooms 5 double, 2 with bath, 3 with shower; one single with shower; all rooms have central heating, phone, TV, radio, tea/coffee kit, hairdrier, trouser-press
Facilities dining-room, sitting-room, bar, patio room
Credit cards AE, DC, MC, V
Children not accepted
Disabled access difficult
Pets not accepted
Closed Jan
Proprietors Bernie and John Clarke

East Anglia and Region

Converted windmill, Cley-next-the-Sea

Cley Mill

Imagine staying in a 'real' windmill. That is the sense of adventure that Cley Mill can induce even in the most world-weary. Memories of 'Swallows and Amazons' or the 'Famous Five' crowd in as you climb higher and higher in the mill, finally mounting the ladder to the look-out room on the fourth floor. Superb views over the Cley Marshes, a Mecca for bird-watchers.

The sitting-room on the ground floor of the Mill is exceptionally welcoming – it feels well used and lived-in, with plenty of books and magazines, comfortable sofas, TV and an open fire. Bedrooms in the Mill feel rather like log cabins – much wood in the furniture and fittings. They are pretty rooms, with white lace bedspreads, and bathrooms ingeniously fitted in to the most challenging nooks and crannies that the old building provides.

Jeremy Bolam took over the running of the Mill last year. He used to own his own restaurant in Battersea, so greater emphasis is put on food and dining in, now, but he won't mind a bit if you simply take B&B.

A recent reporter was happy to find Cley Mill every bit as enchanting as our description suggests, but we welcome further comments. See also our other windmill (page 24).

Nearby Sheringham Hall, 6 miles (10 km); Cromer Lighthouse, 10 miles (16 km); Norwich within reach.

Cley-next-the-Sea, Holt, Norfolk NR25 7RP
Tel (01263) 740209
Location 7 miles (11 km) W of Sheringham on A149, on N edge of village; in garden, with ample car parking
Food & drink full breakfast; dinner on request; licence
Prices B&B £28-£35; dinner £15; reductions for 3 to 7 nights
Rooms 7 double, 1 single, 4 with bath and shower; 2 with bath, 1 with shower
Facilities sitting-room, dining-room
Credit cards MC, V
Children welcome
Disabled access difficult
Pets accepted
Closed never
Managers Jeremy Bolam

Country guest-house, Great Snoring

Old Rectory

Though presumably the words have a quainter etymology, Great Snoring lives up to its name. There is no shop, the last pub has closed, and it is easy to drive through the village without noticing the Old Rectory, hidden behind high stone walls beside the church. This seclusion is the pride of Rosamund Scoles, her husband and family, who have been running the red-brick parsonage – of very mixed vintage, but dating in part from the 16th century – as a hotel since 1978.

'Hotel' is scarcely the right word for this relaxed retreat. There is no reception desk, no row of keys, no signs. After early morning tea, which is brought to each of the richly and individually furnished bedrooms, you are left to your own devices, and you can settle in the large sitting-room with its hotch-potch of comfortable old chairs.

In the dining-room, heavy velvet drapes hang at the stone mullioned windows, and fresh flowers are arranged on each of the tables. The dinner menu is traditional English in style; some may find it restricted, but guests are consulted before the one main course dish is chosen and there are plenty of mouth-watering home-made puddings to choose from.

Nearby Walsingham Abbey, 1.5 miles (2.5 km); Holkham Hall, 8 miles (13 km); Norfolk Heritage Coast; Norwich within reach.

Barsham Road, Great Snoring, Fakenham, Norfolk NR21 0HP
Tel (01328) 820597
Fax (01328) 820048
Location 3 miles (5 km) NE of Fakenham, in hamlet; in 1.5-acre garden with ample car parking
Food & drink full breakfast, dinner; restaurant and residential licence
Prices B&B £45.50-£75; dinner from £23; serviced cottages (the Sheltons) £95-£115

Rooms 6 double, all with bath; all rooms have central heating, colour TV, phone
Facilities sitting-room, dining-room
Credit cards AE, MC, V
Children by arrangement
Disabled access difficult
Pets not accepted
Closed Christmas Day and Boxing Day
Proprietors Rosamund and William Scoles

East Anglia and Region

Country house hotel, King's Lynn

Congham Hall

'Quintessentially English' is how some guests describe their stay here. Practically everything about this white 18thC Georgian house, set amid 40 acres of lawns, orchards and parkland, impresses.

The spacious bedrooms and public areas are luxuriously furnished, the service is solicitous and efficient, and the Forecasts themselves extend a warm welcome. Cooking (in the modern British style) is adventurous and excellent, making much use of home-grown herbs. The restaurant is a spacious, airy delight, built to look like an orangerie, with full-length windows over-looking the wide lawns of the parkland, where the herb gardens are an attraction in their own right. Visitors stop to admire the array of 600 herb varieties and to buy samples, from angelica to sorrel. The restaurant doors open onto the terraces for pre-dinner drinks and herb garden strolls. Dressing for dinner is requested.

Personal attention is thoughful. For walkers and cyclists, the hotel will arrange to collect luggage from guests' previous destination and deliver it onwards, too. The Forecasts have devised a book of their own special walks.

They can also arrange for tuition at the Sandringham Shooting School.

Nearby Sandringham, 4 miles (6 km); Ely and Norwich.

Grimston, King's Lynn, Norfolk PE32 1AH
Tel (01485) 600250
Fax (01485) 601191
Location 6 miles (10 km) NE of King's Lynn near A148; in 40-acre grounds with parking for 50 cars
Food & drink full breakfast; lunch (except Sat); residential and restaurant licence
Prices B&B £60-£135; dinner from £25; breaks

Rooms 11 double, all with bath; one single with shower; 2 suites; all rooms have central heating, TV, phone, radio
Facilities 2 sitting-rooms, bar, dining-room; spa bath, swimming-pool, tennis, croquet, putting **Credit cards** AE, DC, MC, V **Children** welcome over 12 **Disabled** access easy to restaurant **Pets** not accepted
Closed never **Proprietors** Christine and Trevor Forecast

East Anglia and Region

Restaurant with rooms, Lavenham

The Great House

The ancient timber-framed houses, the fine Perpendicular 'Wool Church' and the high street full of antiques and galleries makes Lavenham a high point of any tourist itinerary of the pretty villages of East Anglia.

The Great House in the market place was built in the heyday of the wool trade but was extensively renovated in the 18thC and looks more Georgian than Tudor – at least from the outside. It was a private house (lived in by Stephen Spender in the 1930s) until John Spice, a Texan with family roots in Suffolk, had the bright idea of turning it into a restaurant with rooms. It is now owned by chef, Régis Crépy, and the food (predominantly French) is the best for miles – 'stunningly good' enthuses one visitor (a fellow hotelier). If you can secure one of its four bedrooms it is also a delightful place to stay. All are different, but they are all light, spacious and full of old-world charm, with beams and antiques. Each has its own fireplace and sitting-area, with sofa or upholstered chairs. The dining-room is dominated by an inglenook fireplace which formed part of the original house. In winter, log fires blaze; in summer, French doors open on to a pretty stone-paved courtyard for drinks, lunch or dinner.
Nearby Little Hall, Guildhall Priory (Lavenham); Melford Hall, 4 miles (6 km); Gainsborough's House, Sudbury, 5.5 miles (9 km).

Market Place, Lavenham, Suffolk CO10 9QZ
Tel (01787) 247431
Fax (01787) 248007
Location 16 miles (26 km) NW of Colchester, in middle of village; garden at rear, with public car parking
Food & drink full breakfast, lunch, tea, dinner; full licence
Prices B&B £35-£88; dinner from £17.95; reduction for 3 nights or more, and for children sharing parents'
room
Rooms 4 family-size suites, all with bath; all rooms have central heating, phone, colour TV, tea/coffee kit
Facilities sitting-room/bar, dining-room, patio
Credit cards AE, MC, V
Children very welcome; cot and high chair provided, free baby-listening
Disabled access difficult
Pets welcome **Closed** Jan
Proprietor Régis Crépy

East Anglia and Region

Country hotel, Long Melford

The Countrymen

Long Melford is a famously attractive Suffolk village, and The Countrymen is at the heart of it, overlooking the green. It is an elegant early 19thC building, which is decorated and furnished with great sympathy, taste and lightness of touch. The Erringtons now use the restaurant name for the hotel as well (it was The Black Lion). It offers 'modern cuisine with a strong classical influence' and a wide-ranging wine list. The recently opened Wine Bar serves bistro food. They can now also offer a high standard of accommodation. Our latest reporter thought it was 'a delight'. Bedrooms are comfortable and 'non slick: nothing much matches in a charming sort of way'. She noticed the half-open trunk on a landing, spilling out hats and costumes; an antique typewriter on a desk; and bookcases groaning with old books, in the wine bar.

It is obvious that the Erringtons like what they do from the numerous events they organize, from wine tastings or live jazz in the bar to murder dinners and midsummer balls. They welcome anyone from businessmen to families of four. 'There is a great gung-ho feeling – an enormous energy and sense of fun, though this doesn't detract from the Errington's professionalism.'

Nearby Long Melford church, Melford Hall and Kentwell Hall.

The Green, Long Melford, Suffolk CO10 9DN
Tel (01787) 312356
Fax (01787) 374557
Location in village 3 miles (5 km) N of Sudbury, overlooking village green; with car parking
Food & drink full breakfast, lunch, dinner; full licence
Prices B&B £35-£75; dinner £9.95-£38; bargain breaks
Rooms 7 double, one suite, one family room; all with bath; all have central heating, phone, TV, tea/coffee kit
Facilities sitting-room, 2 dining-rooms, bar
Credit cards AE, MC, V
Children welcome; baby-listening, highchair and cot provided **Disabled** no special facilities **Pets** not in public rooms **Closed** Jan **Proprietors** Janet and Stephen Errington

East Anglia and Region

Country guest-house, Melbourn

Melbourn Bury

This gracious manor house, dating mainly from Victorian times although of much earlier origin, offers an intimate retreat only 20 minutes' drive from Cambridge. The whitewashed and crenellated house, with roses round the door, has a delightful setting in mature parkland with its own lake and gardens.

All the public rooms are furnished with antiques, but have just the right degree of informality to make the house feel like a lived-in home and not a museum – not surprising, when you learn that Sylvia Hopkinson's family have been here for 150 years. As well as an elegant drawing-room, there is a splendid Victorian billiard room (full-size table) incorporating a book-lined library, and a sun-trap conservatory. The three bedrooms are spacious and comfortably furnished in harmony with the house; particularly delightful is the 'pink room' which looks out over the lake and the garden; it is a profusion of Sanderson prints and antiques, and has a large bathroom.

The Hopkinsons' dinner-party food (by prior arrangement) is home-made, down to the ice-creams and sorbets and served dinner-party-style around a large mahogany table in the dining-room.

Nearby University colleges and Fitzwilliam Museum, in Cambridge; Duxford Air Museum, 8 miles (13 km); Wimpole Hall and Audley End within reach.

Melbourn, near Royston, Hertfordshire SG8 6DE
Tel (01763) 261151
Fax (01763) 262375
Location 10 miles (16 km) SW of Cambridge, on S side of village off A10; in 5-acre gardens with ample car parking
Food & drink full breakfast, dinner; residential licence
Prices B&B £45-£60; dinner £17.50
Rooms 2 double, one single, all with bath or shower; all rooms have central heating, TV, clock/radio
Facilities 2 sitting-rooms, dining-room, billiard room, conservatory
Credit cards AE, MC, V
Children welcome over 8
Disabled not suitable **Pets** not accepted **Closed** Christmas, New Year and Easter
Proprietors Anthony and Sylvia Hopkinson

East Anglia and Region

Country guest-house, Otley

Bowerfield House

Its quiet village location is appealing – Bowerfield House is up a secluded drive overlooking fields and an orchard. Lise (who is Danish) and Michael Hilton first opened the doors of their listed 17thC stable and barn conversion in March 1995, and when we last inspected Bowerfield, we were impressed enough to promote it to a full entry in the guide.

The Hiltons have created a billiard room, a wonderful drawing room with grand piano for guests' use, and a croquet lawn. There is a large, pretty garden with a fountain and a natural pond, where Koi Carp and Golden Orf swim among the water lilies, and a terrace with outside seating.

'You'd actually want to spend time in the house rather than use it as a base,' noted our reporter, who got the feeling of a friendly, efficiently run household. She liked the tasteful country style of the decoration – 'old pine, plain carpeting, clean floral fabrics and immaculate bathrooms. It is generously furnished with antiques and 'it feels like a real home – which it is. Golf and riding can be arranged.' Young children are not encouraged here because of the number of breakables, and smoking is banned.

No licence, but guests are welcome to bring their own wine; and there is a good choice of restaurants and inns in the area.

Nearby Woodbridge, 6 miles (10 km); Suffolk Coast.

Otley, near Ipswich, Suffolk
IP6 9NR
Tel (01473) 890742
Fax (01473) 890059
E-mail lise@bowerfld.demon.co.uk
Location 7 miles (11 km) N of Ipswich on B1079; ample car parking
Food and drink full breakfast
Prices B&B £25-£36
Rooms 3 double, one with sitting-room, one with four-poster, 1 single, all with bath; all rooms have central heating, TV, radio, hairdrier
Facilities drawing-room, dining-room, billiard room; terraces, croquet
Credit cards not accepted
Children welcome over 12
Disabled difficult
Pets by arrangement
Closed Nov to mid-March
Proprietors Lise and Michael Hilton

East Anglia and Region

Country hotel, Swaffham

Strattons ★

Strattons epitomizes everything we are looking for in this guide. Perhaps it's because Les and Vanessa Scott are such natural hosts who love entertaining; perhaps it's because of their genuine artistic flair (they met as art students) or perhaps it's because they had a very clear vision of what they wanted to create when they bought this elegant listed villa in 1990. A reader writes: '20 out of 20 for staff attitude, value for money, quality of accommodation; 17 out of 20 for scenery and ambience – the three points deducted only because of the setting in the town. An absolute delight.'

Bedrooms are positively luxurious. Plump cushions and pillows jostle for space on antique beds, books and magazines fill the shelves, and the same coordinated decoration continues into smart bathrooms – one resembling a bedouin's tent. The two beautifully furnished sitting-rooms and *trompe l'oeil* hallway are equally impressive. Yet it is emphatically a family home and you share it with the Scott cats and children. The food is special, too. Vanessa, a cookery writer, continues to gain awards for her cooking. The daily changing menu is inventive and beautifully presented. It is cheerfully served by Les in the cosy basement restaurant.

Nearby Norwich, 30 miles (48 km); north Norfolk coast.

Ash Close, Swaffham, Norfolk
PE37 7NH
Tel (01760) 723845
Fax (01760) 720458
Location down narrow lane between shops on main street; with garden and ample car parking
Food & drink full breakfast, lunch, dinner; restaurant and restaurant licence
Prices B&B £45-£95; dinner £25.50
Rooms 6 double, 4 with bath, 2 with shower; 1 suite with bath (suitable for a family); all rooms have central heating, phone, TV, tea/coffee kit, hairdrier
Facilities 2 sitting-rooms, bar, dining-room; no smoking
Credit cards MC, V
Children welcome; cots and cotbeds available available
Disabled access difficult
Pets welcome
Closed Christmas
Proprietors Vanessa and Les Scott

East Anglia and Region

Ounce House

The Pott family have lived in one half of this tall, brick-built Victorian house in central Bury St Edmunds for some time, and in the mid-1980s they bought the other half and skilfully refurbished it for guests. Warm feedback from a reporter, who thought the house 'splendid'.

The four bedrooms – the best of them very spacious – are done out in a smart, restful style, with fully tiled bathrooms. Downstairs there is a palatial formal drawing-room where dinner is a no-choice dinner-party affair, served around one table.

Nearby Cathedral, abbey, Gershom-Parkington collection.

Northgate Street, Bury St Edmunds, Suffolk IP33 1HP
Tel (01284) 761779
Fax (01284) 768315
E-mail pott@globalnet.co.uk
Location close to town centre; with walled garden and ample car parking
Food & drink breakfast, dinner by arrangement; residential licence
Prices B&B £35-£60; dinner £18-£20
Rooms 3 double, all with bath; all have central heating, phone, TV, hairdrier, trouser-press, tea/coffee kit
Facilities dining-room, 2 sitting-rooms, bar, library
Credit cards MC, V
Children tolerated; cot, high-chair, baby-sitting by arrangement **Disabled** access difficult
Pets not accepted **Closed** never **Proprietors** Simon and Jenny Pott

Maison Talbooth

For lavish comfort this rather plain-looking Victorian house is hard to beat. The bedrooms have flamboyant fabrics, luxury drapes, king-size beds; and the bathrooms have thick fluffy towels, gold taps and circular sunken baths. The French doors of an elegant sitting-room open out on to a beautiful landscaped garden. Down the road, Le Talbooth, also under the Milsom ownership, provides the gastronomic highlight of the area. But a light snack will be willingly served in your room. When we last inspected we were again impressed by the stylish boldness of the decoration.

Nearby Castle House (in Dedham); Dedham Vale.

Stratford Road, Dedham, Colchester, Essex CO7 6HN
Tel (01206) 322367
Location 5 miles (8 km) NE of Colchester, W of village; in 2-acre grounds with parking for 12 cars
Food & drink breakfast and light snacks in rooms
Prices B&B £100-£175; dinner from £24 (courtesy car to Le Talbooth)
Rooms 10 double, all with bath (2 with spa bath); all have central heating, TV, minibar
Facilities sitting-room; croquet, lawn chess
Credit cards AE, MC, V
Children welcome if well behaved **Disabled** easy access: 5 ground-floor rooms
Pets not accepted
Closed never
Proprietors Gerald, Paul and Diana Milsom

East Anglia and Region

Restaurant with rooms, Great Dunmow

The Starr

A striking black and white former coaching inn, the Starr stands in a commanding position in this attractive old market town. With a pleasing interior which combines olde worlde with Home Counties polish, it is run as a well-reputed restaurant with great Welsh gusto by Brian and Vanessa Jones, who are chatty and affable, according to a recently satisfied inspector. The barn at the back has bedrooms, one with a huge and prettily clad four-poster and a cast-iron bath in the room; others simpler but neat and spotless. New conservatory. Imaginative menu, with vegetarian dishes.

Nearby Stansted Airport, 8 miles (13 km); Audley End House.

Market Place, Great Dunmow, Essex CM6 1AX
Tel (01371) 874321
Fax (01371) 876337
Website www.zynet.co.uk/menu/starr
Location In the town centre, on the old market place, 10 miles E of Bishop's Stortford
Food & drink breakfast, lunch (except Sat) dinner (except Sun); restaurant licence
Prices B&B £55-£85; dinner from £21.50
Rooms 7 double 1 twin, all with bath; all rooms have central heating, TV, radio/alarm, direct dial phone, tea/coffee kit, hairdrier
Facilities bar, restaurant
Credit cards AE, DC, MC, V
Children welcome
Disabled no special facilities but access possible
Pets welcome if well-behaved
Closed Sun eve
Proprietors Brian and Vanessa Jones

Town guest-house, Hadleigh

Edgehill

Mrs Rolfe has achieved a happy combination of old and new in her handsome red-brick Georgian town house: a flagstoned hall, open fireplaces and chandeliers downstairs, bedrooms (some of which are surprisingly spacious) decorated with modern floral wallpaper, matching fabrics and thick pile carpets. The sitting-room opens on to a walled flower-garden and croquet lawn. Dinner is a cosy affair – 'nothing trendy or complicated,' says our latest reporter, and with home-produced ingredients. It is right on the main street, but our reporter found it quiet.

Nearby Castle House, 6 miles (10 km); Dedham.

2 High Street, Hadleigh, Ipswich, Suffolk IP7 5AP
Tel (01473) 822458
Location 9 miles (14.5 km) W of Ipswich, in middle of town; with walled garden and car park at rear
Food & drink breakfast, dinner if pre-booked; residents licence
Prices B&B £25-£45; dinner £18; bargain breaks
Rooms 7 double, 4 with bath, 3 with shower; 2 single; 2 family rooms, one with bath, one with shower; all rooms have central heating, TV
Facilities sitting-room, dining-room **Credit cards** not accepted **Children** welcome; high-chair provided
Disabled access difficult
Pets welcome **Closed** one week Christmas to New Year
Proprietors Angela and Rodney Rolfe

East Anglia and Region

The Pier at Harwich

Also part of Gerald Milsom's East Anglian empire, and a sharp contrast to Maison Talbooth (page 161) – a seaside fish-and-chip restaurant – the Ha'Penny Bistro below, and The Harbourside, a rather more ambitious seafood restaurant (alternative dishes available), on the floor above, with pianist on Saturday evenings and Sunday lunchtimes. Both the bar and reception area have undergone a facelift to become more spacious, but retain their nautical theme. In the bedrooms, plain colour schemes are relieved by brightly floral duvet covers.

Nearby Car ferry port; Dedham Vale.

The Quay, Harwich CO12 3HH
Tel (01255) 241212
Location on quayside at Harwich; parking for 10 cars
Food & drink breakfast, lunch, dinner
Prices from £52.50-£85; dinner £18.50 (3 courses)
Rooms 6 double, all with bath; all rooms have central heating, TV, tea/coffee kit
Facilities 2 restaurants, bar
Credit cards AE, DC, MC, V

Children welcome
Disabled access possible to restaurant; only 2 small steps
Pets not accepted
Closed Christmas Day eve
Proprietor Gerald Milsom

Old Ferry Boat Inn

Weekend crowds beat a path to this venerable thatched inn (another 'oldest in England') on the banks of the Great Ouse. But when day visitors leave it's a peaceful and picturesque spot. Inside are all the requisite pub trappings – log fires, oak beams, and an interesting range of good-value bar food and real ales. In summer families spill out to the tables and lawns to let children romp unhindered, or view the small animals farm. Following a serious fire bedrooms have been refurbished. A reader's letter praised the 'extremely friendly staff and happy atmosphere.'

Nearby Cambridge 12 miles (19 km).

Holywell, St Ives, Huntingdon, Cambridgeshire PE17 3TG
Tel (01480) 463227
Location on banks of Ouse, signed from Holywell, 2 miles E of St Ives; with garden and car parking
Food & drink full breakfast, lunch, dinner; full licence
Prices B&B £54.50-£73; dinner £10-£15
Rooms 7 double (2 with four-posters, one twin),

4 with bath or shower, 1 single; all rooms have central heating, phone, TV, tea/coffee kit
Facilities dining room, bar
Credit Cards MC, V
Children welcome
Pets not accepted
Disabled access difficult
Closed Christmas dinner
Proprietors Richard and Shelley Jeffrey

East Anglia and Region

Country bed-and-breakfast, Manningtree

Aldhams

Aldhams is a fine sight as you approach: a Queen Anne farmhouse converted and enlarged in 1933 in the Lutyens style by contemporary architect Maurice Webb. He added the two huge brick chimneys and the elm floors and doors inside. Coral McEwen is a dedicated and welcoming hostess whose breakfasts are worth waiting for. She serves them whenever guests wish. 'If you are catching a plane and want breakfast at 5 am that's fine by me,' she says. No dinner, but plenty of places to eat nearby and an air of peace in the well-equipped rooms and large grounds with countryside beyond.
Nearby Colchester, 10 miles (16km).

Bromley Road, Lawford, Manningtree, Essex CO11 2NE
Tel & Fax (01206) 393210
E-mail coral.mckewen3@which.net
Location On A120 between Colchester and Harwich; road signposted to Little Bromley; 3 acres of grounds; parking
Food & drink full breakfast
Prices B&B £20-£30
Rooms 3 double, 1 with king-size bed and bath; 1 twin with dressing room with single bed and bath; 1 double; all rooms have central heating, TV, radio/alarm, tea/coffee kit, hairdrier
Facilities sitting-room, dining-room; large garden
Credit cards not accepted
Children welcome
Disabled access difficult
Pets not accepted
Closed Christmas
Proprietors Christopher and Coral McEwen

Manor house hotel, Needham Market

Pipps Ford

We have received more enthusiastic reports lately for this glorious half-timbered Tudor house in flowery gardens, which Raewyn Hackett-Jones has been running as a guest-house since the early 1980s. She lays great stress on the quality of her meals, producing her own bread, honey, vegetables and countless other ingredients.

The bedrooms at Pipps Ford are delightful and full of character, with log fires burning downstairs in the winter. There is tennis and fishing.
Nearby Blakenham Woodland Garden, 3 miles (5 km).

Needham Market, near Ipswich, Suffolk IP6 8LJ
Tel (01449) 760208
Location in countryside one mile (1.5 km) E of Needham Market, down private road off roundabout where A140 meets A14; with car parking
Food & drink full breakfast, dinner; residential licence
Prices DB&B £38.50-£61; B&B by arrangement
Rooms 6 double, all with bath and shower; all rooms have central heating, tea/coffee kit, radio/alarm
Facilities 3 sitting-rooms, conservatory, dining-room
Credit cards not accepted
Children accepted over 5
Disabled in Stable Annexe on one floor **Pets** not accepted in house **Closed** Christmas to mid-Jan; no dinner on Sun
Proprietor Raewyn Hackett-Jones

East Anglia and Region

The Swan

Enthusiastically recommended by a reader, the Swan is the finest of Southwold's Medieval inns, and, like the Crown, now owned by Adnams Brewery, on to which it backs. It's a handsome building, with two columns of broad, white-painted windows, the Union Jack flying proudly in between. The interior is pleasing and comfortable, using checks and chintzes and open fires to create the English country house look. Bedrooms in the main building are preferable to the newer Garden Rooms. Somewhat formal atmosphere, but staff are friendly and service is helpful.

Nearby Suffolk churches; Aldeburgh, 20 miles (32 km).

Southwold, Suffolk IP18 6EG
Tel (01502) 722186
Fax (01502) 724800
Location in town centre, 14 miles (22 km) S of Lowestoft; ample parking
Food & drink breakfast, lunch, dinner; full licence
Prices B&B £44.50-£160; lunch £16; dinner from £22
Rooms 45 double, twin, single and suites, all with bath or shower; all rooms have central heating, phone, TV, hairdrier

Facilities sitting room, reading room, bar, dining room, meeting room, lift, garden, croquet
Credit cards AE, DC, MC, V
Children welcome
Disabled access possible to public rooms and garden rooms
Pets accepted in garden rooms only
Closed never
Manager Carole Ladd

The Angel Inn

This low-slung timber and brick building on a fairly busy junction has an impressive local reputation. An imaginative menu is chalked up daily in the main bar, and a tall hat or two indicates the serious nature of the food. This may be eaten casually in the bars or at a table reserved in the dining-room, a lofty converted barn with an enormous brick chimney and a fern-lined brewery well-shaft (discovered during renovation and now a spotlit talking point). Above it a gallery leads to the bedroom wing, with half a dozen unevenly shaped rooms smartly kitted out.

Nearby Constable country.

Stoke-by-Nayland, Nr Colchester, Essex CO6 4SA
Tel (01206) 263245
Fax (01206) 263373
Location on T-junction in village, 2 miles (3 km) off A134 between Colchester and Sudbury; with car parking
Food & drink full breakfast, lunch, dinner; full licence
Prices B&B £30.50-£47.50; meals £7-£20
Rooms 6 double (one twin), all with bath
Facilities sitting-room, restaurant, bars
Credit Cards AE, DC, MC, V
Children not accepted
Pets not accepted
Disabled not suitable
Closed Christmas
Proprietors Richard Wright and Peter Smith

Lake District and Region

Inn, Bassenthwaite Lake

The Pheasant

'A very special place,' says the inspector we sent in 1996. Tucked away behind trees just off the A66, the Pheasant was originally an old coaching inn, and there are many reminders of this within, particularly in the little old oak bar, which is full of dark nooks and crannies – a real piece of history, little changed from its earliest days. The building is a long, low barn-like structure that has been exceptionally well maintained. There is a small but well-kept garden to the rear and grounds which extend to 60 acres.

One of the great attractions is the generous sitting space. There are two residents' sitting-rooms to the front, both low ceilinged with small windows and plenty of small prints on the walls. A third, with easy chairs before an open log fire, has the advantage of its own serving hatch to the bar. Bedrooms are modern, light, and individual. The dining-room has been reorganized to make the best of its slightly uncomfortable shape; the food – no-nonsense, with few concessions to modern fashions – is competently cooked, and service is outstandingly friendly. No telephones or TVs in the bedrooms, notes our inspector, but we value The Pheasant's originality and character far too much for that to signify.

Nearby Bassenthwaite Lake; Keswick, 5.5 miles (9 km).

Bassenthwaite Lake, near Cockermouth, Cumbria CA13 9YE
Tel (017687) 76234
Fax (017687) 76002
Location 5 miles (8 km) E of Cockermouth, just off A66
Food & drink breakfast, lunch, tea, dinner, bar snacks; full licence
Prices B&B £45-£55; DB&B £67; reduced weekly rates
Rooms 15 double, all with bath; 5 single, 3 with bath, 2 with shower; all rooms have central heating, hairdrier
Facilities bar, sitting-rooms, dining-room
Credit cards MC, V
Children welcome, but not allowed in main bar
Disabled access easy only to public rooms, and one room in bungalow annexe
Pets not allowed in bedrooms
Closed Christmas Day
Manager Christopher L. Curry

Lake District and Region

Farm guest-house, Blawith

Appletree Holme

The Carlsens came here in 1979 after years of running a much bigger and glossier (and in its way very successful) hotel on the shores of Ullswater – because they wanted, in Roy's words, 'to go back to looking after people again'.

The farm enjoys a lovely and totally secluded setting on the fringe of Lakeland, with nothing but fells in view. The low, stone-built house has been lovingly restored and sympathetically furnished with antiques; pictures and books abound, and open fires on stone hearths supplement the central heating. Two of the equally welcoming bedrooms have the unusual luxury of double-size whirlpool baths.

Roy believes in tailoring his menus (whether for breakfast or dinner) to suit guests' tastes and the local fruits of the land – home-grown vegetables, meat, poultry and dairy produce from neighbouring farms. Sadly, Pooch the sheepdog is not around now to accompany, but anyone whose appetite needs a lift can take his favourite walk over the fells to Beacon Tarn (map provided).

In the interests of their guests the Carlsens discourage casual callers, so do phone ahead if you want to look around.

Nearby Rusland Hall, 4 miles (6.5 km); Coniston Water, Lake Windermere.

Blawith, near Ulverston, Cumbria LA12 8EL
Tel (01229) 885618
Location 6 miles (10 km) S of Coniston off A5084, in open countryside; in extensive grounds, with ample car parking
Food & drink full breakfast, picnic lunch on request, dinner; residential and restaurant licence
Prices DB&B £61.50-£65.50

Rooms 3 double, all with bath and shower; all rooms have central heating, phone, radio, tea/coffee kit, colour TV
Facilities 2 sitting-rooms, dining-room
Credit cards AE, MC, V
Children not suitable
Disabled access difficult
Pets not allowed in the house
Closed never
Proprietors Roy and Shirley Carlsen

Lake District and Region

Seatoller House

It should be said at the outset that a stay at Seatoller House is something quite different from the run-of-the-mill hotel experience. You eat communally at set times, and to get the best out of the place you should take part in the social life of the house. If you do, the 'country house party' effect, much vaunted elsewhere, really does come about.

Seatoller House is over 300 years old and has been run as a guest-house for over 100 years; the first entry in the visitors' book reads 23 April 1886. The long, low house, built in traditional Lakeland style and looking like a row of cottages, is in the tiny village of Seatoller, at the head of Borrowdale and the foot of Honister Pass. Bedrooms are simple and comfortable, and all now have their own bathrooms (although some are physically separate from the bedrooms). The dining-room is in a country-kitchen style, with a delightfully informal atmosphere – one that spills over into the two sections of the low-ceilinged sitting-room. Food is excellent; and if you are thirsty, just wander to the fridge, take what you like and sign for it in the book provided.

Several times a year the house is taken over by members of the Lakes Hunt, who enjoy running up and down the surrounding fells in pursuit not of foxes (the traditional quarry), but of one another. A change of management recently; so reports please.

Nearby Derwentwater, 4 miles (6 km); Buttermere, 6 miles (10 km); Keswick, 8 miles (13 km).

Borrowdale, Keswick, Cumbria CA12 5XN
Tel (017687) 77218
Location 8 miles (13 km) S of Keswick on B5289; parking for 12 cars
Food & drink full breakfast, packed lunch, dinner (not Tue); residential licence
Prices DB&B £37.50-£38.50
Rooms 5 double, 4 family rooms; all with bath and shower, or separate bathroom; all rooms have central heating

Facilities sitting-room, library, dining-room, tea room, drying-room
Credit cards not accepted
Children welcome over 5
Disabled access easy; 2 downstairs bedrooms
Pets welcome but not in public rooms
Closed Dec to Feb
Managers Christine and Graham Welch

Lake District and Region

Country house hotel, Bowness

Miller Howe

A mainstay of the guide for many years, Miller Howe changed ownership in 1998, so we revisited. The food, pioneered back in the 1970s by its owner-chef John Tovey, quite a celebrity chef in his heyday, has always been its *raison d'etre*, and today, under new proprietor Charles Garside, formerly a national newspaper editor, the show still goes on. Dinner is still served promptly at 8 pm, with guests ushered in by name and the lights dimmed a touch as everyone sits down. However, Tovey's uncompromising no-choice set menu is now supplemented with alternative starters and main courses.

Will it work? Has Miller Howe lost its magic? How long will the hotel's reputation continue to weave its spell? We leave it to you, but the bare facts, as we saw them, are that Miller Howe is a solid, respectable hotel with wonderful views over Lake Windermere, charming and attentive staff, comfortable, if somewhat passé, bedrooms (the bathrooms are currently being overhauled), and above-average cooking. The price you pay for dinner, bed and breakfast, approximately double that of The Old Vicarage, page 175, reflects all these factors.

The same care and attention that goes into the food seems also to go into the housekeeping; and the staff are a dedicated team, some having been here two decades or more. Already the conservatory and the grounds have been improved and other changes are on the way.

Nearby Windermere Steamboat museum; Lake Windermere.

Rayrigg Road, Bowness-on-Windermere, Cumbria LA23 1EY
Tel (015394) 42536
Fax (015394) 45664
Location on A592 between Bowness and Windermere; in 4-acre landscaped garden with ample car parking
Food & drink full breakfast, picnic lunch, tea, dinner; residential and restaurant licence
Prices DB&B £80-£125; weekend breaks

Rooms 13 double, 12 with bath, one with shower; all rooms have central heating, TV, phone, radio, trouser- press, hairdrier, hi-fi
Facilities 4 sitting-rooms, dining-rooms
Credit cards AE, DC, MC, V
Children welcome over 8
Disabled access difficult
Pets accepted if well behaved, but not allowed in public rooms
Closed 3 Jan to 11 Feb
Proprietor Charles Garside

Lake District and Region

Country house hotel, Brampton

Farlam Hall

'Exceptional,' says an inspector – 'perfect in every way'.

For over twenty years now the Quinion and Stevenson families have assiduously improved their solid but elegant Border country house. It has its roots in Elizabethan times, but what you see today is essentially a large Victorian family home, extended for a big family and frequent entertaining – the Thompsons, wealthy local industrialists – presided over its heyday. No coincidence that it makes such a good hotel.

'Absolutely beautiful very large country house set in stunning grounds,' continued our inspector. 'Beautifully furnished throughout in wonderful taste, many fine pieces of furniture. All the bedrooms are luxurious and charmingly done out. The dining-room and public rooms are discreet and the atmosphere is one of traditional English service and comfort. The family is most welcoming.'

Another reporter could find no flaw: 'charming family, quiet surroundings, excellent food, tastefully furnished bedroom'. Bedrooms vary widely and some are decidedly large and swish.

Barry Quinion's dinners range from plain country dishes to mild extravagances, and there is a notable cheeseboard.

Farlam Hall is well placed for the Lakes, Dales and Northumberland Coast.

Nearby Naworth Castle, 2.5 miles (4 km); Hadrian's Wall.

Brampton, Cumbria CA8 2NG
Tel (016977) 46234 **Fax** 46683
Location 3 miles (5 km) SE of Brampton on A689, NE of (not in) Farlam village); ample car parking
Food & drink full breakfast, dinner; restaurant and residential licence
Prices DB&B £110-£130; winter and spring reductions
Rooms 12 double, 11 with bath and shower, one with bath; all have central heating, TV, phone, hairdrier, radio, trouser-press
Facilities 2 sitting-rooms; croquet **Credit cards** MC, V
Children accepted over 5
Disabled access reasonable; 2 ground-floor bedrooms
Pets welcome but not in dining-room or left alone in bedrooms **Closed** Christmas week **Proprietors** Quinion and Stevenson families

Lake District and Region

Hipping Hall ★

'More like staying with friends than in a hotel' is the typical reaction to a weekend at Hipping Hall. We visited again recently and were much impressed – it's fairly priced, too.

Ian and Jos Bryant's laid-back style might come as a surprise to new guests; but, they are very experienced, and know exactly what they are doing. They have adopted the house-party approach – expect to make friends with strangers: you help yourself to drinks from the sideboard, and dinner is eaten at one table under the minstrel's gallery in the spectacular beamed Great Hall. Jos creates a daily five-course feast (there is no choice, but preferences are taken account of) using home-grown and local produce with emphasis on 'enhancing, not drowning, natural flavours'.

Parts of the Hall date back to the 15th century when a hamlet grew up around the 'hipping' or stepping stones across the beck. After a strenuous day on the fells, you can sink into sofas in front of a wood-burning stove at the other end of the Great Hall and binge on Jos's home-made cookies. Bedrooms (no smoking allowed) are spacious, comfortable and furnished with period pieces

Nearby Yorkshire Dales, Lake District; Settle to Carlisle railway.

Cowan Bridge, Lancashire
LA6 2JJ
Tel (015242) 71187
Fax (015242) 72452
Website http://www.dedicate.co.uk/hipping-hall
Location on A65, 2.5 miles (4 km) SE of Kirkby Lonsdale; in 3-acre walled gardens with ample car parking
Food & drink full breakfast, dinner; full licence
Prices B&B £44-£72; dinner £24, or £32 with wines; reductions for 3 days and over, and for children sharing
Rooms 5 double, 4 with bath, one with shower; two suites with bath; all rooms have central heating, TV, phone, radio, tea/coffee kit, hairdrier
Facilities dining-room, breakfast room, sitting-room, conservatory with bar; croquet, boules
Credit cards AE, MC, V
Children welcome over 12
Disabled not suitable
Pets dogs accepted in bedrooms by arrangement
Closed Nov to mid-Mar, except for private weekend parties **Proprietors** Ian and Jocelyn Bryant

Lake District and Region

Inn, Wasdale

Wasdale Head

The Wasdale Head is in a site unrivalled even in the consistently spectacular Lake District. It stands on the flat valley bottom between three major peaks – Pillar, Great Gable and Scafell Pike (England's highest) – and only a little way above Wastwater, England's deepest and perhaps most dramatic lake.

Over the last decade and a half the old inn has been carefully and thoughtfully modernized, adding facilities but retaining the characteristics of a traditional mountain inn. The main lounge of the hotel is comfortable and welcoming, with plenty of personal touches. The pine-panelled bedrooms are not notably spacious but are adequate, with fixtures and fittings all in good condition; There are also 6 self-catering apartments in a converted barn, and 3 hotel apartments. The dining-room is heavily panelled, and decorated with willow pattern china and a pewter jug collection. Food is solid English fare, served by young, friendly staff. There are two bars. The one for residents has some magnificent wooden furniture, while tasty bar meals are served in the congenial surroundings of the public bar, much frequented by walkers and climbers.

Nearby Hardknott Castle Roman Fort, 5 miles (8 km); Ravenglass and Eskdale Railway, 5.5 miles (9 km); Wastwater; Scafell.

Wasdale Head, Gosforth, Cumbria CA20 1EX
Tel (019467) 26229
Fax (019467) 26334
E-mail wasdaleheadinn@msn.com
Website www.wasdale.com
Location 9 miles (14.5 km) NE of Gosforth at head of Wasdale; ample car parking
Food & drink full breakfast, bar and packed lunches, dinner; full licence
Prices B&B from £34; dinner from £18
Rooms 7 double (2 twin), all with bath; 3 single, one with bath, two with shower; 3 suites

with bath and shower; all rooms have central heating, tea/coffee kit, phone. Also 6 self-catering apartments; 3 hotel apartments
Facilities sitting-room, dining-room, 2 bars; drying room; outdoor shop
Credit cards AE, MC, V
Children welcome, but under-8s not allowed in dining-room after 8 pm
Disabled access easy to ground floor, but not to bedrooms
Pets not in public areas
Closed never
Manager Howard Christie

Lake District and Region

Country hotel, Watermillock

Old Church

There are many hotels with spectacular settings in the Lakes but for our money there are few to match that of this whitewashed 18thC house on the very shore of Ullswater.

Since their arrival in the late 1970s, Kevin and Maureen Whitemore have developed the hotel carefully and stylishly. The three sitting-rooms, one of which is formed by the entrance hall, are all very well furnished with clever touches in their decorations that give some hint of Maureen's interior design training. They also have the natural advantage of excellent views across the lake. The bedrooms are all different in decoration but they too show a confident but harmonious use of colour. Most have lake views and are pleasantly free of modern gadgetry.

Ex-accountant Kevin does more than keep the books in order; his daily changing dinners are both enterprising and expertly prepared, with a reasonable choice at each course.

'Everything one expects of a Charming Small Hotel,' says one completely satisfied visitor, 'with not a single jarring note.'

Nearby Dalemain, 3 miles (5 km); Penrith Castle, 5.5 miles (9 km); Brougham Castle, 7 miles (11 km); Ullswater.

Watermillock Penrith, Cumbria CA11 0JN
Tel (017684) 86204 **Fax** 86368
Location 5.5 miles (9 km) S of Penrith on A592; in own grounds on lakeshore with ample car parking
Food & drink breakfast, dinner; residential licence
Prices B&B £47.50-£99; DB&B £67.50-£120
Rooms 10 double, all with bath; all rooms have central heating, phone, TV, hairdrier
Facilities bar, 2 sitting-rooms, dining-room; boat, fishing
Credit cards AE, MC, V
Children welcome; not allowed at dinner under 8 – cots, high-chairs, high tea available **Disabled** access difficult **Pets** not accepted
Closed Nov to Mar; restaurant only, Sun eve
Proprietors Kevin and Maureen Whitemore

Lake District and Region

Country house hotel, Windermere

Holbeck Ghyll

A classic Victorian lakeland house, ivy-clad with steep slate roofs and mullioned windows – plus oak panelling and art noveau stained glass. Our latest reporter had a 'friendly welcome' and was impressed by its superb set-back position providing both privacy from the bustle of Windermere and grand lake views from the immaculate gardens; also indeed by the two comfortable sitting-rooms, both homelike and beautifully furnished with plenty of contrasting harmonious fabrics.

The Nicholsons, professional hoteliers both, took over in 1988 and have refurbished to very high standards in a traditional, slightly formal style – though proprietors and staff alike are friendly and relaxed. Bedrooms and bathrooms are beautifully and individually decorated, very spacious, some with their own sitting-room. At the top of the house is a 'very special' four-poster room. In the Lodge nearby are six further rooms (four are self-catering), with breathtaking views. The food is a clear attraction: pre-dinner canapés are served while you select from the inventive daily changing menu, which also includes a vegetarian option. No smoking in the dining-rooms. The grounds are being developed – we hope not overmuch: there is now a jogging trail from which you can spot deer and red squirrels, as well as a tennis court, croquet and putting. **Nearby** Lake Windermere.

Holbeck Lane, Windermere, Cumbria LA23 1LU
Tel (015394) 32375
Fax (015394) 34743
Location 3 miles (5 km) N of Windermere, E of A591; 5-acre grounds with ample parking
Food & drink breakfast, light lunch, dinner; residential and restaurant licence
Prices DB&B £60-£120; reductions for children and for 5 nights or more

Rooms 13 double (6 twin), one family room, all with bath and shower; all have central heating, phone, TV, radio, hairdrier **Facilities** 2 dining-rooms, 2 sitting-rooms; health spa; tennis court **Credit cards** AE, DC, MC, V **Children** welcome; baby-listening, high tea for under 8s **Disabled** access difficult **Pets** in bedrooms only **Closed** never **Proprietors** David and Patricia Nicholson

Lake District and Region

Country hotel, Witherslack

The Old Vicarage

Revisiting recently, our happy impressions of The Old Vicarage were reconfirmed. The key to the charm is its peace and seclusion, with large, mainly wooded grounds, at the edge of a tiny, half-asleep Lakes village – yet some of the area's major tourist sights and thoroughfares are only minutes away by car. There are views out to some low fells.

The building is no more, nor less, than a Georgian vicarage: some of the reception rooms are smallish, but it's all pleasantly but unexceptionally furnished, with some interesting touches here and there, to create a relaxing atmosphere. The bedrooms are not swanky, but comfortable, and usually prettily done, the priciest, especially in the annexe, spacious and well-equipped with CD players and verandas. And here's more charm: the prices are certainly fair, if not good value.

The owners are relaxed and welcoming. The food is impressive, all prepared to order on the premises using fresh ingredients: which is more than can be said of some reputable Lakes hotels, where dinner is delivered to the back door by caterer's van. The wine list is unusually well chosen and explained.

Nearby Levens Hall and Topiary Garden, 3 miles (5 km); Sizergh Castle, 5 miles (8 km); Holker Hall, 6 miles (10 km).

Church Road, Witherslack, near Grange-over-Sands, Cumbria LA11 6RS
Tel (015395) 52381
Fax (015395) 52373
E-mail hotel@oldvic.demon.co.uk
Location 5 miles (8 km) NE of Grange off A590; in 5-acre garden and woodland with ample car parking
Food & drink full breakfast, dinner, Sun lunch; residential and restaurant licence
Prices DB&B £70-£100; dinner £29.50 (4 courses); 3-day bargain breaks
Rooms 14 double, 10 with bath, 4 with shower; all rooms have central heating, radio/alarm, phone, colour TV, hairdrier, tea/coffee kit
Facilities breakfast room, dining-room, 2 sitting-rooms; tennis court **Credit cards** MC, V **Children** welcome (high tea at 5.30pm) **Disabled** not suitable **Pets** dogs accepted by arrangement, but not allowed in public rooms or left unattended
Closed never
Proprietors Jill and Roger Burrington-Brown, Irene and Stanley Reeve

Lake District and Region

Country hotel, Ambleside

Rothay Manor

This 1830s building in French colonial style seems far removed from the bustle of Ambleside. The reputation of Rothay Manor was built up over 20 years by the late Bronwen Nixon, and it is a relief (though no surprise) to report that the standards she achieved are maintained by her two sons Nigel and Stephen.

Bedrooms are neatly and subtly furnished with a full range of facilities unobtrusively accommodated, the public rooms are calm and polished. Food remains a key part of the hotel's appeal.
Nearby Townend, 1.5 miles (2.5 km); Rydal Mount, 2.5 miles (4 km); Dove Cottage, 3 miles (5 km); Lake Windermere.

Rothay Bridge, Ambleside, Cumbria LA22 0EH
Tel (015394) 33605
Fax (015394) 33607
E-mail hotel@rothaym.demon.co.uk
Location 0.5 miles (0.75 km) S of Ambleside; in 2-acre grounds with ample parking
Food & drink full breakfast, lunch, tea, dinner; residential and restaurant licence
Prices B&B £61-£87; dinner £24-£30; reduction for 3 nights or more; winter breaks

Rooms 8 double, 2 single, 6 family rooms, 2 suites; all with bath and shower; all rooms have central heating, TV, phone, hairdrier **Facilities** 3 sitting-rooms, dining-room; croquet **Credit cards** AE, DC, MC, V **Children** welcome; high tea, cots, baby-listening service **Disabled** ground-floor bedrooms **Pets** not accepted in hotel building **Closed** Jan to early-Feb **Proprietors** Nigel and Stephen Nixon

Country hotel, Blackburn

Northcote Manor

In a part of the world where there are few satisfactory alternatives, this late-Victorian red-brick mill-owner's house stands out for a combination of good food and comfortable surroundings. The young partners, Craig Bancroft and Nigel Haworth, built up the reputation of the hotel during the early 1980s. They have thoroughly revamped the place, making the bedrooms and public rooms a fitting match for what seems, still, to be the main attraction: Nigel's cooking – frequently changing menus of modern, innovative dishes – wins him awards, including a Michelin star.
Nearby Browsholme Hall; Gawthorpe Hall, 8 miles, (13 km).

Northcote Road, Langho, near Blackburn, Lancashire BB6 8BE
Tel (01254) 240555
Fax (01254) 246568
Location north of village, off A59; with ample car parking
Food & drink full breakfast, lunch, dinner; full licence
Prices B&B £55-£90; suite £130; dinner from £40; gourmet breaks £130-£165 per person

Rooms 14 double, all with bath, 10 with shower; one suite with four-poster; all have central heating, phone, TV, radio **Facilities** 2 sitting-rooms, bar, dining-room, restaurant **Credit cards** AE, DC, MC, V **Children** welcome **Disabled** access easy **Pets** not accepted **Closed** Christmas Day, New Year's Day **Proprietors** Craig Bancroft and Nigel Haworth

Lake District and Region

Crosthwaite House

Crosthwaite is a quiet village (and 'not particularly attractive' according to one visitor), spread along a minor road at the head of the Lyth Valley, close to Windermere. Crosthwaite House has a fine position at one end of the village. It is a handsome Georgian house, furnished and decorated with a panache that is far from universal in Lake District guest-houses. The Dawsons are friendly hosts. Marnie cooks excellent dinners. Our reporter thought the dining-room charming; the bedrooms and bathrooms unpretentious, though comfortable; and the atmosphere informal.

Nearby fell walking, the Lakes; Sizergh Castle 7 miles (11 km).

Crosthwaite, Nr Kendal, Cumbria LA8 8BP
Tel & Fax (015395) 68264
Location in countryside just off A5074 5 miles (8 km) W of Kendal; with garden and private car parking
Food & drink breakfast, dinner; residential licence
Prices B&B £22; DB&B £34
Rooms 6 double all with shower; all rooms have central heating, TV, tea/coffee kit

Facilities sitting-room, dining-room
Credit cards AE
Children welcome
Pets accepted
Disabled access difficult
Closed mid-Nov to Feb
Proprietors Marnie and Robin Dawson

White Moss House

We have received mixed reports on this country house, owned by the Wordsworth family until the 1930s. It is close to the busy A591 (so noise in the front garden), but also to some stunning countryside around Rydal Water. It has an enviable reputation for its food. Peter Dixon, who cooks virtually single-handed, is considered to be in the forefront of 'modern English cooking'. The main house has bright and prettily decorated bedrooms; there are two more in a secluded cottage. The sitting-room is light and elegant. A Lake District hotel with the feel of a private house.

Nearby Rydal Mount; Dove Cottage, one mile (1.5 km).

Rydal Water, Grasmere, Cumbria LA22 9SE
Tel (015394) 35295
Fax (015394) 35516
Location one mile (1.5 km) S of Grasmere on A591; ample car parking
Food & drink full breakfast, dinner; full licence
Prices DB&B £55-£90; reductions for 3 nights plus and for children in Jul/Aug
Rooms 7 double, 6 with bath, one with shower; all have central heating, phone, TV, radio, hairdrier, trouser-press
Facilities sitting-room, bar, dining-room; fishing, use of local leisure club **Credit cards** MC, V **Children** welcome; no young children in dining-room after 8 pm; cot **Disabled** access difficult **Pets** cottage suite only; may stay in cars
Closed Dec to Feb **Proprietors** Susan and Peter Dixon

Lake District and Region

Ees Wyke

'Ees Wyke is the realisation of our dreams,' says John Williams, a catering lecturer until (in 1989) he and Margaret took over this house. The Georgian gent who built it may have expressed similar satisfaction; he certainly picked a glorious spot – above Esthwaite water, with grand views. It is old-fashioned in the best sense and lovingly cared for, with light rooms and modestly elegant furniture. Bedrooms are simply decorated, spacious and airy. The Williamses make everyone feel at home. A recent inspector gives it a warm report.

Nearby Hill Top – Beatrix Potter's house; Windermere.

Near Sawrey, Hawskhead, Ambleside, Cumbria LA22 0JZ
Tel (015394) 36393
Location in hamlet on B5285 2 miles (3 km) SE of Hawkshead; in garden with car parking
Food & drink breakfast, dinner; restaurant and residential licences
Prices B&B £44-£46; DB&B £56-£58
Rooms 8 double (3 twin), 3 with bath, 5 with shower; all rooms have central heating, hairdrier, TV, tea/coffee kit
Facilities 2 sitting-rooms, dining-room
Credit cards AE
Children accepted over 8
Pets allowed in bedrooms only
Disabled access difficult
Closed Jan, Feb
Proprietors John and Margaret Williams

Old Dungeon Ghyll

At the very heart of the Lake District – overshadowed by the Langdale Pikes, and perfectly placed for a walking break. The slate-and-stone main building is in typical local style and is flanked by a Climber's Bar. The sitting-room is comfortably chintzy, with an open fire. Bedrooms have a pleasant, cottagey feel, some distinctly small, some a little worn. Food is wholesome, in enormous portions to suit walkers' appetites. Guests return for the unchanging nature of the place. 'No fuss, practical and solid – dogs, children and hiking boots all perfectly acceptable,' says a reporter.

Nearby high fell walks into the heart of the Lakes.

Great Langdale, Ambleside, Cumbria LA22 9JY
Tel & Fax (015394) 37272
Location 7 miles (11 km) NE of Ambleside off B5343; in countryside; ample parking
Food & drink breakfast, packed lunch, dinner, bar meals; full licence
Prices B&B £28-£33.50; dinner from £16; mid-week breaks; reductions for children; free under 3 sharing parents' room
Rooms 9 double, 4 with shower; 3 single; 2 family rooms, 3 with shower; all rooms have central heating
Facilities sitting-room, 2 bars, dining-room
Credit cards AE, MC, V
Children welcome
Disabled access difficult
Pets welcome, but not allowed in dining-room **Closed** 24 to 26 Dec **Proprietors** Neil and Jane Walmsley

Lake District and Region

The River House

'A rare example of old-fashioned, small-scale high quality', says a reporter of this comfortable red brick Victorian house on the banks of a tidal creek. It is full of fun prints and characterful antiques and furniture. Bedrooms are individually furnished and pretty; two have extraordinary 19thC hooded baths. Public rooms are furnished eclectically and the *pièce de résistance* is the cast-iron conservatory. Food centres on local game. The place 'reflects Bill Scott's exuberance,' comments another satisfied visitor. Guests are encouraged to relax and 'do as they please'.

Nearby Blackpool; many golf courses.

Skippool Creek, Little Thornton, near Blackpool, Lancashire FY5 5LF
Tel (01253) 883497
Fax (01253) 892083
Location one mile (1.5 km) SE of Thornton, off A585; parking for 20 cars
Food & drink full breakfast, lunch, dinner; fully licenced
Prices B&B £65-£80; dinner about £35
Rooms 4 double, with bath; all rooms have central heating, TV, phone, radio, tea/coffee kit, trouser-press, hairdrier
Facilities sitting-room, bar, dining-room, conservatory; garden
Credit cards MC, V
Children welcome if well behaved
Disabled access difficult
Pets if well behaved **Closed** never; booking essential; restaurant closed Sun evenings
Proprietor Bill Scott

The Mill

The Mill (not to be confused, as it often is, with the Mill Inn next door) is a cottagey, small hotel in wooded grounds, offering good value for money and run in a quiet unassuming fashion by the Quinlan family. The main sitting-room is chintzy, relaxing and well cared for, and thirty original watercolours and oil paintings adorn the walls of the bedrooms and public rooms. Eleanor Quinlan's cooking is traditional, with bread baked daily; she gets special praise for vegetarian dishes and tempting puddings. Packed lunches can be prepared for guests. Bedrooms are light and airy.

Nearby Derwentwater, Ullswater; Hadrian's Wall.

Mungrisdale, Penrith, Cumbria CA11 0XR
Tel (017687) 79659
Location 9.5 miles (15 km) W of Penrith close to A66, in village; parking for 15 cars
Food & drink breakfast, dinner; fully licenced
Prices B&B £29-£39, dinner £26; reductions for 5 nights or more, and for children sharing parents' room
Rooms 8 double, 5 with bath; one single; one family room; all rooms have tea/coffee kit, TV **Facilities** sitting-room, TV room, dining-room, games room, drying-room
Credit cards not accepted
Children welcome; cots, high-chairs; laundry facilities
Disabled access difficult
Pets dogs accepted if well behaved; not in public rooms
Closed Nov to Feb **Proprietors** Richard and Eleanor Quinlan

Lake District and Region

Swinside Lodge

A recent inspector gives this typical Victorian lakeland house a warm report; and a reader writes of it in equally glowing terms – 'well maintained, tastefully decorated, with pleasant, efficient service and excellent four-course set dinners; there is a friendly and relaxed atmosphere, and the hotel is keenly priced'. Not the least of its attractions for another reporter is the position: excellent walks right from the door. It is carefully furnished and immaculately decorated, with personal ornaments, books and so on. Dinners are mildly adventurous – take your own wine. No smoking.
Nearby Derwent Water, Bassenthwaite Lake.

Grange Road, Newlands, Keswick, Cumbria CA12 5UE
Tel & Fax (017687) 72948
Location 3 miles (5 km) SW of Keswick, 2 miles (3 km) S of A66; with garden, and parking for 10 cars
Food & drink breakfast, dinner; no licence
Prices B&B £42-£56; DB&B £67-£81; reductions for 2 nights or more
Rooms 7 double (2 twin), 6 with bath, one with shower;

all have central heating, TV, radio, hairdrier, tea/coffee kit
Facilities dining-room, 2 sitting-rooms
Credit cards MC, V
Children accepted over 12
Disabled not suitable
Pets not accepted
Closed mid-Dec to mid-Feb
Proprietor Graham Taylor

Mortal Man

A classic friendly Lakeland inn – white walls, slate roof, black trimmings – off the road linking two of the loveliest lakes, Windermere and Ullswater. The bar, too, is traditionally black-and-white, the dining-room inoffensively neat. Bedrooms are compact and functional, but they are well equipped and most share the good views of the Troutbeck valley.

Dinners are above-average – satisfying and mildly adventurous five-course affairs offering a reasonable choice, always including a vegetarian option.
Nearby Windermere, 3 miles (5 km), Ullswater, 9 miles (15 km).

Troutbeck, nr Windermere, Cumbria LA23 1PL
Tel (015394) 33193
Fax (015394) 31261
Location in hamlet off A592, 2.5 miles N of junction with A591, just N of Windermere village; with ample car parking
Food & drink breakfast, Sun lunch, dinner; full licence
Prices DB&B £55-£62; reductions for 3 nights or more

Rooms 12 double (6 twin), 2 single, all with bath; all have phone, hairdrier, TV, radio
Facilities bar, sitting-room, dining-room
Credit cards AE, MC, V
Children welcome
Disabled access to bedrooms very difficult
Pets welcome
Closed never
Manager Mrs Audrey Brogden

Yorkshire Dales and Region

Country hotel, Arncliffe

Amerdale House

Since they took it over in 1987, the Crappers (ex-restaurateurs) have gradually transformed this hotel and the bedrooms have all been refurbished over the last few years. The setting is one of the most seductive in all the Dales; on the fringe of a pretty village in a lonely valley, wide meadows in front, high hills behind.

We visited a few years ago and decided to promote it to a long entry on the strength of the location ('total peace and serenity'); the comfortable and beautifully decorated bedrooms and bathrooms – the top-floor four-poster bedroom is particularly charming and romantic with stunning views; and the exceptional welcome given by Nigel Crapper who is also the chef. Its food, in the modern English style, is, to quote a visitor, 'unbelievably good'. Dishes singled out by our inspector included local lamb; minted fillet of sea bass; avocado pear salad with a lightly curried mayonnaise; and a terrine of oranges in Campari and orange jelly. His imaginative menus change frequently and the food had an ecstatic review in one national paper recently.

Usefully situated for a number of Dales sights – and well priced, too. Please note that there are, however, no telephones in the bedrooms – not a significant drawback as far as this guide is concerned.

Nearby Wharfedale, Grassington, Pennine Way.

Arncliffe, Littondale, Skipton, North Yorkshire BD23 5QE
Tel & Fax (01756) 770250
Location in a rural setting; 7 miles (10 km) NW of Grassington, 3 miles (5 km) off B6160; ample car parking
Food & drink full breakfast, dinner; residential and restaurant licence
Prices DB&B £59.50-£62.50; reductions for children sharing parents' room; 4-night breaks
Rooms 11 double, 7 with bath, 4 with shower; all rooms have colour TV, tea/coffee kit, hairdrier
Facilities sitting-rooms, bar, dining-room **Credit cards** MC, V **Children** welcome **Disabled** access easy to ground floor only **Pets** not accepted
Closed Nov to Mar
Proprietors Nigel and Paula Crapper

Manor house hotel, Gainford

Headlam Hall

'Extraordinary house, fine grounds, reasonable rates' was the message that came back from one of our scouts about this mansion in a peaceful hamlet just north of the Tees. And so it is: a grand Jacobean house on three floors, its mellow stone all but hidden by creepers, with substantial Georgian additions – standing in four acres of beautiful formal gardens, with mellow stone walls, massive hedges and a canalised stream. As for the rates – although they have crept up (no doubt partly because of the new leisure facilities added in 1990), they are still reasonable. But it is equally true that Headlam is not among the best-furnished country hotels in the land – and therein lies part of its appeal, for us at least. Although there are abundant antiques alongside the reproductions (the Robinsons furnished the place from scratch after they took it over in the late 1970s) there is a comfortable ordinariness about the place which is refreshing. According to a recent report, standards in the restaurant are being raised.

Nearby Barnard Castle, 8 miles (13 km); Yorkshire Dales.

Gainford, Darlington, Durham DL2 3HA
Tel (01325) 730238
Fax (01325) 730790
E-mail admin@headlamhall.co.uk
Website www.headlamhall.co.uk
Location 7 miles (11 km) W of Darlington, off A67; in 4-acre gardens surrounded by own farmland; with ample car parking; cottage annexe
Food & drink breakfast, lunch, dinner; full licence
Prices B&B £61-£105; dinner £18-£26

Rooms 36 double, all with bath and shower; all rooms have central heating, TV, phone, tea/coffee kit
Facilities sitting-room, bar, dining-room, restaurant, snooker room; tennis, fishing, indoor swimming-pool, sauna
Credit cards AE, DC, MC, V
Children welcome **Disabled** access to ground floor only; 3 bedrooms **Pets** welcome; not in bedrooms **Closed** Christmas Eve, Christmas Day
Proprietor John Robinson

Yorkshire Dales and Region

Country house hotel, Hawes

Simonstone Hall

We visited recently to see the major changes at Simonstone following a recent change of ownership. Outside, it is the same dignified, slightly forbidding, large Dales country house; but as you enter you will probably hear the lively chatter coming from the extensive new bar area which is intended to re-create the hotel as a place that will attract local non-residents as well as overnight guests. To have this popular country pub within an essentially dignified old country hotel is something of a novelty – and not unpleasant. The pub is handsomely done out; bar meals and the range of wines by the glass are imaginative; waiters in black tie and apron, French bistro-style, bustle about. It gives the place an injection of life, but if you've come here for peace, or a romantic twosome, just cross the hall and slump in the stylish drawing room. Beyond is the panelled Game Tavern, serving Sunday lunch and an excellent three-course dinner for only £22.50.

Just as interesting are the bedrooms: even the cheapest, at £37.50 including breakfast, are as spacious as you'll find for this price; the superior rooms are handsomely done out, country house style – again, a notable bargain.

Since our last edition the management has changed again. We welcome further reports.

Nearby Pennine Way, Wharfedale, Ribblesdale.

Hawes, North Yorkshire
DL8 3LY
Tel (01969) 667255
Fax (01969) 667741
Location 1.5 miles (2.5 km) N
of Hawes on Muker road;
ample car parking
Food & drink breakfast, bar
lunch Sunday lunch), tea,
dinner; full licence
Prices B&B from £37.50; dinner £22.50; reductions for
short breaks

Rooms 18 double, all with
bath and shower; all rooms
have central heating, TV,
tea/coffee kit
Facilities bar, 2 sitting-rooms,
garden room **Credit cards** AE,
DC, MC, V **Children** welcome
Disabled easy access to ground
floor, but no lift/elevator
Pets welcome; small charge
Closed never
Managers Iain and Elaine
Russell-Jarvie

Yorkshire Dales and Region

The Hawnby Hotel

After a spectacular drive through rolling valleys and the unspoilt stone village of Hawnby, the hotel may come as something of a let-down. It is not until you are ushered into the elegant sitting-room that you realize how deceptive first appearances can be.

The 'village pub' façade hides an exquisite small hotel which was decorated with obvious flair by the Countess of Mexborough. The hotel used to be part of the 13,000-acre Mexborough estate and Lady Mexborough gave it much personal attention, refurbishing the six bedrooms which are named after colour schemes (Cowslip, Coral, Jade and so on), choosing Laura Ashley wallpaper and fabrics throughout the cosy rooms and immaculate bathrooms. Some of the bedrooms have received a further facelift from the Archbells, who took over The Hawnby in 1997. Their next project is to provide accommodation in a two-bedroomed, self-catering cottage opposite the hotel.

The hotel does suffer slightly from a lack of space. The sitting-room is at one end of the dining-room, and although it does not feel cramped and can be curtained off at guests' request, it might be noisy and crowded at peak times. The hotel caters for shooting parties, and is popular with walkers. Reports welcome.

Nearby Rievaulx Abbey, 4 miles (6 km), North York Moors.

Hawnby, near Helmsley, York YO6 5QS
Tel (01439) 798202
Location at top of hill in village 7 miles (11 km) NE of Helmsley; with garden and car parking
Food & drink full breakfast, bar snacks, dinner; full licence
Prices B&B from £27.50; dinner from £14; cottage from £300 (sleeps 4)
Rooms 6 double, all with bath; all rooms have central heating, radio, TV, hairdrier, tea/coffee kit, iron
Facilities sitting-room/dining-room, bar
Credit cards MC, V
Children welcome over 10 years
Disabled access difficult
Pets not accepted; boarding kennel in village by arrangement
Closed Christmas; Feb
Proprietors C.C and B.A Archbell

Yorkshire Dales and Region

Country house hotel, Lastingham

Lastingham Grange

Lastingham Grange – a wistaria-clad former farmhouse – nestles peacefully in a delightful village on the edge of the North York Moors. Unlike many country house hotels, it manages to combine a certain sophistication – smartly decorated public rooms, friendly unobtrusive service, elegantly laid gardens – with a large dash of informality, which puts you immediately at ease. From the moment you enter, you feel as if you are staying with friends. We had a favourable reaction from a 1996 inspector: 'Family feeling; very child friendly; charming rooms; however, dining-room a little dour.'

The main attraction is the garden. You can enjoy it from a distance – from the windows of the large L-shaped sitting-room (complete with carefully grouped sofas, antiques and a grand piano) – or, like most guests, by exploring. There is a beautifully laid rose garden, enticing bordered lawns and an extensive adventure playground for children.

In comparison, bedrooms are more ordinary. They are perfectly comfortable, with well-equipped bathrooms, but some people may find the decoration unsophisticated in places. Jane cooks straightforward English meals.

Nearby North York Moors.

Lastingham, York Y06 6TH
Tel (01751) 417345/402
Fax (01751) 417358
Location at top of village, 6 miles (10 km) NW of Pickering; with garden and ample car parking
Food & drink full breakfast, tea, dinner; lunches available on request; residential and restaurant licence
Prices B&B £89.50-£101; DB&B £97.50-£149; £95 (week)
Rooms 10 double, 2 single, all with bath; all rooms have central heating, phone, TV, radio, tea/coffee kit, hairdrier, trouser-press, baby-listening device
Facilities sitting-room, dining-room, terrace
Credit cards not accepted
Children welcome
Disabled access difficult
Pets by prior arrangement in bedrooms only
Closed Dec to mid-Mar
Proprietors Dennis and Jane Wood

Yorkshire Dales and Region

The Millers House

Judith and Crossley Sunderland recently completed the addition of a large conservatory to this elegant Georgian house, set back from Middleham's cobbled market square. The public rooms have smart furniture and sumptuous drapes. The bedrooms and bathrooms are spacious and comfortable – one bedroom has a richly festooned four-poster and a splendid Victorian bath. 'For me, the perfect small hotel – homely, neat and welcoming,' says a recently delighted inspector.

The cooking combines the traditional with the unusual, so main courses can include an ostrich casserole in red wine, or sea bass with cous cous and lemon pepper sauce. Starters include smoked chicken with a raspberry and walnut dressing.

It is not surprising that gourmet wine-tasting weekends are among the many special interest breaks the hotel offers, and well-stocked picnic hampers are also available for guests exploring the Yorkshire Dales. 'Very welcoming owners.'

Nearby Middleham Castle; Jervaulx Abbey; Wensleydale, Coverdale, Bishopsdale.

Middleham, Wensleydale, North Yorkshire CL8 4NR
Tel (01969) 622630
Fax (01969) 623570
E-mail millershouse.demon.co.uk
Location just off market square, 2 miles (3 km) S of Leyburn; parking for 8 cars
Food & drink breakfast, picnic lunch, dinner; residential licence
Prices B&B £37-£46; dinner £20.50; various breaks
Rooms 6 double, all with bath, 3 with shower; one single, with bath; all rooms have central heating, colour TV, tea/coffee kit, phone, radio/alarm
Facilities sitting-room, dining room; croquet
Credit cards MC, V
Children welcome over 11
Disabled no special facilities
Pets not accepted
Closed Jan
Proprietors Judith and Crossley Sunderland

Yorkshire Dales and Region

Canalside hotel, Mytholmroyd

Redacre Mill

Canals provide some of the most attractive and interesting locations, as proved by this well-converted, 150-year-old cotton mill in two acres of landscaped gardens, which has featured in a TV holiday programme about the Calderdale country- side. Owners Judith and Tony Peters have retained the original features in the comfortable, spotless bedrooms, including the old office panelling in the Ashton Room. The Winch Room has a hoist mechanism once used to lift cotton bales, as well as pretty floral wallpaper trimmings, curtains and bed coverings on the antique brass bedstead.

Judith cooks traditional home-made food, with some exotic dishes, eaten at a large table in the antique filled dining-room, with views over the canal and surrounding hills. Reports welcome.

Nearby Brontë country; dales; south Pennines.

Mytholmroyd, Hebden Bridge, West Yorkshire HX7 5DQ
Tel & Fax (01422) 885563
Location beside the Rochdale Canal. Follow the Halifax to Burnley road, turn right at fire station in Mytholmroyd to cross a hump-backed bridge, then turn first right; ample car parking; 5 min walk for frequent bus service and rail station
Food & drink full breakfast, dinner; restaurant licence
Prices B&B £29-£39; four-course dinner £17.50;
bargain breaks
Rooms 4 double, 3 with shower, 1 with bath; all rooms have central heating, TV, tea/coffee kit, hairdrier
Facilities sitting-room, dining-room; garden; no smoking allowed **Credit cards** MC, V
Children welcome; cot and high chair available
Disabled access limited
Pets not accepted
Closed Christmas to New Year; early Mar for 3 weeks
Proprietors Judith and Tony Peters

Yorkshire Dales and Region

Sportsman's Arms

A recent inspection confirms that the Sportsman's Arms is going from strength to strength. The long, rather rambling building dates from the 17th century, and the setting is as enchanting as the village name sounds; the river Nidd flows across the field in front; Gouthwaite reservoir, a bird-watchers' haunt, is just behind; glorious dales country spreads all around.

Jane and Ray Carter have been running the Sportman's Arms, with the help of a young enthusiastic team, for over twenty years now, and continue to make improvements. Bedrooms (two with four-posters) have been redecorated and are light and fresh, with brand-new bathrooms. Six more rooms, four with views across open countryside, have been created in the barn and stable block. All the public rooms have been recently refurbished as well.

And then there is the food. The Sportsman's Arms is first and foremost a restaurant, and the large dining-room is the inn's focal point, sparkling with silver cutlery and crystal table lights. The lively menu embraces sound, traditional local fare, as well as fresh fish and seafood brought in daily from Whitby, To back it up, there is a superb wine list – and an extremely reasonable bill.

Nearby Wharfedale, Wensleydale; Fountains Abbey, Bolton Abbey.

Wath-in-Nidderdale, Pateley Bridge, near Harrogate, North Yorkshire HG3 5PP
Tel (01423) 711306
Fax (01423) 712524
Location 2 miles (3 km) NW of Pateley Bridge, in hamlet; in 0.5-acre gardens, with ample car parking in front
Food & drink full breakfast, bar lunch, dinner (residents only on Sun); full licence
Prices B&B £25.50-£39; dinner £21-£25; reductions for more than 3 nights
Rooms 7 double, 2 with shower; 6 in annexe; all rooms have central heating, tea/coffee kit, TV
Facilities 3 sitting-rooms, bar, dining-room; fishing
Credit cards MC, V
Children welcome
Disabled access easy, but no ground-floor bedrooms
Pets welcome, not in restaurant; own bedding must be provided
Closed Christmas Day, Boxing Day and New Year's Day
Proprietors Jane and Ray Carter

Yorkshire Dales and Region

Country house hotel, Walkington

The Manor House

This late-Victorian house may not be what most people expect a manor house to be, but that can be forgiven. Under the practised eye of chef-patron Derek Baugh and his wife, it has made an exceptionally civilized hotel. The furnishings are opulent, with a sprinkling of antiques and plenty of rich fabrics in carefully harmonized colours. The drawing-room is spacious, dividing naturally into several different sitting areas, but still manages to have a human scale. On sunny days there is plenty of light from a tall bow window, and the whole room is drawn together by a pale carpet with a geometric pattern. The original conservatory serves as a dining-room – a particularly pleasant place to eat on a summer evening.

When our inspector re-visited, she particularly liked the 'perfect, tranquil location just outside the village'. She thought the bedrooms (great views) a little modern given the character of the house – but comfortable and smart. Bathrooms are equipped with very large, fluffy towels and an 'amazing' range of extras, such as body lotions.

Food is elaborate and modern; the wine list long and interesting, mainly European.

Nearby Beverley Minster, 4 miles (6 km); Skidby Windmill Museum, 4 miles (6 km).

Northlands, Walkington,
North Humberside HU17 8RT
Tel (01482) 881645
Fax (01482) 866501
Location on the Newbald road
NW of Walkington, 4 miles (6
km) SW of Beverley
Food & drink breakfast,
dinner; lunch by arrangement;
residential licence
Prices B&B £42-£75; full breakfast £8.50; dinner
from £16.50

Rooms 7 double, all with bath;
all have central heating, TV,
phone, tea/coffee kit, minibar
Facilities sitting-room,
dining-room, conservatory
Credit cards MC, V
Children accepted
Disabled no special facilities
Pets by arrangement
Closed Christmas Day
Proprietors D and L Baugh

Yorkshire Dales and Region

Country hotel, Bainbridge

Riverdale House

Anne Harrison's converted row of cottages on the green of this quiet little Wensleydale village is in the best tradition of the unpretentious country hotel – bedrooms freshly decorated, in simple tasteful style (those in the main building more spacious than the rather cramped ones which have been added at the back), and first-class country cooking (Anne used to be a home economics teacher) served in a tea-shop-style dining-room at polished tables. Packed lunches are available on request. We assume service remains friendly, but we lack recent reports.
Nearby Aysgarth Falls, 4 miles (6 km); Upper Dales Folk Museum.

Bainbridge, Leyburn, North Yorkshire DL8 3EW
Tel (01969) 650311
Location off A684 on village green; with small garden and parking on road
Food & drink full breakfast, packed lunch, dinner (except Thurs)
Prices B&B £25-£30; reductions for children
Rooms 12 double, 10 with bath, or shower; all rooms have central heating, colour TV, tea/coffee kit
Facilities 2 sitting-rooms (one with TV), bar/dining-room
Credit cards not accepted
Children welcome
Disabled access very difficult
Pets not welcome
Closed Dec to Feb; weekends Nov to Mar
Proprietor Mrs A Harrison

Country guest-house, Crookham

The Coach House

Lynne Anderson is a charming hostess (and fluent in Spanish), who devotes herself to the care of guests in this group of converted farm buildings. Some bedrooms are in outbuildings around a sunny courtyard, others in a separate stone house. Most have their own fridge. The four-course dinners are wholesome affairs employing much local produce, as are the exceptional breakfasts. Special diets are well catered for too. When we last inspected The Coach House we were impressed with the thoughtful service, the food and the comfortable, well-equipped rooms (seven with fridges).
Nearby Northumberland National Park.

Crookham, Cornhill-on-Tweed, Northumberland TD12 4TD
Tel (01890) 820293
Fax (01890) 820284
Location 4 miles (6 km) E of Cornhill-on-Tweed on A697; with ample car parking
Food & drink breakfast, tea, dinner; licenced
Prices B&B from £23-£36; DB&B from £39.50-£52.50; dinner £16.60; reductions for children under 10
Rooms 9 double, 7 with bath and shower; 2 singles with bath and shower; all rooms have central heating, phone, TV, radio, tea/coffee kit
Facilities sitting-room, dining-room, TV room with videos
Credit cards MC, V
Children accepted; cots, highchairs
Disabled excellent facilities
Pets welcome; not in public rooms
Closed Nov to Easter
Proprietor Lynne Anderson

Yorkshire Dales and Region

Country guest-house, Grassington

Ashfield House

Originally three 17thC cottages, Ashfield House is now a guest-house (or small hotel) with a surprisingly large walled garden, tucked behind Grassington's main square. The bedrooms are all different – a white lacy duvet cover here, an antique pine wardrobe there – all quite small but 'clean, tidy and pleasantly simple,' according to a recent reporter. In the two sitting-rooms are comfortable chairs and blazing log fires. In the evenings, guests socialize as they anticipate Linda Harrison's Aga cooking. No smoking.

Nearby Skipton Castle, 7 miles (11 km); Yorkshire Dales.

Grassington, near Skipton, North Yorkshire BD23 5AE
Tel & fax (01756) 752584
Location close to main square; parking for 7 cars
Food & drink full breakfast, dinner; residential licence
Prices B&B £30-£45; DB&B £40-£50; half-price for children aged 5-10 sharing with an adult; special breaks
Rooms 4 double, 3 twin, 7 with bath or shower; all rooms have central heating, colour TV, radio, tea/coffee kit, hairdrier
Facilities 2 sitting-rooms, one with bar, dining-room
Credit cards MC, V
Children welcome over 5
Disabled not suitable
Closed Jan
Proprietors Keith and Linda Harrison

Country hotel, Hunmanby

Wrangham House

This Georgian vicarage still retains the feel of an unpretentious family-run place, with plenty of home-like touches – bookshelves line the cosy bar, ornaments and water colours decorate the public rooms, bedrooms are positively cottagey, with brass beds and lacy trimmings.

Dinner consists of simple tasty dishes, served in the elegant dining-room, with French windows that lead to the tree-lined garden. Manageress Joanna Shaw and her staff offer a warm welcome and friendly service.

Nearby beaches, walking; Scarborough Castle 9 miles (16 km).

Stonegate, Hunmanby, North Yorkshire
Tel (01723) 891333
Location behind church in village, one mile (1.5 km) SW of Filey; with garden and ample car parking
Food & drink full breakfast, dinner; lunch on Sun; residential and restaurant licence
Prices B&B £30-£47.50; DB&B £42.50-£60; dinner £14.75-£25
Rooms 11 double, 5 with bath, 6 with shower; 2 single with shower; all have central heating, hairdrier, TV, radio, tea/coffee kit
Facilities dining-room, sitting-room, bar
Credit cards AE, DC, MC, V
Children over 12 only
Pets not accepted
Disabled access easy; ground-floor rooms
Closed never
Manageress Joanna Shaw

Yorkshire Dales and Region

Country guest-house, Kettlewell

Langcliffe Country House

Kettlewell is a Dales village with its fair share of hotels and B & Bs. Langcliffe stands on the edge, and is its only 'country house', a distinction which Jane and Richard Elliott like to stress. Although this is essentially a private house organized to receive guests, and Jane and Richard run it with little help, it is more than a guest-house. The six bedrooms are recently decorated and properly equipped. The conservatory-dining room is charming, with great views down the dale. Jane's dinners are good value and enjoyable. Above all, this is place with a heart: you'll get unaffected, personal attention.
Nearby Malham Cove & Tarn; Bolton Abbey; Aysgarth Falls.

Kettlewell, Skipton, North Yorkshire, BD23 5RJ
Tel (01756) 760243
Location just outside Kettlewell village, off B6160, N of Grassington
Food & drink full breakfast, dinner; fully licenced
Prices B&B £30-£40; DB&B £40-£49; dinner from £16; special breaks
Rooms 6 double all en suite; family suite; all rooms have central heating, TV, phone, radio tea/coffee kit
Facilities sitting-room, dining-room, conservatory
Credit cards MC, V
Children welcome
Disabled fully adapted ground-floor room
Pets dogs acceptedby prior arrangement
Closed never
Proprietors Richard and Jane Elliott

Country hotel, Nunnington

Ryedale Country Lodge

This former village railway station makes a calm and well-ordered retreat, which new owners, the Handleys, are continuing to improve. Once past the urns full of flowers by the door, you find yourself in the sitting-room, with its rich assortment of flowers and plants, its comfortable sofas, restful blue-and-pink colouring and pleasing tapestries. The dining-room and conservatory look out over the former platform and farmland beyond. 'Small, homely, friendly. Charming dining-room.' says an inspector.
Nearby Nunnington Hall; Duncombe Park, 3 miles (5 km); Rievaulx Abbey, 6 miles (10 km); Castle Howard, 8 miles (13 km).

Nunnington, near Helmsley, York, North Yorkshire YO6 5XR
Tel (01439) 748246
Fax (01439) 748346
Location 4 miles (6 km) SE of Helmsley off B1257, one mile (1.5 km) W of village; in open countryside; large car park
Food & drink full breakfast, dinner; fully licenced
Prices B&B £35; dinner from £15; bargain breaks **Rooms** 7 double (2 twin), all with bath; all rooms have central heating, TV, phone, radio alarm, tea/coffee kit, hair-drier, trouser-press **Facilities** sitting-room, dining-room, bar servery, conservatory; fishing **Credit cards** MC, V **Children** welcome **Disabled** not suitable **Pets** not accepted, but may stay in cars **Closed** never **Proprietors** Peter and Gerd Handley

Yorkshire Dales and Region

Village Hotel, Reeth

The Burgoyne Hotel

Reeth lies at the heart of Swaledale, and the Burgoyne Hotel – once the private home of a prestigious local family – dominates the village green. Within its severe stone walls Derek Hickson and Peter Carwardine have created a superior base for touring or walking the region (walking weekend breaks can be arranged). Seven of the bedrooms have beautiful views over Swaledale, one overlooks the garden. Public rooms, including the sitting-room with its open fire, are handsome, as is the four-course set dinner prepared by Peter Carwardine. We have a warm report from a recent visitor.

Nearby Richmond Castle, 10 miles (16 km); Yorkshire Dales

On the Green, Reeth, Richmond, North Yorkshire, DL11 6SN
Tel & Fax (01748) 884292
Location 10 miles (16 km) W of Richmond on the B6270; garden; car parking
Food & drink full breakfast; packed lunch or private lunch on request; dinner; restaurant licence
Prices B&B £35-£140; dinner £23; winter breaks
Rooms 8 double (3 twin),

5 en-suite, 3 with bath or shower; all rooms have central heating, TV, radio/alarm, tea/coffee kit, phone, hairdrier
Facilities sitting-room, diningroom
Credit Cards MC, V
Disabled ground floor room
Pets by arrangement
Closed 4th Jan to 14th Feb
Proprietors Derek Hickson and Peter Carwardine

Country inn, Romaldkirk

Rose and Crown

Built in 1733, and thoroughly renovated by the Davys nine years ago, the Rose and Crown is thriving in their hands. The bars are typically rustic with log fires, old photographs and copper and brass ornaments. Pub food with 'blackboard specials' is served in the bistro-style 'Crown room'; traditional four-course dinners in the panelled dining-room feature moorland game and fish from the East Coast, served with locally grown vegetables.

Seven bedrooms (comfortable, with antique furniture) in the main building; five others (larger, modern) around rear courtyard.

Nearby Barnard Castle, 6 miles (10 km).

Romaldkirk, Barnard Castle, Co. Durham DL12 9EB
Tel (01833) 650213
Fax (01833) 650828
Location in middle of village, on B6277, 6 miles NW of Barnard Castle; with ample car parking
Food & drink breakfast, dinner, Sun lunch; full licence
Prices B&B £42-£62; Sun lunch £12.95; dinner £24
Rooms 11 double, 8 with bath,

3 with shower; one family room with bath; all have central heating, phone, TV, radio, tea/coffee kit
Facilities dining-room, sitting-room, bar **Credit cards** MC, V
Children welcome; baby-listening **Disabled** access good; ground-floor bedroom **Pets** accepted in bedrooms **Closed** 25th and 26th Dec; restaurant only, Sun eve **Proprietors** Christopher and Alison Davy

Yorkshire Dales and Region

Country inn, Rosedale Abbey

Milburn Arms

Rosedale Abbey is a favourite spot for weekend outings, and part of its appeal is this pretty stone inn at the centre of the village. The bar is traditionally pub-like, but the other areas are properly hotel-like – a polished dining-room, tables laid with silver, glass and fine china, a welcoming sitting-room. Bedrooms have all the comforts but lack character; bathrooms are small. 'The main attractions are definitely the pub and garden.' The food has won chef Alister Passley several awards for his modern British food. Extensive wine list, featuring many from the New World.

Nearby Pickering Castle, 10 miles (16 km); North York Moors.

Rosedale Abbey, nr Pickering, North Yorkshire YO18 8RA **Tel & fax** (01751) 417312 **Location** in middle of village, 10 miles (16 km) NW of Pickering; with gardens and ample car parking **Food & drink** breakfast, dinner, Sun lunch, bar meals; full licence **Prices** B&B £34-£54.50; dinner £20-£25; reductions midweek and for children sharing **Rooms** 9 double, 2 family rooms, all with bath; all rooms have central heating, phone, TV, radio, tea/coffee kit **Facilities** dining-room, sitting-room, bar **Credit cards** DC, MC, V **Children** accepted **Disabled** access fairly easy; 4 ground floor bedrooms **Pets** dogs accepted by arrangement (£3 per day) **Closed** Christmas Day (except for lunch) **Proprietors** Terry and Joan Bentley

Country guest-house, Sheriff Hutton

Rangers House

The Butlers have adopted an unusual formula for their converted stables, built of mellow stone. Although the dining-room has elegant dark-wood tables and the lofty hall-cum-sitting-room is filled with antiques, the house has a lived-in, casual feel which should suit families well. High teas are available for children and teddy bears are provided in the bedrooms. The Butlers are a charming, down-to earth couple who are entirely flexible – breakfast any time you like, bring your own drink if you prefer.

Nearby Sheriff Hutton Castle; Castle Howard, 5 miles (8 km).

The Park, Sheriff Hutton, York, North Yorkshire YO6 1RH **Tel & Fax** (01347) 878397 **Location** 9 miles (14.5 km) N of York between B1363 and A64; in garden with ample car parking **Food & drink** full breakfast, afternoon tea, dinner; full licence **Prices** B&B £32-£34; DB&B £45.50; dinner £23; special breaks **Rooms** 4 double, one with bath, one with shower; one single with shower; one family room; all rooms have central heating, tea/coffee kit, hairdrier **Facilities** sitting-room, con-servatory, dining-room **Credit cards** not accepted **Children** welcome **Disabled** access difficult **Pets** not accepted **Closed** never **Proprietors** Sid and Dorianne Butler

Yorkshire Dales and Region

Restaurant with rooms, Staddlebridge

McCoy's

This Victorian coaching inn at the junction of two busy roads is run by three eccentric brothers and filled with an eclectic mix of antiques and junk – not everyone's cup of tea. But you may be surprised; the loud colour schemes and odd furniture somehow work, and live music drifting up from the packed basement bistro adds to the atmosphere. The roomy bedrooms have pine antiques and striking fabrics. 'A real one-off'; 'really fun'; 'funky' writes a recently enchanted visitor. But the star attraction is head chef Marcus Bennett's cooking – the best for miles.

Nearby North York Moors, Mount Grace Priory; Thirsk Museum.

The Tontine, Staddlebridge, Nr Northallerton, N Yorkshire
Tel (01609) 882671
Fax (01609) 882660
Location in countryside, at junction of A19 and A172, 5 miles (8 km) N of Northallerton; with garden and private car parking
Food & drink breakfast, lunch, dinner; full licence
Prices B&B £45.50-£75; dinner £25-£30 **Rooms** 6 double, all with bath; all rooms have central heating, radio, TV, air-conditioning, phone
Facilities 2 sitting-rooms, breakfast room, bistro, restaurant, bar
Credit cards AE, DC, MC, V
Children very welcome
Pets welcome
Disabled access difficult
Closed Christmas, New Year; restaurant only, Sun & Mon
Proprietors Peter, Thomas and Eugene McCoy

Manor house hotel, Winteringham

Winteringham Fields

The name is as romantically bleak as anything conceived by the Brontë sisters, but the house is quite different: an amiable stone manor house dating from the sixteenth century, decoratively Victorian inside. Germain Schwab is a Swiss master chef; he and his wife Ann, who runs the front of house, have created an exceptionally alluring formula since they moved here in 1988. Bedrooms are spacious and beautifully furnished, one with a four-poster; food earns high praise.

Nearby Normanby Hall, 6 miles (10 km); Thornton Abbey, 13 miles (21 km); Lincoln, 30 miles (48 km).

Winteringham, North Lincolnshire DN15 9PF
Tel (01724) 733096
Fax (01724) 733898
Location in middle of village on south bank of Humber, 4 miles (6 km) W from Humber bridge on A1077; ample car parking
Food & drink breakfast, lunch, dinner; full licence
Prices B&B £40-£89; lunch £20; dinner £29-£52
Rooms 7 double, all with bath and shower (one suite); all rooms have central heating, colour TV, phone
Facilities sitting-room, 2 dining-rooms, conservatory
Credit cards AE, MC, V
Children babes-in-arms and children over 12 **Disabled** access difficult **Pets** local kennels **Closed** Sun, Mon; 2 weeks at Christmas; 1 week Aug, Mar
Proprietors G and A Schwab

Southern Scotland

Inn, Canonbie

Riverside Inn

For over twenty years now the Phillipses have been improving this country-house-turned-inn to the point where it scores highly whether viewed as a pub, a restaurant or a hotel. We guess that motorists travelling between England and Scotland remain the mainstay of trade, despite the fact that the A7 from Carlisle to Edinburgh has been shifted westwards to by-pass Canonbie. For those who do pause there, Canonbie and the Riverside are, not surprisingly, more attractive now that very little traffic separates the Riverside from the public park it faces, and from the river Esk – offering sea trout in summer and salmon in autumn – which it overlooks fifty yards away.

Inside, the comfortable bar and cosy sitting-rooms have the occasional beam and are furnished in traditional chintz, country style, while the dining-room is less pub-like. Both in the bars and dining-room, the food is way above normal pub standards, both in ambition, and execution, using fresh local produce and home-grown vegetables.

Nearby Hadrian's Wall and the Borders.

Canonbie, Dumfries and Galloway DG14 0UX
Tel (013873) 71512
Location 11 miles (18 km) N of M6 on A7, in village by river; with garden and ample car parking
Food & drink full breakfast, lunch, dinner; full licence
Prices B&B £39-£45; Sun lunch £11.95; dinner £19.50 (3 courses); winter breaks
Rooms 7 double, 4 with bath, 3 with shower; all rooms have storage heater, tea/coffee kit, TV
Facilities 2 sitting-rooms, bar, dining-room; fishing, tennis, green bowls
Credit cards MC, V
Children welcome
Disabled access easy – one ground-floor bedroom
Pets accepted by arrangement
Closed Boxing Day, New Year, 2 weeks Feb and Nov
Proprietors Robert and Susan Phillips

Southern Scotland

Country house hotel, Portpatrick

Knockinaam Lodge

Galloway is very much an area for escaping the hurly-burly, and Knockinaam Lodge complements it perfectly (as well as being the ideal staging post for anyone bound for the ferry to Northern Ireland). Succeeding proprietors of the Lodge have had a reputation for fine food and warm hospitality, and the tradition is still thoroughly maintained with the help of an enthusiastic young staff and the proprietors, Michael Bricker from Alberta, Canada, and Pauline Ashworth, from Lancashire.

The house, a low Victorian villa, was built as a hunting lodge in 1869 and extended a few years later. Its rooms are cosy in scale and furnishings, the bedrooms varying from the stylishly simple to the quietly elegant. A key part of the appeal of the place is its complete seclusion – down a wooded glen, with lawned garden running down to a sandy beach.

Dinner is an interesting and adventurous 4-course menu; and the cooking is competent and stylish – modern British with international touches.

Nearby Logan Botanic Gardens, 16 miles (25.6 km); Castle Kennedy Gardens, 9 miles (14.5 km); Glenluce Abbey, 11 miles (17.5 km).

Portpatrick, Wigtownshire,
Dumfries and Galloway
DG9 9AD
Tel (01776) 810471
Fax (01776) 810435
Location 3 miles (5 km) SE of Portpatrick, off A77; in large grounds, parking for 25 cars
Food & drink full breakfast, lunch, dinner, high tea for children; full licence
Prices DB&B £80-£150; dinner £38; reductions for stays of 3 nights plus, and for children sharing parents' room; winter breaks

Rooms 9 double with bath; one single with shower; all have central heating, TV, video, hairdrier, phone
Facilities bar, 2 sitting-rooms, dining-room; croquet; helipad
Credit cards AE, DC, MC, V
Children welcome; cots and baby-sitting available
Disabled access easy, but no ground-floor bedrooms
Pets accepted, but not in public rooms
Closed never
Proprietors Michael Bricker and Pauline Ashworth

Southern Scotland

Nivingston House

We inspected this amiable country house last year and experienced exceptionally friendly, helpful service from the young and competent staff. It has a pleasant outlook, close to the Cleish Hills, and the grounds are impressive.

Food in the Orchard Restaurant was expensive for what it was – even allowing for Scottish prices, but we remain happy to recommend Nivingston as quite a charming place to stay north of Edinburgh, even if the bar area furnishings are not what we like. We are assured that former laundry problems have been resolved.

Nearby Loch Leven, 3 miles (5 km); Edinburgh within reach.

Cleish, Kinross-shire, Tayside KY13 7LS
Tel (01577) 850216
Fax (01577) 850238
Location 4.5 miles (7 km) SW of Kinross, off B9097 (2 miles W of M90, junction 5); 12-acre gardens; ample parking
Food & drink breakfast, lunch, dinner; full licence
Prices B&B £53-£82.50; DB&B £70 (3 nights or more and 2 people sharing
Rooms 13 double, 2 single, 2 family rooms, all with bath or shower; all rooms have central heating, satellite TV, phone, radio/alarm, tea/coffee kit, hairdrier
Facilities 2 sitting-rooms, bar; snooker; pitch and putt, croquet **Credit cards** AE, MC, V
Children welcome
Disabled 6 ground-floor bedrooms **Pets** welcome in bedrooms (not unattended)
Closed first 2 weeks in Jan
Proprietor Allan Deeson

Auchenskeoch Lodge

For over ten years now, Christopher and Mary Broom-Smith have welcomed guests to their granite-built home, where you can soak in the atmosphere of a Victorian shooting lodge without having to shoot a thing. Settled in a comfortable chair in the sitting-room, you can peruse the turn-of-the-century game books before partaking of a four-course dinner at the long oak dining-table, and then trying your hand at billiards. Bedrooms are spacious, comfortable, old fashioned. Outside, the thickly wooded and lawned grounds include a vegetable garden, gravel maze, and small fishing loch .

Nearby Threave Gardens 9 miles (15 km).

by Dalbeattie, Kirkcudbrightshire, DG5 4PG
Tel (01387) 780277
Fax (01387) 780277
Location 5 miles SE of Dalbeattie on B793; woodland; garden; ample car parking
Food & drink breakfast, dinner; residential licence
Prices B&B £28-£39; dinner £16.00
Rooms 3, all double with bath; all rooms have central heating, colour TV, tea/coffee kit
Facilities sitting-room, dining-room, billiard room, croquet lawn, fishing loch
Credit cards MC, V
Children welcome over 12
Disabled one ground floor room specially adapted
Pets accepted
Closed Nov to Easter
Proprietors Christopher and Mary Broom-Smith

Southern Scotland

Albany

A short distance from the hubbub of Princes Street, the Albany is a peaceful retreat in three houses of a Georgian terrace, with flowers spilling from windowboxes at the front. The sitting-room is pleasant, with dusky pink walls and squashy sofas. Bedrooms, named after streets and areas in Edinburgh, are all comfortably furnished; bathrooms are sparkling. Downstairs, Haldanes Restaurant serves traditional Scottish food (open to non-residents). Opened in 1997 by the owner of Nivingston House (page 198), the Albany is a newcomer to the guide, so reports please.
Nearby Castle, museums; Holyrood House; Arthur's Seat.

39 Albany Street
Edinburgh, EH1 3QY
Tel (0131) 556 0397
Fax (0131) 557 6633
E-mail 100414.1237@compuserve.com
Location close to Princes St and St. James shopping centre; easy access by bus, rail or car
Food & drink breakfast, lunch, dinner; full licence
Prices B&B £77.50-£165; special breaks
Rooms 13 double, 5 single, 2 family rooms, all with bath or shower; all rooms have central heating, TV, phone, tea/coffee kit, hairdrier; most with minibar, safe
Facilities sitting-room; restaurant
Credit cards AE, MC, V
Children welcome
Disabled not suitable
Pets by arrangement; not in public rooms
Closed Christmas
Proprietor Allan Deeson

Babbity Bowster

An original name (from a rude-sounding Scottish dance) for an original little hotel, created in the shell of an 18thC mansion in Glasgow's old merchant quarter. Fraser Laurie, bearded, with eye-patch, has created a lively atmosphere and holds classical concerts, poetry readings, and exhibitions in the first-floor Schottische restaurant/gallery. Food in the café-bar downstairs ranges from haggis to oysters, accompanied by traditional folk music on Saturday evenings and Sundays. Bedrooms are small and simpler with pine furniture and fine prints on the walls. 'Magnificent' breakfasts.
Nearby Cathedral, Hunterian Museum and other sights.

16/18 Blackfriars St, Glasgow
G1 1PE
Tel (0141) 552 5055
Location in pedestrian street, on eastern edge of city centre, near High Street station; with parking for 7 cars
Food & drink breakfast, lunch, dinner; full licence
Prices B&B £45-£65; dinner from £10.50
Rooms 5 double, one single, all with shower; all rooms have central heating
Facilities dining-room, bar/café, patio
Credit cards AE, MC, V
Children not accepted; building unsuitable
Disabled no special facilities
Pets not accepted
Closed 1 Jan; Christmas Day
Proprietor Fraser Laurie

Southern Scotland

Country house hotel, Gullane

Greywalls

Greywalls is right at the top of our price-range and size-range, but we cannot resist such a distinctive place. It is a classic turn-of-the-century product of Sir Edwin Lutyens with a garden laid out by Gertrude Jekyll, overlooking the 10th green of the famous Muirfield golf links. The feel is still very much one of a private house, furnished largely with period pieces; the large panelled library is a particularly appealing room. Some three hundred yards from the hotel is the Colonel's House which has its own sitting-room, dining area, terrace and garden – ideal for a group of eight to ten people.
Nearby Countless golf courses; stately homes; sandy beaches.

Muirfield, Gullane, East Lothian EH31 2EG
Tel (01620) 842144
Fax (01620) 842241
Location 17 miles (27 km) E of Edinburgh on A198 to North Berwick; car parking
Food & drink breakfast, lunch, dinner; full licence
Prices B&B £95-£100; The Colonel's House £620 (8 people); dinner £35
Rooms 18 double, all with bath and shower; 4 single, all with bath, 3 also with shower; all rooms have central heating, TV, phone, radio, hairdrier
Facilities 2 sitting-rooms, library, bar; croquet, tennis
Credit cards AE, DC, MC, V
Children welcome **Disabled** access good; 8 ground-floor bedrooms **Pets** accepted, but not in public rooms
Closed Nov to Mar
Manager Sue Prime

Manor house hotel, Kentallen

Ardsheal House

It would be hard to find a more beautiful setting: on the edge of Loch Linnhe, with a backdrop of heather. Ardsheal House is a rambling grey-and-white manor with gabled windows and a square tower. It is the Sutherland's family home and has a country-house atmosphere. 'Slightly old-fashioned, but a genuine charming small hotel,' writes a visitor. 'The car park somewhat detracts from the location.' Guest rooms are decorated with family antiques and have wonderful views. Daily changing 4-course menu with vegetarian specialities, served in the conservatory.
Nearby Glencoe 8 miles (13 km); Fort William 17 miles (27 km).

Kentallen of Appin, Argyll PA38 4BX
Tel (01631) 740227
Fax (01631) 740342
E-mail ardsheal97@aol.com
Website www.milford.co.uk/scotland/accom/h+1767.html
Location on shorefront off A828, 17 miles (27 km) SW of Fort William; large grounds and car parking
Food & drink breakfast, tea, dinner; residential licence
Prices DB&B £60; dinner £23 (residents) **Rooms** 5 double with bath and shower; 1 single with shower; all have radio, phone **Facilities** dining-room, conservatory, 3 sitting-rooms, bar; billiard table **Credit cards** AE, MC, V **Children** welcome **Disabled** no special facilities **Pets** dogs welcome except in dining-room **Closed** Christmas and New Year **Proprietors** Neil and Philippa Sutherland

Highlands and Islands

Country hotel, Drumnadrochit

Polmaily House

Thoughtful improvements have been taking place at this tall, secluded Edwardian-style house since the proprietors took over in 1993. They do not hold with traditional formality and are aiming for a relaxed atmosphere within the luxury of a country house hotel. Sonia comes from three generations of hotel owners and brings her experience at Langan's Brasserie together with John's (ex Park Lane Hotel) to ensure top comfort. Plenty for families to do here, with a heated indoor swimming pool, indoor and outdoor children's play areas, skippered sailing on Loch Ness, riding, and a conservatory overlooking a trout pond. Local specialities abound, and menus include game, Tay salmon and Aberdeen beef.

Nearby Urquhart Castle, 2.5 miles (4 km); Loch Ness.

Drumnadrochit, Inverness-shire, Highland, IV3 6XT
Tel (01456) 450343
Fax (01456) 450813
E-mail
polmailyhousehotel@BTinternet.com
Location 2 miles (3 km) W of Drumnadrochit on A831; in 18 acres with ample car parking
Food & drink breakfast, lunch, dinner; residential and restaurant licence
Prices B&B from £38-£64; dinner from £15-£24; reductions for children and 2 nights or more

Rooms 6 double, (2 twin); 5 family suites all with bath and shower; 3 single with bath; all rooms have central heating, radio, phone
Facilities 3 sitting-rooms, bar, restaurant; tennis, heated indoor swimming-pool; riding, croquet, sailing **Credit cards** MC, V **Children** welcome; indoor and outdoor play area **Disabled** access to dining-room good; one bedroom with garden access
Pets welcome **Closed** never
Proprietors John and Sonia Whittington-Davis

Highlands and Islands

Minmore House

Minmore House was new to the guide a few years ago and we were impressed by the friendly, relaxed atmosphere. It has since been taken over by Brett and Christine Holmes.

It is a solid mid-Victorian family home set in four and a half acres of landscaped gardens. It stands adjacent to the famous Glenlivet whiskey distillery, and was the home of George Smith, the distillery's founder. Not surprisingly, whiskey plays its part in the hotel, and the fine oak panelled bar displays an impressive range of single malts. From the hotel, enthusiasts can follow the signposted Whiskey Trail, visiting renowned Speyside whiskey distilleries.

'Proper' Scottish breakfasts, with kippers and smoked haddock, are on offer, as well as complimentary afternoon tea. In the award-winning restaurant, the 5-course set dinners (with vegetarian options) have a Scottish bias. The hotel has a tranquil, relaxed atmosphere, with open fires in all the public rooms. With the exception of the two single rooms, the bedrooms and bathrooms are spacious. The Holmes are happy to arrange all manner of activities – golf, shooting, stalking, salmon and trout fishing, walking, and castle and distillery visits.

Minmore House is being upgraded ; more reports please.

Nearby Glenlivet Distillery; Ballindalloch Castle 5 miles (8 km).

Glenlivet, Banffshire
AB37 9DB
Tel (01807) 590378
Fax (01807) 590472
Location on the B9008; next to the Glenlivet Distillery; in 4.5 acres garden with ample parking
Food & drink breakfast, picnic lunch on request, afternoon tea, dinner; residential licence
Prices B&B £45; DB&B £65; dinner £25; special rates for 3 days plus
Rooms 8 double, 2 single, all with bath; all rooms have central heating, phone, tea/coffee kit **Facilities** 2 sitting-rooms, bar, dining room, croquet lawn, tennis court, swimming-pool **Credit cards** MC, V **Children** welcome **Disabled** access difficult **Pets** accepted **Closed** mid-Oct-1st May **Proprietors** Brett and Christine Holmes

Highlands and Islands

Country guest-house, Harris

Scarista House

Harris has little in the way of hotels, but Scarista would stand out even among the country houses of the Cotswolds. It is not uncommon to discover that several of the guests at Scarista have re-arranged their holiday itineraries to be sure of a stay.

The converted Georgian manse stands alone on a windswept slope overlooking a wide stretch of tidal sands on Harris's western shore. The decoration is quite formal, with antiques throughout, but the atmosphere is relaxed, and by the open peat fires, conversation replaces television. The bedrooms, all with private bathrooms, have selected teas, fresh coffee, as well as home-made biscuits. Most of them are in a new single-storey building; the one in the house itself is non-smoking.

The Callaghans quit banking and antiques to take over at the beginning of 1990 and have since refurbished the public areas and most of the bedrooms. They aim to be welcoming and efficient, but never intrusive, and to preserve that precious private home atmosphere.

One of Scarista's greatest attractions, particularly rewarding after a long walk over the sands, is the meals. The imaginatively prepared fresh local and garden produce and an impressive wine list ensure a memorable dinner in the candle-lit dining-room.

Nearby swimming, walking, bird-watching, golf, boat trips.

Harris, Western Isles
HS3 3HX
Tel (01859) 550238
Fax (01859) 550277
E-mail scarista@compuserve.com
Location 15 miles (24 km) SW of Tarbert on A859, overlooking sea; in 2-acre garden, with ample car parking
Food & drink full breakfast, packed/snack lunch, dinner; residential licence
Prices B&B £55-£72;

dinner £30
Rooms 5 double, all with bath; all rooms have central heating, tea/coffee kit
Facilities library, 2 sitting-rooms, dining-room **Credit cards** MC, V **Children** welcome over 8 **Disabled** access easy, but no ground-floor toilets **Pets** welcome in annexe if well behaved **Closed** Oct to April **Proprietors** Ian and Jane Callaghan

Highlands and Islands

Town hotel, Mull

Strongarbh House

The seafood restaurant and grill have put this small family-run hotel firmly on the gourmet map, thanks to the award-winning cooking of head chef and proprietor, Ian McAdam, who trained in Glasgow, America and Australia. Superbly fresh prawns, scallops, mussels, oysters, and lobster are guaranteed as guests can see the fishermen unloading the catch in the busy harbour, with its brightly painted houses, below the hotel. It is a solid Victorian building with large bedrooms which are plainly decorated and pristinely kept. Outstanding views are the strongest point of the bedrooms. The two Bay Rooms overlook Tobermory Bay, and the two Garden Rooms look towards the distant hills. In the evenings, the sitting-room with sofas around an open log fire, makes a cosy base for planning sightseeing trips, helped along by the guide books on the shelves. Ian follows a family tradition as his father, Derek McAdam, is also a well-known local hotelier who runs the suitably named Fairways Lodge, a modern building located between the third and fourth fairways of Tobermory Golf Couse. Guests staying here have priority booking for Ian's seafood restaurant.

Nearby Loch Scridain; Ben More 3,169 ft (966 m); Iona; Staffa.

Tobermory, Isle of Mull
PA75 6PR
Tel (01688) 302328
Fax (01688) 302238
Location top of the town overlooking fishermen's harbour; ample parking
Food & drink breakfast, lunch (served on Sun only in winter months), dinner; residential licence
Prices B&B £33.50-£57.50; lunch £9.95; dinner from £15; bargain breaks
Rooms 2 double, 2 twin, all with bath and shower; all rooms have central heating, TV, tea/coffee kit, hairdrier

Facilities sitting-room, restaurant
Credit cards MC, V
Children welcome
Disabled access difficult
Pets well-behaved dogs in bedroom (not in sitting-room or restaurant)
Closed early Jan
Proprietors Ian and Mhairi McAdam

Highlands and Islands

Town hotel, Nairn

Clifton ★

It is not unusual to come upon small hotels with a theatrical touch, but the Clifton is in a different league; it actually is a theatre, staging plays and recitals in the dining-room during the winter months, to the delight of locals and visitors alike. Gordon Macintyre has lived here all his life, 40 of those years as a hotel-keeper, and his act is by now thoroughly polished.

The Victorian house is richly furnished to ensure not only the comfort but also the amusement of guests; paintings fill the walls (themselves works of art), flowers fill antique vases, books fill shelves, knick-knacks fill every other nook and cranny. Whatever your mood, one of the public rooms should suit – the Drawing-room has stunning red, gold and black wallpaper with pomegranite motif, originally designed by Pugin for the Robing Room in the Palace of Westminster. Bedrooms are individually decorated and furnished in what Gordon (with characteristic modesty and humour) calls 'a mixture of good antiques and painted junk'.

The cooking imposes French provincial techniques on the best local produce – particularly seafood, upon which lunch in the smaller Green Room is largely based – and there is a fine, long wine-list. Typically, breakfast is served without time limit.

Nearby Cawdor Castle, 5 miles (8 km); Brodie Castle, 5 miles (8 km); Fort George, 8 miles (13 km); Inverness within reach

Nairn, Highland IV12 4HW
Tel (01667) 453119
Fax (01667) 52836
Location on sea-front in middle of town, close to A96; with own parking
Food & drink full breakfast, lunch, dinner; full licence
Prices B&B £50-£60; dinner £20-£25
Rooms 8 double, 4 single, all with bath; all rooms have heating

Facilities 2 sitting-rooms, TV room, 2 dining-rooms
Credit cards AE, DC, MC, V
Children welcome, but no special facilities
Disabled access difficult – no ground-floor bedrooms
Pets well behaved dogs accepted but not allowed in restaurant
Closed mid-Dec to end Jan
Proprietor J Gordon Macintyre

Highlands and Islands

Kinloch Lodge

When we revisited Kinlock Lodge we were as impressed as ever. This white-painted stone house, in an isolated position with uninterupted sea views, at the southern extremity of the Isle of Skye, was built as a farmhouse around 1700 and later became a shooting lodge. But it escaped the baronial treatment handed out to many such houses – 'thank goodness,' says Lady Macdonald, whose style is modern interior-designer rather than dark panelling and tartan. The house has that easy-going private-house air: indeed it is the Macdonalds' home – they have separate quarters at one side of the house. The guests' sitting-rooms are comfortably done out in stylishly muted colours; family oil paintings grace the walls. The dining-room is more formal, with sparkling crystal and silver on polished tables. All but three of the bedrooms are undeniably on the small side, but this does not deter fans, who go here for an unaffectedly warm welcome and for the excellent food – four courses with a choice at each stage, cooked by Lady M along with Peter Macpherson. Lady Macdonald has written cookery books and gives cookery demonstrations.

Nearby Clan Donald Centre, 6 miles (10 km).

Sleat, Isle of Skye, Highland
IV43 8QY
Tel (014713) 214
Fax (014713) 277
Location 6 miles (10 km) S of
Broadford, one mile (1.5 km)
off A851; in 60-acre grounds
with ample car parking
Food & drink full breakfast,
lunch by arrangement, dinner;
residential and restaurant
licence
Prices B&B £40-£85;
dinner £35
Rooms 10 double, 8 with bath;
all rooms have central heating,
tea/coffee kit, hairdrier

Facilities 2 sitting-rooms,
dining-room; fishing
Credit cards MC, V
Children welcome if well
behaved; special meals
provided for those under 8
Disabled access reasonable –
one ground-floor bedroom
Pets dogs accepted by
arrangement but not
allowed in public rooms
Proprietors Lord & Lady
Macdonald

Highlands and Islands

Country guest-house, Skye

Viewfield House

We inspected recently and decided to give Viewfield House a long entry, mainly because it is so unusual. 'It won't suit everyone,' writes our reporter, 'but for those seeking an age gone by, the experience would be memorable.'

It is an imposing Victorian country mansion, as the name suggests, has some fine views from its elevated position. The need for costly repairs to the roof prompted Evelyn Macdonald, Hugh's grandmother, to open Viewfield to guests. The delight of it is that the distinctive character of the house was preserved; and though you will not lack for comfort or service, a stay here is likely to be a novel experience. The house is full of colonial memorabilia: stuffed animals, and birds; priceless museum relics; and a magnificent collection of oil paintings and prints.

The rooms are original, right down to the wallpaper in one instance (though all but a couple now have *en suite* bathrooms in the former dressing-rooms); there is a classic Victorian parlour and a grand dining-room with two huge wooden tables. Guests are entertained house-party style, although individual seating can be arranged – we admire this flexibility. There is a fixed menu, but individual needs can be met. On the day our reporter called, good old bread and butter pudding was on the menu.

Nearby Trotternish peninsula.

Portree, Isle of Skye, Highland IV51 9EU
Tel (01478) 612217
Fax (01478) 613517
Location on outskirts of town, 10 minutes walk S of centre
Food & drink full breakfast, packed lunch, dinner
Prices B&B £30-£45; DB&B £45-£60; 3-night and weekly reduction
Rooms 8 double, 7 with bath; 2 single, one with bath; one family room; all rooms have radio alarm, tea/coffee kit
Facilities sitting-room, dining-room, TV room
Credit cards MC, V
Children welcome
Disabled access difficult
Pets welcome; not in public rooms
Closed mid-Oct to mid-Apr
Proprietors Mr and Mrs Hugh Macdonald

Country hotel, Ullapool

Altnaharrie Inn

There are good hotels in many unlikely-sounding places in Britain, but this one takes first prize. Ullapool itself is pretty remote, but to get to Altnaharrie you have to make a 10-minute crossing of Loch Broom in the inn's private ferry – or tackle it from Little Loch Broom and hike 2 miles over the mountains.

Such complete seclusion has a powerful appeal in itself; at least to some, there can hardly be a better way to appreciate the wild grandeur of this north-western extremity of the British mainland than to explore it on foot from this remote spot. But the really remarkable thing about staying here is that it involves no compromises whatever. The inn is as welcoming a house as you will find anywhere; what is more, the food is widely acknowledged to be stunningly good.

Gunn does the cooking and brings to it the same originality she employs in painting and weaving. Fresh local ingredients – including superb seafood and game in season – form the basis of her set menus, which defy classification but have achieved wide acclaim. There are no better restaurants in the Highlands, and few in the whole of Britain, as the many awards verify.

The centuries-old white-painted stone house, only a stone's throw from the loch, is warmly and prettily decorated with woven wall-hangings, Middle Eastern rugs and a sprinkling of antiques. Note that prices are among the highest in these pages.

Nearby walking, birdwatching; Loch Broom Highland Museum, Ullapool; Inverewe gardens.

Ullapool, Highland IV26 2SS
Tel (01854) 633230
Location SW of Ullapool across Loch Broom – reached by private launch; private car park in Ullapool
Food & drink full breakfast, light lunch (residents only), dinner; residential and restaurant licence
Prices DB&B £170-£200
Rooms 8 double, all with bath
Facilities 2 sitting-rooms, dining-room
Credit cards MC, V
Children welcome if well behaved, but not suitable for small children
Disabled access difficult
Pets dogs may be accepted by prior arrangement
Closed part of winter
Proprietors Fred Brown and Gunn Eriksen

Highlands and Islands

Summer Isles

Mark and Geraldine Irvine run this very remote, cottagey hotel which has belonged to the family since the 1960s. The decorations and furnishings remain simple but satisfactory, the food wholesome and interesting (a different five-course set dinner is served each night), the views across Loch Broom and the Summer Isles themselves riveting.

The emphasis at Summer Isles is on eating well, sleeping well and relaxing in beautiful surroundings – 'there is a marvellous amount of nothing to do'.

Nearby walking, beaches, boat cruises.

Achiltibuie, by Ullapool, Ross-shire, Highland IV26 2YG
Tel (0185482) 622282
Location close to village post office; car parking
Food & drink full breakfast, lunch, dinner; full licence
Prices B&B £37-£71; dinner £36; reductions for 6 nights or more
Rooms 10 double, one single, two suites, all with bath; all rooms have central heating
Facilities dining-room, sitting-room, 2 bars, sun room; fishing
Credit cards MC, V
Children welcome over 6
Pets dogs allowed, but not in dining- or sitting-rooms
Closed mid-Oct to Easter
Proprietors Mark and Geraldine Irvine

Arisaig

Not to be confused with the much grander Arisaig House nearby, this lochside inn, set on the edge of Arisaig village, has been meeting the needs of travellers on the road to the isles for almost 200 years. Malcolm and Jacqueline Ross offer high standards of service, hospitality and an *à la carte* menu based on fresh local produce, with particular emphasis on fish and seafood, which comes in by boat. A wide range of beers and over sixty malt whiskies are offered in the bar.

Nearby Mallaig (for ferries to Skye); white sands of Morar. Cruises to Eigg, Rum and Muck in summer; 9-hole golf course.

Arisaig, Inverness-shire PH39 4NH
Tel (01687) 450210
Fax (01687) 450310
E-mail Arisaighotel@dial.pipex.com
Location 35 miles (56 km) W of Fort William, 10 miles (16 km) S of Mallaig on A830; with ample car parking
Food & drink breakfast, bar lunch, tea, dinner; full licence
Prices B&B £30-£35;
Rooms 9 double (3 twin), 6 with bath, 3 with shower; 2 single with shower; 2 family rooms, all rooms have radio, TV, tea/coffee kit, phone,
Facilities 2 bars, sitting-room, TV area **Credit cards** MC, V
Children welcome; playroom; cots, baby-listening **Disabled** access easy to public rooms
Pets dogs not in public rooms
Closed Christmas and Boxing Day **Proprietors** Malcolm and Jacqueline Ross

Highlands and Islands

Country house guest-house, by Banff

Eden House

Eden House is an elegant Grade II listed building with a fine portico and sweeping bay windows from which there are wide views of the surrounding countryside and the curling River Deveron in the valley below. The Sharps can arrange fishing on the river, as well as shooting, and there are some excellent golf courses within easy reach. The ambience is warm and relaxing and the friendly owners join their guests at the communal dining table, where Di serves traditional dishes often featuring salmon and raspberries in summer.

Nearby Duff House, Banff, 4 miles (6.5 km); Aberdeen 40 miles (64 km).

by Banff, Aberdeenshire AB45 3NT
Tel (01261) 821282
Fax (01261) 821283
Location off A947, 4 miles (6.5 km) S of Banff; in own grounds with ample parking
Food & drink breakfast, dinner; no licence; guests may bring their own wine
Prices B&B £36-£38; dinner £20 including a glass of wine
Rooms 3 double and twin, one family, all with bath or shower;

all rooms have central heating
Facilities sitting-room/library, drawing room, dining room, billiard room, drying rooms, garden, tennis court
Credit cards not accepted
Children welcome over 12
Disabled not suitable
Pets accepted, but not in bedrooms
Closed Christmas and New Year
Proprietors Anthony and Di Sharp

Inn, Colonsay

Isle of Colonsay Hotel

Colonsay is not one of the most remote Scottish isles, but it is nevertheless a two- to three-hour steamer trip from Oban. The island's old inn is a warmly civilized place set in its own large grounds. The Reysenn's took over in 1998 – Claude is a Masterchef from Belgium and makes good use of fresh, island produce for his daily changing four-course menus.

You can leave your car at Oban if you don't need one on the island. Bicycles are available, as well as sea and loch fishing, golf and sailing. Reports welcome.

Nearby Colonsay House gardens; walking, wildlife, fishing, golf.

Scalasaig, Isle of Colonsay, Argyll, Strathclyde PA61 7YP
Tel (01951) 200316 **Fax** (01951) 200353 **E-mail** colonsay.hotel@pipemedia.co.uk
Location on E coast of island; car parking **Food & drink** breakfast, bar lunch, high tea, dinner or bar supper; full licence **Prices** DB&B £50-£75; reductions for 1 week or more; for children sharing with parents **Rooms** 6 double,

all with shower; 3 single; 2 family rooms with bath and shower; all rooms have central heating, tea/coffee kit, phone, TV **Facilities** sitting-room, sun room, 2 bars **Credit cards** AE, MC, V **Children** welcome **Disabled** ground-floor rooms **Pets** dogs welcome; not in public rooms **Closed** Nov to Feb except 2 weeks at New Year **Proprietors** Claude and Christine Reysenn

Highlands and Islands

Kilcamb Lodge

'Beautifully situated, welcoming staff, a homely atmosphere, excellent food, large comfortable rooms with big beds, generous towels and thoughtful extras.' Thus a reader describes Kilcamb Lodge, a Georgian house with Victorian additions, which stands on the outskirts of Strontian at the head of Loch Sunart. The hotel's grounds, filled with azaleas and rhododendrons, run down to the water, from where there are fine views. 'Perfect peace – a haven to return to after a day's walking.' Self-catering two-bedroomed cottages are also available on a weekly basis. More reports please.
Nearby Fort William 22 miles (35 km).

Strontian, Argyll PH36 4HY
Tel (01967) 402257
Fax (01967) 402041
Location on outskirts of Strontian, off A861, 22 miles (35 km) SW of Fort William; in own grounds with ample parking
Food & drink breakfast, lunch, dinner; full licence
Prices DB&B £70-£100; room only £70-£100; dinner £29.50; cottage £500 per week
Rooms 11; 10 double/twin, 1 single, all with bath; all rooms have central heating, TV, hairdrier
Facilities drawing room, sitting room/bar, dining-room, garden
Credit cards MC,V
Children welcome
Disabled not suitable
Pets accepted by arrangement
Closed Dec to Feb (except New Year)
Proprietors Peter and Anne Blakeway

Bunchrew House

If you have one of the bedrooms with a sea view, you might be lucky enough to see an osprey swooping for salmon in the Beauly Firth, which laps at the garden wall of this pink sandstone turreted mansion, built in the 17thC. Log fires liven up the dark wood panelled bar and sitting-room. Dinner is a candlelit affair consisting of traditional dishes served in the rather formal dining-room. Bedrooms are large and comfortable.

As this edition went to press, we learned that Janet and Graham Cross had just taken over. Reports please.
Nearby fishing, shooting, golf; Cawdor Castle, 10 miles (16 km).

Bunchrew, Inverness IV3 8TA
Tel (01463) 234917
Fax (01463) 710620
Location in countryside, one mile (1.5 km) W of Inverness on A862; with gardens and ample car parking
Food & drink breakfast, lunch, dinner, snacks; full licence
Prices B&B £65-£150; lunch £15; dinner £25
Rooms 11 double, all with bath and shower; all rooms have central heating, phone, hairdrier, TV, minibar
Facilities drawing room, bar; salmon fishing
Credit cards AE, MC, V
Children welcome; baby-sitting available
Pets accepted by arrangement
Disabled access to restaurant only
Closed never
Proprietors Janet and Graham Cross

Highlands and Islands

Argyll Hotel

Fiona Menzies fell in love with the tiny remote island of Iona as a child and was able to take over the Argyll Hotel in 1977 – her husband runs the local pottery. The 19thC inn has upgraded all its bedrooms, mostly all now with *en suite* facilities, and has a dining-room wing. Set right on the shores of the island – its lawn runs down to the rocks and sand – the public rooms all have superb views over the Sound of Iona to Mull. Food is freshly prepared and satisfying; a meat or fish course and a vegetarian main dish are always offered. Cars are left on Mull.

Nearby Beaches; abbey, Heritage Centre; Fingal's cave.

Isle of Iona, Argyll PA76 6SJ
Tel (016817) 334
Location in village street, facing Sound of Iona; reached by ferry from Mull
Food & drink breakfast, lunch, tea, dinner; residential and restaurant licence
Prices B&B £43-£47; DB&B £58-£63; lunch £4-£9; dinner £20.50
Rooms 8 double, 8 with bath; 8 single, 6 with bath; 1 family rooms with bath; all have
tea/coffee kit, electric blankets
Facilities dining-room, 2 sitting-rooms, sun lounge, TV/conference lounge
Credit cards MC, V
Children welcome, and catered for
Disabled access difficult
Pets accepted, but not in restaurant
Closed mid-Oct to Easter
Proprietor Fiona Menzies

Osprey ★

This modest hotel without any grounds stands on a corner of the village street at a distance from the main road to Aviemore, so it is not too noisy. The sitting-room is small but welcoming, the bedrooms clean and cosy, decorated with light floral wallpapers and furnished in various styles. Like so many 'amateur' hoteliers in these pages, the Burrows, who have been running Osprey for seven years now, succeed in offering a warm informal welcome combined with excellent home-cooked meals, using local produce with vegetarian alternatives, served in the tiny dining-room.

Nearby Highland Folk Museum (in Kingussie).

Ruthven Road, Kingussie, Inverness-shire, Highland PH21 1EN
Tel & Fax (01540) 661510
Location in middle of village on A86; herb garden and parking for 10 cars
Food & drink breakfast, packed lunch, dinner; full licence
Prices B&B £24-£39; DB&B £42-£59
Rooms 7 double, 3 with bath
and shower, 4 with shower; one single with shower; all have central heating , TV, hairdrier **Facilities** 2 sitting-rooms (1 well stocked with wine and spirits), dining-room
Credit cards AE, DC, MC, V
Children welcome **Disabled** wheelchair access difficult; 2 ground-floor rooms **Pets** dogs by arrangement **Closed** never
Proprietor Robert and Aileen Burrow

Highlands and Islands

The Cross

Ruth Hadley's inspired cooking had long made her award-winning restaurant with rooms in Kingussie a must for gourmets. In a secluded four-acre waterside setting, down a private drive, The Cross is in a former nineteenth century tweed mill which the Hadleys converted five years ago. Rough stone walls and heavy beams have been retained to create a Nordic and rustic look, and there is an attractive riverside terrace. No smoking is permitted in the dining-room or bedrooms. There is a wide choice of healthy, home-baked food at breakfast.

Nearby Highland Folk Museum; Highland Wildlife Park

Tweed Mill Brae, Kingussie, Inverness-shire, Highland PH21 1TC
Tel (01540) 661166
Fax (01540) 661080
Location off the Ardbroilach Road, close to town centre; ample parking
Food & drink breakfast, dinner; restaurant and residential licence
Prices DB&B £85-£105; dinner £35
Rooms 7 double, 2 twin, all with bath, 6 also with shower; all rooms have central heating, phone, hairdrier; TV and radio on request
Facilities 2 sitting-rooms
Credit cards MC, V
Children welcome over 12
Disabled access to restaurant
Pets not accepted
Closed 8 Jan to 28 Feb; 1 to 26 Dec; restaurant only, Tue eve
Proprietors Tony and Ruth Hadley

Baile-na-Cille

Discovered in a ruinous state by the Gollins who have been here for more than twenty years, this beautifully set 18thC manse has been lovingly restored, and the adjacent stables converted into light, pretty rooms. Many discarded antiques were restored and given new life in this friendly, relaxed guest-house. The home-cooked meals, which include freshly baked bread, are served around communal tables in a lofty dining-room. It is essential to book well ahead. There are plenty of outdoor activities in the area, and there is now a new tennis court in the village.

Nearby walking, climbing, birdwatching, fishing.

Timsgarry, Uig, Isle of Lewis, Outer Hebrides PA86 9JD
Tel (01851) 672242
Fax (01851) 672241
E-mail RandJGollin@compuserve.com
Location 32 miles (51 km) W of Stornaway, close to end of B8011, in countryside, with ample car parking
Food & drink full breakfast, dinner, packed lunch; residential licence
Prices B&B £24-£39; dinner £24; children in bunk bed £12 including supper **Rooms** 9 double, 7 with bath; 3 single; 2 family rooms; all rooms have storage heater /radiator
Facilities 3 sitting-rooms, dining-room, TV room; boat trips
Credit cards MC, V **Children** welcome; playroom **Disabled** unsuitable **Pets** welcome
Closed 5th Oct to 5th Mar (not cottages) **Proprietors** Richard and Joanna Gollin

Highlands and Islands

Ardfenaig House

Originally the Duke of Argyll's factor's house, Ardfenaig was expanded as a shooting lodge before its conversion into a hotel, in the hands of the Davidsons since 1991. The house, with panoramic views from the conservatory, stands at the head of a narrow sea-loch, its lawns stretching down towards the water; in the other direction leading off into splendid moorland. Furnishings are traditional and comfortable; the lighter loch-view rooms naturally have an edge. Jane cooks satisfying dinners using local produce and home-grown vegetables. Self-catering in the Coach House.
Nearby walking, beaches; islands of Iona and Staffa.

By Bunessan, Isle of Mull, Argyll PA67 6DX
Tel & fax (01681) 700210
Location on A849 between Bunessan and Fionnphort; with 15-acre grounds and ample car parking
Food & drink breakfast, dinner; residential and restaurant licence
Prices DB&B £78-£92; reductions for 2 nights or more; Coach House £360-£520 per week

Rooms 5 double (3 twin), all with bath; all rooms have central heating
Facilities conservatory dining-room, 2 sitting-rooms; croquet, sailing **Credit cards** MC, V **Children** welcome, over 12 **Disabled** access easy but no ground-floor bedrooms
Pets welcome, but not in house **Closed** Nov to Mar, except by arrangement
Proprietors Malcolm and Jane Davidson

The Tobermory Hotel

This long-established guest-house, set on the waterfront on Tobermory Bay, was relaunched as a hotel in 1985, and the Suttons arrived in 1990. Extensive refurbishment and decoration of the bedrooms and bathrooms has taken place. The house is pretty as well as comfortable.

There is a proper emphasis on quality ingredients in the cooking (seafood is the speciality – lobsters and oysters), making use of wild salmon, venison, Scottish beef and lamb; vegetarian dishes are also available. Wide selection of single malt whiskies.
Nearby walking, golf, fishing, sailing; beaches.

53 Main Street, Tobermory, Isle of Mull, Argyll, Strathclyde PA75 6NT
Tel (01688) 302091
Fax (01688) 302254
Location ample car parking on street and quayside
Food & drink full breakfast, dinner; fully licenced
Prices DB&B £58.50-£68.50; reductions for children sharing parents' room; 2-day breaks

Rooms 12 double, 2 single, 2 family rooms, all en suite; all rooms have tea/coffee kit, phone
Facilities 2 sitting-rooms (one with TV), dining-room
Credit cards MC, V
Children welcome
Disabled access easy to public rooms and 2 ground-floor bedrooms **Pets** not accepted
Closed Christmas **Proprietors** Kay and Martin Sutton

Highlands and Islands

Auchnahyle Farmhouse

This is a small, secluded 18thC farmhouse in large gardens and within walking distance of the popular tourist town of Pitlochry where the Howmans have been taking guests since 1982. Game and sheep are reared on the farm and there are several family pets. Rooms in the main house are simple and comfortable – there is also a stone cottage across the courtyard suitable for families. Penny Howman's satisfying four-course dinners are served by candle-light – since there is no licence, you are welcome to bring your own wine.

Nearby Falls of Tummel; Blair Castle; Pitlochry Festival Theatre.

Pitlochry, Perthshire PH16 5JA
Tel (01796) 472318
Fax (01796) 473657
Location on E edge of town, towards Moulin; ample car parking
Food & drink full breakfast, picnic lunch, dinner; no licence
Prices B&B £32-£36; dinner £21
Rooms 3 double (twin), all with bath; family cottage available; all rooms have central heating, tea/coffee kit, TV
Facilities sitting-room with TV, conservatory
Credit cards MC, V
Children welcome over 12
Disabled access good – one ground-floor bedroom
Pets well-behaved dogs welcome
Closed Christmas and New Year
Proprietors Alastair and Penny Howman

Burrastow House

The good news from this remotely located guest-house, with a simple, honest style, is that an extension for more bedrooms has replaced the barn. It also houses the dining-room/conservatory, and has a kitchen for guests who come for the workshops, including painting, writing, music and massage.

Burrastow, a calm, solid, stone house set in its own spacious grounds, is located on a rocky shore, reached down a long, single-track road.

Nearby walking, swimming, boating, birdwatching, fishing.

Walls, Shetland lslands ZE2 9PD
Tel (01595) 809307
Fax (01595) 809213
Location 2 miles (3 km) W of Walls; ample car park
Food & drink breakfast, high tea; dinner, restaurant licence
Prices DB&B £80; reduction for 4 nights or more; spring weekend breaks; big reductions for children
Rooms 3 double en suite, 1 with 4-poster, 1 with half-tester bed; 2 twin en suite; all rooms have central heating, hair-drier, tea/coffee kit; TV on request **Facilities** dining-room, 2 sitting-rooms; dinghy, fishing **Credit cards** AE, MC, V
Children welcome
Disabled access easy to barn extension **Pets** dogs accepted, but not in public rooms
Closed Oct to end Feb
Proprietor Bo Simmons

Highlands and Islands

Ardvasar Hotel

When we last inspected we gave it low marks for welcome. Some exterior paint was peeling and our reporter thought the furnishing 'utilitarian'. However, its reputation for good food is confirmed by locals, and re-decoration has now spruced up this busy 18thC Highland coaching inn.

It is solid and low-built, with wonderful views across the Sound of Sleat (pronounced 'Slate'). So we continue to recommend it as a useful address on Skye, with fair prices charged for accommodation and food..

Nearby Clan Donald Centre, 1 mile (1.5 km).

Ardvasar, Sleat, Isle of Skye, Highland, IV45 8RS
Tel (01471) 844223
Location in tiny village, 0.5 miles (one km) SW of Armadale ferry; on roadside, with parking for 30 cars
Food & drink breakfast bar, lunch and supper, fixed-menu dinner, bar meals; full licence
Prices B&B £29-£35; dinner from £13
Rooms 9 double, 7 with bath, 2 with shower; one single with shower; all rooms have phone, TV, tea/coffee kit
Facilities sitting-room, TV room, two bars, dining-room
Credit cards AE, MC, V
Children welcome
Disabled access easy to public rooms but not to bedrooms
Pets well-behaved dogs accepted; not in public rooms
Closed Nov to Mar
Proprietors Bill and Gretta Fowler

Flodigarry Country House Hotel

An ungainly 19thC mansion house with modern additions, built by a descendant of Flora Macdonald, and converted to a hotel in the 1920s. The low adjacent cottage, now housing seven of the hotel's bedrooms, was the marital home of Flora, where she settled with her husband five years after helping Bonny Prince Charlie to escape after his defeat at Culloden. Views are spectacular, with the pinnacles of the Quiraing above and vistas of the distant mountains of Gairloch on the mainland. Inside, the hotel is traditional in style, with log fires, and has a quiet, informal atmosphere.

Nearby Staffin, 3 miles (4.5 km); Portree 24 miles (38 km)..

Staffin, Isle of Skye, IV51 9HZ
Tel (0147) 055 2203
Fax (0147) 055 2301
Location on the north-east coast of Skye, in 5 acres of woodland grounds with ample car parking; courtesy car for those arriving by train or ferry
Food & drink breakfast, lunch, dinner; full licence
Prices B&B £42-£80; dinner from £24.50
Rooms in hotel: 11 double, 2 with shower, 1 with hip bath; 1 single with shower; all rooms have central heating, phone, radio, tea/coffee kit. Cottage: 7 double, 6 with bath, 1 with shower **Facilities** conservatory, bar, lounge, dining-room
Credit cards MC, V **Children** welcome **Disabled** 1 specially adapted room in cottage **Pets** well behaved dogs **Closed** never **Proprietors** Andrew and Pam Butler

Highlands and Islands

Country guest-house, Ullapool

Ceilidh Place

A 'ceilidh' (pronounced kaylee) is a sort of impromptu gathering – an evening of music, song, dance and story-telling; and the name gives a clue to the vitality of this friendly 'hotel'. Started by the late actor, Robert Urquhart in 1970 as a coffee shop in a shed, it spread into adjacent cottages to provide bedrooms, and then into other 'clubhouse' buildings nearby, where there is a bookshop, gallery and a venue for some of Scotland's finest musicians, singers, actors and dancers. Simple, comfortable rooms with plenty of pictures, wholesome cooking, and 'no telly, no teasmaids'.
Nearby mountains; walks.

West Argyle Street, Ullapool, Wester Ross, Highland IV26 2TY
Tel (01854) 612103
Fax (01854) 612886
E-mail reception@ceilidh.demon.co.uk
Location in middle of village; 0.5-acre garden with parking for 25 cars
Food & drink breakfast, lunch, all day buffet, dinner; full licence
Prices B&B £22-£55; dinner from £16; reductions for 5 nights or more
Rooms 10 double, 8 with bath; 3 single, 2 with bath; 11 family rooms (bunk beds); all rooms have central heating
Facilities sitting-room, bar, coffee shop, dining-room
Credit cards AE, DC, MC, V
Children welcome
Disabled access difficult
Pets welcome, but not in public rooms
Closed never
Proprietor Jean Urquhart

Country house hotel, Whitebridge

Knockie Lodge

Since taking over in 1997, recent owners Louise Dawson and Nicholas Bean have added three new bathrooms and refurbished bedrooms at this two-hundred-year-old shooting-lodge with a romantic setting in open countryside overlooking Loch nan Lann. While adding to the comfort of Knockie Lodge, their intention is to retain the welcoming atmosphere created by its former owners, the Millwards. Dinner is a set meal of five courses from the Dorchester-and-Savoy trained chef.

Ideal for hill walking, bird watching, and sporting pursuits.
Nearby Loch Ness.

Whitebridge, Inverness, Highland IV1 2UP
Tel (01456) 486276
Fax (01456) 486389
Location 8 miles (13 km) NE of Fort Augustus on B862; ample car parking
Food & drink breakfast, bar lunch, dinner; residential licence
Prices B&B £50-£60
Rooms 8 double, all with bath, 4 also with shower; 2 single, both with bath; all rooms have central heating
Facilities sitting-room with bar, dining-room, billiard-room; fishing
Credit cards AE, DC, MC, V
Children welcome over 10
Disabled access difficult
Pets dogs accepted, by prior arrangement
Closed Nov to Apr
Proprietors Louise Dawson and Nicholas Bean

Irish Republic

Converted farmhouse, Aglish

Ballycormac House

Set amid north Tipperary farmland, almost exactly in the middle of Ireland, this is a 300-year-old-farmhouse which has long been well known as a guest house, but which was taken over from the previous occupants in 1994 by an energetic American couple, Herbert and Christine Quigley. They cater to guests who simply wish to relax, or small groups who want to take advantage of their specialist holidays based on riding, fox hunting, golfing, fishing and shooting. Bookings for outdoor activities can be tailor-made to suit individual requirements.

Since their arrival, Herb and Christine have painstakingly upgraded the pretty but compact house, Ballycormac, creating a warm and cosy retreat. There are log fires in winter, and in summer guests can see the organic herb, fruit and vegetable gardens which provide produce for meals. And this is where the Quigleys' real prowess lies: in the kitchen. Herb is a superb baker, and so breakfast might feature traditional Irish soda bread, or his own version of *pain au chocolat*, chocolate cherry soda bread, while dinner at the communal table might be accompanied by anything from homemade Swedish limpa to Indian naan. One delicious meal featured roast rack of lamb, a tart of carrot and Swiss chard and a delicious gratin of potato and goat's cheese.

Nearby Terryglass; 3 miles (4.5 km); Birr, 7 miles (11 km).

Aglish, Borrisokane, Co Tipperary **Tel** (067) 21129 **Fax** (067) 21200 **Location** in 2 acres of gardens, 0.5 mile (one km) north of Borrisokane, signposted on right; ample car parking **Food & drink** breakfast, picnic lunch on request, dinner; wine licence **Prices** B&B £35-£40; dinner weekdays £20, weekends £24	**Rooms** 3 double, 1 suite, 1 single, all with bath; all rooms have central heating **Facilities** sitting-room, dining-room; garden **Credit cards** MC, V **Children** welcome over 6 years **Disabled** access difficult **Pets** accepted but not in rooms; lodging available **Closed** never **Proprietors** Herbert and Christine Quigley

Irish Republic

Country house hotel, Ballinderry

Gurthalougha House

By the time you reach the end of the mile-long drive which twists and turns through the forest on the way to this hotel beside Lough Derg, it is easy to believe that you have travelled back to an altogether more peaceful and graceful era. Sadly, Michael and Bessie Wilkinson are leaving Gurthalougha House, after seventeen years here, but with assurances that the civilized and serene atmosphere they created will be retained by new owner, Anne Pettit.

The spacious high-ceilinged public rooms have plenty of pictures and antiques, but the search for style has not got in the way of comfort. The long, well-lit sitting-room, with its two open fireplaces and big cosy armchairs, is notably relaxed, while the enormous panelled library has a substantial collection of books about the locality. This restraint continues through into the bedrooms, which are spacious and carefully (though fairly sparsely) furnished, with no modern trimmings.

A set menu each evening, which may include locally-caught pike and smoked eel. A recent visitor praised the food, and we welcome further reports.

Nearby Birr Castle gardens, 12 miles (19 km); Limerick.

Ballinderry, Nenagh, Co Tipperary
Tel (067) 22080
Fax (067) 22154
Location just W of village, 10 miles (16 km) N of Nenagh off L152; in 100- acre woodland on lakeside, with ample car parking
Food & drink full breakfast, dinner, snack (or packed) lunch; wine licence (though other drinks available)
Prices B&B IR£32-IR£38; dinner IR£15; bargain breaks
Rooms 8 double, 6 with bath, 2 with shower; all rooms have central heating, phone
Facilities dining-room, sitting-room, library; table tennis, croquet, tennis, rowing-boats.
Credit cards AE, MC, V
Children accepted, if well behaved; high tea available
Disabled access not easy – 2 sets of steps on ground floor
Pets accepted if well behaved
Closed Christmas, Feb
Proprietors Anne Pettit

Irish Republic

Country hotel, Ballylickey

Sea View House

Kathleen O'Sullivan grew up in this white Victorian house a stone's throw from Ballylickey bay. In 1978 she turned it into a successful small hotel. Her plan for an extension to give double the number of rooms, was finally realized in 1990. 'Kathleen is a *delightful* hostess,' writes a recent reporter, and Sea View really is a 'very nice, quiet comfortable hotel'.

The new bedrooms are all similar in style, beautifully decorated in pastel colours and floral fabrics with stunning antique furniture – especially the bed-heads and wardrobes, and matching 3-piece suites, collected or inherited from around the Cork area. The rooms in the old part of the house are more irregular and individual. All front rooms have large bay windows and views of the garden and sea (through the trees). The 'Garden Suite' downstairs is especially adapted for wheelchairs.

There are two sitting-rooms – a cosy front room adjoining the bar and a large family room at the back. The dining-room has also been extended (though many regular guests do not believe it). Our reporter thought the food 'excellent and generous'; breakfast was 'wonderful' with a big choice and traditional Irish dishes, such as potato cakes. The menu changes daily, and Kathleen is forever experimenting with new dishes – roast smoked pheasant on the day we visited.

Nearby Bantry, 3 miles (5 km); Beira Peninsula; Ring of Kerry.

Ballylickey, Bantry, Co Cork
Tel (027) 50073
Fax (027) 51555
Location in countryside, just off N71, 3 miles (5 km) N of Bantry; in large grounds with ample car parking
Food & drink breakfast, lunch (Sun only), dinner; full licence
Prices B&B IR£40-IR£55; dinner IR£23.50; reductions for children sharing, and for stays of 3 or 7 days
Rooms 14 double, 13 with bath, one with shower; 3 family rooms, all with bath; all rooms have central heating, phone, TV, hairdrier
Facilities 2 dining-rooms, sitting-room, TV room, bar
Credit cards AE, MC, V
Children welcome; baby-sitting
Disabled access easy – one ground-floor adapted room
Pets dogs accepted in bedrooms only
Closed Nov to Mar
Proprietor Kathleen O'Sullivan

Irish Republic

Country hotel, Caragh Lake

Caragh Lodge

An excellent response to this comfortable house from a recent visitor: 'Full of warmth, and a marvellously peaceful setting' on the edge of Caragh Lake. The 100-year-old house is furnished with antiques and log fires, it has a 300-yard lake frontage, and there are nine acres of parkland with a fine planting of rare and sub-tropical shrubs. You get views of some of Ireland's highest mountains, abundant facilities for relaxation, quick access to the sea and glorious sandy beaches: a heady combination attractive to a great many holidaymakers (including golfers) – so much so that seven new rooms have been built to satisfy demand.

Mary Gaunt, described by our reporter as 'lively and fun', took over in 1989. She thoroughly redecorated the public rooms, bedrooms and the previously rather drab annexe rooms, and has achieved some impressive results. As a result, the hotel is now a happy combination of elegance and informality. Mary's excellent cooking – featuring seafood, wild salmon and local lamb – has earned high praise from recent visitors.

Nearby Killarney, 15 miles (24 km); Ring of Kerry.

Caragh Lake, Co Kerry
Tel (066) 9769115
Fax (066) 9769316
E-mail caraghl@IOL.IE
Location 22 miles (35 km) NW of Killarney, one mile (1.5 km) off Ring of Kerry road, W of Killorglin; in 9-acre gardens and parkland, with ample car parking
Food & drink full breakfast, dinner; restaurant licence
Prices B&B IR£49.50-IR£66; suite £99; dinner IR£29.70

Rooms 13 double, 1 single, 1 suite; all with bath; all rooms have central heating
Facilities 2 sitting-rooms, dining-room; tennis, swimming in lake, fishing, boating, sauna, bicycles
Credit cards AE, MC, V
Children welcome over 7
Disabled access easy – some ground-floor bedrooms
Pets not accepted
Closed mid-Oct to Easter
Proprietor Mary Gaunt

Irish Republic

Restaurant with rooms, Dingle

Doyle's Seafood Restaurant

'Most attractive and unexpected,' says one of our most experienced inspectors. 'A charming homey feeling – they give you your own door key.' It is in fact a delightful small hotel in the middle of a quaint fishing village on the Dingle Peninsula. The visitors' book perches on an antique writing-desk in the elegant sitting-room; it drips with superlatives, and rightly so.

Sean and Charlotte Cluskey have recently taken over from the Doyles, who originally gave their name to the place over two decades ago when they moved to this wild and lovely corner of Kerry. Eight spacious bedrooms and a sitting-room were added next door to the restaurant when the neighbouring house came on the market. The bedrooms are all beautifully decorated: the four back rooms have balconies looking over the tiny garden, and the two downstairs rooms (suitable for disabled guests) open on to it. Fresh flowers and potted plants abound throughout.

The restaurant is as popular and cosmopolitan as ever, and it is easy to see why. The menu is mainly, but not exclusively, fishy, and changes with the seasons. By all accounts the food really is superb, and pretty good value, too. We welcome more reports.

Nearby Dingle Peninsula, Ring of Kerry (beaches, historical sites.

John St, Dingle, Co Kerry
Tel (066) 51174
Fax (066) 51816
Location just off main street of town; with small garden and on-street parking
Food & drink breakfast, lunch, dinner; full licence
Prices B&B IR£38-IR£40; dinner IR£21
Rooms 8 double, all with bath; all rooms have central heating, phone, TV, hairdrier, radio
Facilities dining-room, sitting-room
Credit cards DC, MC, V
Children welcome; babysitting by arrangement
Disabled 2 ground-floor bedrooms
Pets not accepted
Closed mid-Nov to mid-Mar
Proprietors Sean and Charlotte Cluskey

Irish Republic

Innishannon House

Conal O'Sullivan returned to his Irish roots in 1989 when he and his wife Vera moved to this attractive, imposing 18thC house on the banks of the Bandon river. The couple are seasoned hoteliers and travellers, having run hotels all over the world (their last stop the Carribean) but they are particularly excited at this latest challenge.

The hotel has already become a welcoming haven for visitors, its comfortable, attractive rooms hung with the O'Sullivans' extensive collection of modern art (including two possible Gauguins in the dining-room). Vera has a great eye for interior design, and has decorated all the bedrooms with infinite care and flair – number 16 is a cosy attic room with an antique bedspread, number 14 a fascinating circular room with small round windows and a huge curtained bed – Irish hero, Michael Collins' bath is the latest addition to the antiques around the hotel – to join that of Winston Churchill. The enormous suite has a Victorian bathroom.

The O'Sullivan's son, Pearse, does the cooking, with emphasis on seafood, lobster and seasonal produce. Dinner in the lovely pink dining-room is a gastronomic delight. Pre-dinner drinks are served outside in summer, or in the airy lounge, or cosy bar – full of photos of Conal's car rallying days. Innishannon is not the last word in seclusion or intimacy; there are facilities for conferences and wedding receptions.

Nearby Kinsale, 7 miles (11 km); Cork, 15 miles (24 km).

Innishannon, Cork
Tel (021) 775121 **Fax** 775609
Location on banks of river, near village; with gardens and car parking
Food & drink breakfast, lunch, dinner, snacks
Prices B&B IR£50-IR£95; dinner from IR£25; weekly and off-season reductions
Rooms 13 double, 1 suite, all with bath and shower; all rooms have central heating, phone, TV, hairdrier
Facilities dining-room, sitting-room, bar, terrace; fishing, boating
Credit cards AF, DC, MC, V
Children welcome
Disabled ground floor suite
Pets accepted in bedrooms only **Closed** mid-Jan to mid-Mar **Proprietors** Conal and Vera O'Sullivan

Irish Republic

Country house hotel, Kanturk

Assolas Country House

This historic, mellow country house, in a fairy-tale setting of award-winning gardens beside a slow-flowing river, has been in the Bourke family since the early years of this century. The familiar story of escalating maintenance costs and dwindling bank balances led to their taking in guests in 1966, and since then they have never looked back. Assolas is still their family home, and the business of sharing it has obviously turned out to be a pleasure. One recent visitor described her stay there as 'stunning, with wonderful, beautifully served food'.

The house was built around 1590, and had unusual circular extensions added at two corners in Queen Anne's time; beyond the expanses of lawn are mature woods, and then hills and farmland. Inside, the public rooms are richly decorated and elegantly furnished, almost entirely with antiques, and immaculately kept. The bedrooms are notably spacious and many have large luxury bathrooms – the 'circular' rooms at the corners of the house are particularly impressive. Three of the rooms are in a renovated stone building in the courtyard. The food, prepared by Hazel Bourke, is in what might be called modern Irish style – country cooking of fresh ingredients (many home-grown). **Nearby** Killarney (Ring of Kerry), Limerick, Blarney.

Kanturk, Co Cork
Tel (029) 50015
Fax (029) 50795
E-mail assolas@tinet.ie
Location 12 miles (19 km) W of Mallow, NE of Kanturk, signposted from N72; in extensive gardens with ample car parking
Food & drink full breakfast, light or packed lunch, dinner; full licence
Prices B&B IR£55-IR£84; dinner £32; reductions for children under 12 sharing
Rooms 9 double/family rooms, all with bath and shower; all rooms have central heating, phone
Facilities sitting-room, dining-room; fishing, tennis, boating, croquet **Credit cards** AE, DC, MC, V **Children** welcome
Disabled access fair **Pets** welcome, but must stay in stables
Closed Nov to Apr (except by prior arrangement)
Proprietors Bourke family

Irish Republic

Roundwood House

A recent reporter reacted very well to the Kennans' operation. The house is 'not in perfect repair, but for the type of place they run, this didn't seem to matter': it's a 'wonderful place, and the Kennans really are charming and informal hosts'.

The perfectly proportioned Palladian mansion is set in acres of lime, beech and chestnut woodland. The Kennans have whole-heartedly continued the work of the Irish Georgian Society, who rescued the house from near-ruin in the 1970s. All the Georgian trappings remain – bold paintwork, shutters instead of curtains, rugs instead of fitted carpets, and emphatically no TV. Despite this, the house is decidedly lived in, certainly not a museum.

For Rosemarie's plentiful meals, non-residents sit at separate tables; residents must sit together – you don't have a choice – fine if you like to chat to strangers, not ideal for romantic twosomes. After-dinner conversation is also encouraged over coffee and drinks by the open fire in the drawing-room. You may well find the Kennans joining in.

Four pleasant extra bedrooms in a recently converted stable block are perhaps cosier and of a better standard than those in the main house. It's very child-friendly (the Kennans have six), with a lovely big playroom at the top of the house, full of toys.

Nearby walking, horse-riding, fishing; Slieve Bloom mountains.

Mountrath, Co Laois	**Rooms** 7 double (3 twin),
Tel (0502) 32120	2 family rooms, all with bath;
Fax (0502) 32711	all rooms have central heating
Location in countryside, 3	**Facilities** sitting-room, study,
miles (5 km) N of Mountrath	dining-room, hall; croquet
on Kinnitty road; with gardens	**Credit Cards** AE, DC, MC, V
and ample car parking	**Children** very welcome
Food & drink full breakfast,	**Pets** accepted by arrangement
dinner, lunch on Sunday only;	**Disabled** not suitable
wine licence	**Closed** Christmas Day
Prices B&B IR£41-IR£51;	**Proprietors** Frank and
dinner IR£23; Sunday lunch	Rosemarie Kennan
IR£12	

Irish Republic

Country guest-house, Moyard

Crocnaraw

We were somewhat unsure about promoting Crocnaraw to a full page in 1997's expanded edition. Either you will love it, or you will wish you had gone elsewhere. One of our most experienced reporters thought it was wonderful, despite some obvious areas of disrepair – or perhaps because of them. She felt that the place had a great deal of the special quality we look for.

At the same time, we have also received letters from readers who are severely critical of the housekeeping, and who consider Crocnaraw to be poor value for money.

Crocnaraw is certainly the antithesis of the glossy hotel: white is the dominant colour theme, but it is very imaginatively decorated with local 'tweed, rugs, cushions and so on, in gentle colours, with some antique pieces and some modern pieces, wooden and slate floors'. The long, low Georgian building is set on a small hill-top in lush, prize-winning gardens.

The food is 'definitely above average for an Irish hotel', 'imaginative without being fussy'; proper attention is given to breakfast. Lucy Fretwell makes a 'vague but charming hostess'. Come here if you want a 'special atmosphere and a truly peaceful, wonderfully relaxed retreat'. If you want something more conventional in this area, see Rosleague Manor (page 232). Reports welcome.
Nearby Kylemore Abbey, 5 miles (8 km); Joyce Country.

Moyard, Connemara, Co Galway
Tel (095) 41068
Location 6 miles (10 km) N of Clifden, on shores of Ballinakill Bay; in 20-acre grounds, with ample parking
Food & drink full breakfast, lunch, dinner; full licence
Prices B&B IR£25-IR£45; dinner IR£20; reduced DB&B rates for 3 or 7 nights
Rooms 6 double with bath, one also with shower; 2 single; all rooms have central heating
Facilities 2 sitting-rooms, dining-room; fishing, riding and golf nearby
Credit cards AE, DC, MC, V
Children accepted by arrangement **Disabled** access easy to one ground- floor bedroom **Pets** dogs welcome except in dining- room
Closed Nov to Apr
Proprietor Lucy Fretwell

Irish Republic

Coopershill

Brian O'Hara has been running this delightful country house with his wife, Lindy, for the past twelve years now, and has subtly improved the style of the place without interfering with its essential appeal.

It is a fine house – though some may not think it elegant by Georgian standards – with splendidly large rooms (including the bedrooms, most of which have four-poster or canopy beds). It is furnished virtually throughout with antiques; but remains emphatically a home, with no hotel-like formality – and there is the unusual bonus of a table-tennis room to keep children amused.

The grounds are extensive enough not only to afford complete seclusion, but also to accommodate a river on which there is boating and fishing for pike and trout.

Lindy cooks honest country dinners based on English and Irish dishes, entirely in harmony with the nature of the place, while Brian knowledgeably organizes the cellar.

Nearby Sligo, 12 miles (20 km); Lough Arrow, Lough Gara.

Riverstown, Co Sligo
Tel (071) 65108 **Fax** 65466
Location 1 mile (1.5 km) W of Riverstown, off N4 Dublin-Sligo road; in large garden on 500-acre estate, with ample car parking
Food & drink full breakfast, dinner, light or packed lunch; restaurant licence
Prices B&B IR£50-IR£67; dinner IR£26; reductions for 3 or more nights; 75% reduction for children under 12 sharing with parents
Rooms 8 double, 6 with bath, one with separate bath, one with shower; one family room with bath; all rooms have tea/coffee kit
Facilities sitting-room, dining-room; boating, fishing, tennis **Credit cards** AE, DC, MC, V
Children welcome if well behaved **Disabled** no access
Pets welcome if well behaved, but not allowed in public rooms or bedrooms
Closed Nov to end Mar
Proprietors Brian and Lindy O'Hara

Irish Republic

Country house hotel, Shanagarry

Ballymaloe House

Thirty bedrooms normally rules out a hotel for this guide, but we can not resist this amiable, rambling, creeper-clad house – largely Georgian in appearance but incorporating the remains of a 14thC castle keep – set in rolling green countryside. Visitors in 1998 were 'immensely impressed' and found the staff 'as well-drilled as an army, but jolly, with abundant charm'.

The Allens, who have been farming here for over 40 years, opened as a restaurant in 1964 and started offering rooms three years later. Since then they have added more facilities and more rooms – those in the main house now outnumbered by those in extensions and converted out-buildings.

Despite quite elegant and sophisticated furnishings, the Allens have always managed to preserve intact the warmth and natural-ness of a much-loved family home. But not all visitors agree: one reporter judged that Ballymaloe was becoming rather commer-cialized. Even that reporter, however, was impressed by the stan-dard of food. Mrs Allen no longer takes an active role in the cooking. It is now Rory O'Connell who prepares the Classic French and Irish dishes alongside original dishes, all based on home produce and fish fresh from the local quays. (Sunday din-ner is always a buffet.) Just as much care is lavished on breakfast, and the famous children's high tea.

Nearby Beaches, cliff walks, fishing, golf.

Shanagarry, Midleton,
Co Cork
Tel (021) 652531 **Fax** 652021
Location 20 miles (32 km) E of Cork, 2 miles (3 km) E of Cloyne on the Ballycotton road, L35
Food & drink breakfast, lunch, dinner; full licence
Prices B&B IR£60-IR£100; dinner IR£34.50; bargain breaks Nov to mid-Mar
Rooms 32 double, 30 with bath, 2 with shower; 1 single, one with bath; one family room; all have central heating, phone **Facilities** 3 sitting-rooms, conference/TV room, conservatory, library; tennis, golf, heated outdoor swimming-pool (summer)
Credit cards AE, DC, MC, V
Children welcome; high tea provided
Disabled access easy; some rooms built for wheelchairs
Pets tolerated – not in bed-rooms/public rooms
Closed over Christmas
Proprietors I and M Allen

Irish Republic

Gregans Castle

We inspected in 1996 and were impressed with every aspect of Peter and Moira Haden's impeccable and civilized hotel. Bedrooms range from relatively simple to distinctly sumptuous, with lots of space and fine views of the Burren mountains and Galway bay. Pictures of local flora adorn the walls of the cosy, book-filled sitting-room; armchairs, antiques and an open fireplace grace the central hall. The dining-room, with fine views of Galway Bay, has been elegantly and subtly extended; the food is adventurous and satisfying.

Nearby The Burren; Cliffs of Moher, 14 miles (22 km).

Ballyvaughan, Co Clare
Tel (065) 77005
Fax (065) 77111
Location 3.5 miles (5.5 km south of Ballyvaughan, on N67, in open countryside; in large gardens, with ample car parking
Food & drink full breakfast, lunch, dinner; full licence
Prices B&B IR£49-IR£95; DB&B IR£83-IR£129; reduced rates for longer stays
Rooms 18 double, all with bath; 4 suites with bath and sitting-room; all rooms have central heating, hairdrier
Facilities 2 sitting-rooms (one with TV), bar, dining-room
Credit cards MC, V
Children accepted
Disabled access easy – 7 ground-floor rooms
Pets not accepted
Closed Nov to Feb
Proprietors Peter, Moira and Simon-Peter Haden

Cashel House

Despite its size, this immaculate white-painted Victorian establishment, with its own beach and set in 50 acres of luxuriant and exotic gardens on the southern finger of Connemara, has the feel of a comfortable and relaxed country house. The antique-laden sitting-rooms are notably cosy, the greatly extended dining-room has been redecorated and the bar is entirely done out in leather. Some of the bedrooms are quite palatial. Food is based on fresh, local ingredients – lobsters, clams, scallops and Connemara lamb.

Nearby Kylemore Abbey, 21 miles (35 km); Clifden, 12 miles (19 km); Lough Corrib; Connemara National Park.

Cashel, Connemara, Co Galway
Tel (095) 31001 **Fax** 31077
Location 42 miles (67 km) W of Galway, 3 miles (5 km) S off N59; ample car parking
Food & drink breakfast, snack lunch, dinner; full licence
Prices B&B IR£54-IR£80; dinner IR£32-IR£34 (12.5% service charge)
Rooms 16 double, 3 single, 13 mini-suites; all with bath and shower; all have central heating, phone, hairdrier, TV
Facilities 2 sitting-rooms, TV room, library, bar, dining-room; tennis, boat, horse-riding **Credit cards** AE, DC, MC, V **Children** over 5 **Disabled** access easy; several ground-floor bedrooms **Pets** not accepted in public rooms
Closed 4 Jan to 4 Feb
Proprietors Dermot and Kay McEvilly

Irish Republic

Actons

The building is a modern one: long, white-walled, grey-roofed, in a stunning setting overlooking its own private beach, with nothing in front of it except for grass, sand, sea and sky. Readers have told us of the warm welcome they have received here from owners Rita and Martin Acton, of the high standards of housekeeping and the comfort of the bedrooms. These are fairly plain, with modern furnishings and pretty bedspreads. The dining-room is set in the large central bay of the house, with sea views through windows on three sides. Fish and seafood is the speciality; excellent puddings.

Nearby Clifden; Connemara National Park; Kylemore Abbey.

Leegaun, Claddaghduff, Co. Galway
Tel (095) 44339
Fax (095) 44309
Location on N59 Galway to Clifden road; in 15 acres of private land, with ample parking
Meals breakfast, picnic lunch on request, dinner; full licence
Prices B&B £25-£30; special rates for one week's stay; à la carte dinner from £20
Rooms 6 double, 3 with bath, 3 with shower; all rooms have phone, TV, tea/coffee kit, hairdrier
Facilities 2 sitting-rooms, dining room, private beach
Credit cards AE, DC, MC, V
Children welcome
Disabled all bedrooms on ground floor
Pets not accepted
Closed Nov-mid-Mar
Proprietors Martin and Rita Acton

Arbutus Lodge

Arbutus Lodge is a substantial suburban house, well known for its food and for its terraced gardens planted with rare trees and shrubs, including an arbutus tree. Superb shellfish, fish and game are the specialities of the suitably grand restaurant – and there is a top-notch wine list.

The Ryans continue to make improvements – now all the rooms at Arbutus Lodge have undergone smart new decoration, and just recently a nearby house has been converted to provide four extra suites.

Nearby Blarney Castle, 6 miles (10 km).

Middle Glanmire Road, Montenotte, Cork, Co Cork
Tel (021) 501237
Location 0.25 miles (0.4 km) NE of middle of Cork; with garden and ample car parking
Food & drink breakfast, lunch, dinner; full licence
Prices B&B IR£55-IR£125; suites IR£135-IR£200; dinner IR£26.50
Rooms 12 double, all with bath, 4 also with shower; 8 single, 4 with bath, 4 with shower; all rooms have central heating, TV, phone, radio
Facilities sitting-room, bar, dining-room
Credit cards AE, DC, MC, V
Children welcome if well behaved **Disabled** access difficult **Pets** not accepted
Closed 23 to 28 Dec; restaurant only Sun (limited bar menu for residents)
Proprietors Ryan family

Irish Republic

Enniscoe House

Susan Kellett's family home, opened to guests since 1982, is a
Georgian country house with a walled garden, set in wooded parkland on the shores of Lough Conn. The public rooms, with their
open fires and family portraits, are lived-in and welcoming. There
are canopy and four-poster beds in four of the period-style bedrooms. A one-bedroom house with an open fireplace in the sitting-
room has been converted in traditional style for weekly stays. Susan
Kellett produces fine, unfussy Irish country house food (including
Irish cheeses). There are good trout and salmon fishing facilities.
Nearby Moyne Abbey, 10 miles (16 km); Lough Conn.

Castlehill, near Crossmolina,
Ballina, Co Mayo
Tel (096) 31112
Fax (096) 31773
Location 12 miles (19 km) SW
of Ballina, 2 miles (3 km) S of
Crossmolina on Castlebar
road; in parkland on 300-acre
estate, with ample car parking
Food & drink breakfast,
dinner; wine licence
Prices B&B IR£44-IR£76;
DB&B IR£66-IR£86;
reduced weekly, weekend and
family rates
Rooms 3 double, 3 family
rooms, all with bath; all rooms
have central heating
Facilities sitting-room,
dining-room; boating, fishing
Credit cards AE, MC, V
Children welcome
Disabled not suitable
Pets accepted only by special
arrangement
Closed Oct to Mar
Proprietor Susan Kellett

Newport House

Fishing is the preoccupation of most visitors to Newport House,
which overlooks Newport river, though it is by no means the only
attraction. The Georgian house is gracious and elegant, but the
Thompsons encourage a caring, friendly attitude rather than
super-slick professionalism in their staff. Bedrooms are spacious
and individually decorated; a game-keeper's cottage is also available. Simplicity is the hallmark of the food, making full use of
local Clew Bay seafood – and the kitchen does its own butchering
as well as baking. Wines are Kieran's hobby.
Nearby Blarney Castle 12 miles (19 km); Joyce Country; golf

Newport, Co Mayo
Tel (098) 41222
Fax (098) 41613
E-mail KJT1@anu.ie
Location on edge of town;
ample car parking
Food & drink breakfast, light
lunch, dinner; full licence
Prices B&B IR£60-IR£78;
dinner IR£32
Rooms 14 double, 2 single,
2 four-poster rooms, all with
bath; some rooms in courtyard
adjacent to main house; all
rooms have phone
Facilities 2 sitting-rooms, bar,
dining-room; fishing
Credit cards AE, DC, MC, V
Children accepted
Disabled access possible –
ground-floor bedrooms
Pets accepted; not in main
house or public rooms
Closed mid-Oct to mid-Mar;
Christmas **Proprietors** Kieran
and Thelma Thompson

Irish Republic

Country house hotel, Letterfrack

Rosleague Manor

We visited recently and noted the polished decoration and service. It makes an interesting contrast to our other recommendations in the area (Crocnaraw, page 226): come here is you want a charming but more polished experience. Nigel Rush supervises the kichen, which specializes in Connemara lamb and seafood (freshly delivered each evening), and makes much use of home-grown fruit and vegetables. Anne takes charge of the front of house, including the large, elegant dining-room fitted out in keeping with the Georgian building

Nearby Connemara National Park; Kylemore Abbey.

Letterfrack, Connemara, Co Galway
Tel (095) 41101
Fax (095) 41168
Location one mile (1.5 km) W of Letterfrack, on shores of Ballinakill Bay; in 30-acre grounds; ample car parking
Food & drink breakfast, light lunch, tea, dinner; full licence
Prices B&B IR£45-IR£95; dinner from IR£27; also á la carte
Rooms 20 double (4 suites), all with bath; all rooms have central heating, phone
Facilities 3 sitting-rooms, bar, dining-room, conservatory, billiard room **Credit cards** AE, MC, V **Children** accepted
Disabled ramp to public rooms; access at rear to ground-floor bedroom
Pets dogs accepted in bedrooms by arrangement
Closed Nov to Easter
Proprietors Patrick and Anne Foyle

Country house hotel, Mallow

Longueville House

This imposing pink Georgian country house is situated on a 500-acre-wooded estate with plenty of opportunity for walking and fishing. Inside it is full of beautifully ornate plastered ceilings, elaborately framed ancestral oils and graceful period furniture.

The O'Callaghan family are 'charming and informal' says a recent visitor to Longueville House, so there is none of the stiffness you would expect of such a place in Britain. Food is 'sophisticated' and 'superb', served in the stylish Presidents' restaurant or the Victorian conservatory in summer.

Nearby fishing, walks; Blarney castle, 12 miles (19 km).

Longueville, Mallow, Co Cork
Tel (022) 47156
Fax (022) 47459
Location 3 miles (5 km) W of Mallow on Killarney road; ample car parking
Food & drink full breakfast, light snacks, dinner; full licence
Prices B&B IR£60-IR£84; dinner IR£31-IR£40
Rooms 18 double, 2 single, all with bath or shower; all rooms have central heating, TV, radio, phone, tea/coffee kit, hairdrier
Facilities sitting-room, drawing-room, bar, 2 dining-rooms, conference room, billiards, table tennis; fishing
Credit cards AE, DC, MC, V
Children welcome
Disabled access easy to public rooms only **Closed** 20 Dec to 12 Feb **Proprietors** O'Callaghan family

Irish Republic

Currarevagh House

This solid country house on the leafy shores of Lough Corrib has been in the Hodgson family for five generations and its sense of traditional styles and standards meticulously preserved is quite overpowering. Many of the guests return for the fishing on the lough. Afternoon tea in the airy, spacious sitting-room is quite a ritual, as are the 'Edwardian' breakfasts. Rooms vary but all are spotless. Revisiting recently we were struck by its wonderful peaceful location, the charm of the Hodgsons and a certain eccentricity.

Nearby Connemara; Joyce Country; Aran Islands; The Burren.

Oughterard, Connemara, Co. Galway
Tel (091) 552312
Fax (091) 552731
Location 4 miles (6 km) NW of Oughterard; in 150-acre woodlands beside Lough Corrib, with ample car parking
Food & drink breakfast, picnic-lunch, tea, dinner; licence
Prices B&B IR£45-IR£65; dinner IR£21; reductions for 3 nights or more

Rooms 12 double, 10 with bath, 2 with shower; 2 single, one with bath; one family room, with bath
Facilities 3 sitting-rooms (one with TV), bar, dining-room; tennis, boats, croquet, fishing
Credit cards not accepted
Children accepted
Disabled not ideal
Pets accepted
Closed Nov to Mar
Proprietors Harry and June Hodgson

Readers' reports

Reports from readers are of enormous help to us in keeping up to date with the hotels in the guide – and other hotels that should be in it. The most helpful reporters are invited to join our Travellers' Panel, and to stay in listed hotels at little or no cost. More information on p11.

Index of hotel names

In this index, hotels are arranged in order of the most distinctive part of their name; other parts of the name are also given, except that very common prefixes such as 'Hotel' and 'The' are omitted.

Index of hotel names

Index of hotel names

Index of hotel locations

In this index, hotels are arranged by the name of the city, town or village they are in or near. Where a hotel is located in a very small place, it may be under a larger nearby place.

Index of hotel locations